Will Parfitt has worked in the fields of personal and spiritual development for over thirty years. He trained in psychosynthesis and is a registered psychotherapist, leading courses in England and Europe. He also has a private practice in Glastonbury, England, where he lives, offering psychotherapy, mentoring, coaching and professional supervision. He is the author of several books, including *The Complete Guide to the Kabbalah*.

By the same author:

KABBALAH TITLES

The Living Qabalah
The Elements of the Qabalah
The New Living Qabalah
The Complete Guide to the Kabbalah

PSYCHOLOGY TITLES

Walking through Walls
The Elements of Psychosynthesis
Psychosynthesis: the Elements and Beyond

POETRY

Through the Gates of Matter

KABBALAH
FOR LIFE

HOW TO USE THE POWER AND WISDOM
OF THIS ANCIENT TRADITION

WILL PARFITT

RIDER
LONDON · SYDNEY · AUCKLAND · JOHANNESBURG

1 3 5 7 9 10 8 6 4 2

First published in 2006 by Rider,
an imprint of Ebury Publishing, Random House,
20 Vauxhall Bridge Road, London SW1V 2SA

Random House Australia (Pty) Limited
20 Alfred Street, Milsons Point, Sydney,
New South Wales 2061, Australia

Random House New Zealand Limited
18 Poland Road, Glenfield,
Auckland 10, New Zealand

Random House South Africa (Pty) Limited
Isle of Houghton, Corner of Boundary Road & Carse O'Gowrie,
Houghton 2198, South Africa

The Random House Group Limited Reg. No. 954009

Papers used by Rider are natural, recyclable products
made from wood grown in sustainable forests.

Printed and bound in Great Britain by Mackays of Chatham plc, Chatham, Kent

A CIP catalogue record for this book is available from the British Library

ISBN 1-8460-4035-3 (before Jan 2007)
ISBN 9781846040351 (after Jan 2007)

Amandora, always

CONTENTS

LIST OF
ILLUSTRATIONS

LIST OF PRACTICES

ACKNOWLEDGEMENTS

To my partner Patti Howe without whom this would be a much lesser work, mainly because of her being a constant source of inspiration, for her exquisitely detailed reading and correcting of the text, and simply for just being her.

To Susan Lascelles for her fine editing and support throughout the project.

To all my teachers in their various guises and forms.

To all my students and clients for teaching me what I most need to learn.

INTRODUCTION

Kabbalah is a practical system for understanding all aspects of our lives, from the deepest spiritual connections to the everyday experience of life in the modern world. What inspired me most when I first connected to the Kabbalah was that so much wisdom could be expressed through something so apparently simple, and more than thirty years later I still feel the same about it. Things are, of course, rarely as simple as they at first seem. However, while the ramifications and intricacies of the Kabbalah are undoubtedly many, it is nevertheless something that is simple to learn and to start using. I've discovered over the years that keeping the Kabbalah simple leaves space for insights to emerge, and it gives you the opportunity to make the system your own.

Kabbalah has had a tremendous influence on Western thought – people such as Leonardo da Vinci and Shakespeare used it, and even the founding fathers of the United States were influenced by it. Kabbalists teach that each individual person has their own Tree of Life inside them, which has to be directly experienced, not just believed in. To have this inner experience is relevant not only to the evolution of the individual, but also relevant to the evolution of the whole planet.

At the same time, central to Kabbalah is the attitude that, while here, let's enjoy life to the full, appreciate the opportunities it presents to us to learn and grow, and – perhaps most importantly in our modern world – learn to be here with respect for the planet itself and all the life forms it supports. The Kabbalah, with its grounded, pragmatic approach to spiritual growth, is an excellent guide for such practice. We can work at bringing our spiritual insights, connections and experiences to earth, to illuminate not just ourselves but all sentient beings.

Many years have passed since my first Kabbalah book came out, and I am now able to add a lot more breadth and depth than I could have back then. This is partly thanks to my continuing personal work with Kabbalah, but mostly thanks to the wonderful insights and stimulating connections made for me by all the people with whom I work in the fields of Kabbalah and Psychotherapy.

Kabbalah for Life uses the elements of Kabbalah to go beyond the basics, right to the heart of the system where the Tree of Life becomes alive in your consciousness and lives with you in everything you do: increasing your awareness, deepening your connection to soul energy, and giving you assistance in manifesting who you are and what you want to be in your life.

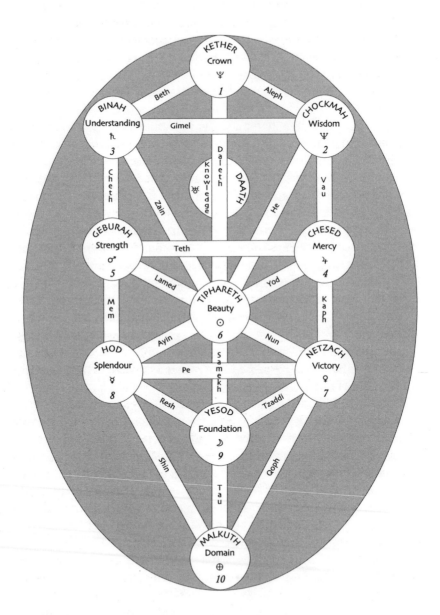

Diagram 1: The Tree of Life

A TREE FOR LIFE

She is more precious than pearls; and all the things you value are not equal
unto her. Length of days is in her right hand; in her left are riches and honour.
Her ways are ways of pleasantness, and all her paths are peace. A tree of life
is she to those that lay hold of her; and every one that firmly grasps her will
be made happy.

King Solomon (Book of Proverbs 3:15–18)

Kabbalah emphasises that we can find the deepest expression of our spirituality in our ordinary, daily lives and is a constant inspiration to seekers after inner wisdom. It offers us a detailed, coherent world view, both of the nature of human existence and the relationship between ourselves, other beings, our planet and even the universe as a whole. Yet, despite being such a potent guide to self-exploration, for many years Kabbalah appeared to be lost in obscurity, particularly in its practical applications. Today, with so many people searching for spiritual roots, and looking for meaning and purpose in their lives, it is undergoing a remarkable comeback. Its influence has not only been in the spiritual realms, however, for it has also exerted a profound and lasting effect on the growth of modern Western Psychology. Although he kept it secret, we now know that Sigmund Freud was interested in Kabbalah, and in his letters Carl Jung made knowledgeable references to the Tree of Life.

Central to Kabbalah is a map of consciousness known as the Tree of Life which, through its cleverly designed visual structure, helps us make connections between apparently unrelated facts that then become gems of meaningful wisdom. This works equally effectively on the most mundane planes and on the most spiritual as the wisdom of Kabbalah can be applied in all areas of life. It aims to help you live life to the full, and – perhaps most importantly in our modern world – learn to be here with respect for the planet itself and all the life forms it supports.

With Kabbalah you don't have to believe in something or not. The Tree of Life is a structure that helps you sort things out for yourself. Once you get the hang of it, which isn't difficult, it becomes second nature to use the Tree of Life to relate different things together. So, for instance, in your work you may come across some new techniques which, through using Kabbalah, you'll be able to understand and utilise more quickly because you can place them in a wider context. Later, back home and feeling stressed after a long work day, Kabbalah can help you to find ways to relax and shift your awareness. Even later, you may want to connect with your deepest artistic abilities, and Kabbalah will aid you to operate on that level, too. Basically, on the mundane level, using Kabbalah helps each of us to make the right choices from the right place and at the right time.

When you look at the more spiritual uses for Kabbalah, it can help you connect to the centre inside yourself where you are closest to the essence of yourself, your divine spark, or simply the deepest and most valuable aspect of yourself. When you connect with this, it vitalises your life, particularly your relationships, because at a deep core level you experience how everything is interrelated. Kabbalah doesn't show you anything new, it's more that as you work with it you uncover what was always there, a distinct individual who is at the same time inextricably linked to everyone else.

Ultimately, Kabbalah stresses that when we care for our environment and all other life forms, both locally and generally, we are also bringing our deepest, spiritual consciousness to earth. Every conscious act that includes such caring is the highest form of Kabbalistic practice, being the work that Kabbalists call *tikkun*, meaning repair or reparation. But more of that later. To fully enter into the depths of Kabbalah we need to first refresh our understanding of the basic elements of the system. Kabbalists never resent time taken in returning to the roots of the system because, like the roots of a tree, these are a constantly renewing source of nourishment for the body, mind and soul.

The Hebrew word Kabbalah means 'to reveal', and it refers to the revelation of our own inner nature that can come from its study and use. The Kabbalistic diagram known as the Tree of Life is a guide to the body, personality, soul and Spirit. It encompasses a philosophy and psychology of great theoretical and practical depth that deals with the whole person, not just the intellect, and it has been called the keystone of Western mysticism.

The word Kabbalah also means 'to receive', referring to our ability to receive inner wisdom and understanding. A distinction is made between 'knowledge', which is primarily theoretical, and 'understanding', which is primarily practical. Nothing can replace the experience of Kabbalah in its practical applications. To appreciate this fully, we have to engage all aspects of our being – our thinking, feeling and sensing functions – and not just the intellect.

Kabbalah can be classified in five divisions. Firstly, there is the 'oral' Kabbalah, aspects of the teaching received orally, either from a teacher of some kind or from another traveller on the journey of self-development. In fact, once we start using Kabbalah practically, it is quite amazing how even chance remarks made by other people can offer us meaningful and timely insights into our own nature. Secondly, there is the 'written' Kabbalah, which traditionally aims to describe the structure and nature of the universe. Thirdly, there is the 'literal' Kabbalah, which is concerned with the decoding of information within Kabbalistic texts, particularly the Bible. In later chapters of this book, we will see how, from a Kabbalistic viewpoint, the Bible reads very differently from the orthodox Jewish or Christian viewpoints.

The fourth division is called the 'symbolic' Kabbalah and is concerned with the understanding and integration of our own experiences in life, where everything with which we relate is viewed as a symbolic representation of something deeper. The symbolic Kabbalah is primarily based on the Tree of Life diagram, which, at its most basic, can be described as a network of spheres linked by pathways. Finally, the fifth division is called the 'practical' Kabbalah and is concerned with the utilisation of all the various aspects of Kabbalah to promote evolution and to create changes on all levels.

As well as being a system of personal development and self-realisation, Kabbalah, more particularly, can be seen as:

- a map of levels of awareness and energy
- a means for the correlation and expression of experience
- a tool for communication
- a method for the expansion of consciousness
- a way to connect inner and outer awareness
- a method for understanding other people's experiences
- a way of formulating ideas with more clarity
- a way of relating to all symbols, whatever their source
- a method for testing the 'truth' of any experience
- a means for communicating with other beings, even those that may seem to inhabit other worlds or planes of existence.

Kabbalah is relevant to our modern world in that it fosters personal, interpersonal and spiritual development. It can be used for any or all of these purposes, either singly or in combination. In fact, what we find is that when we start developing ourselves individually, interpersonal and spiritual repercussions inevitably follow; if we start on a path of spiritual development it affects our personal and interpersonal life, and so on. One cannot be truly separated from the other. We are not individual personalities who somehow 'have' or 'don't have' a soul, a Spirit, relationships with other people. The practical everyday reality of our lives, once we become aware of ourselves in this way, is that we are an interconnected web of different aspects with a 'centre' or 'soul'. It is nearer the truth, therefore, to say that we are individual souls, connected through a common, universal Spirit. Each soul has a personality composed of thoughts, feelings and sensations with which to experience the world and express itself.

In terms of individual development and growth, Kabbalah can be seen as a 'guidebook' to what is happening to us at each and every moment. We can use this guidebook to help us define where we are with reference both to where we come from and where we wish to go. From this perspective we can then work on developing all parts of our being – our physical being, including our body and our senses, our mental being, including both our more abstract and our concrete thinking processes, and our emotional reactions. We will see this possibility applied in various ways throughout this book.

By using the Tree of Life as a guidebook to ourselves, we can clarify what 'makes us what we are'. When we analyse ourselves in this way, it is then possible to begin a process of conscious synthesis, putting our different aspects together in a more coherent, holistic way. An analogy has been made between the Tree of Life and a filing cabinet (or a computer database). Every new experience or piece of information that we receive can be related to our existing body of knowledge and understanding. For example, if I am studying a book about philosophy, I can be pretty sure that most of the insights therein correspond to the sphere on the Tree of Life that represents the mind and intellect (and which is called 'Hod'). Or if I am working on clearing and changing some of the past events in my life that have restricted my free expression, I will probably be working with the sphere called 'Yesod', which has to do with the depths of the unconscious.

When we can relate to information and experience in this way, it helps our interpersonal life, for it allows us to relate to the experiences of other people, however apparently diverse. You may worship the god 'Thoth' and I may worship 'Hermes' – through Kabbalah we will find a strong identity between these two deities. Your god may not be the same as my god, but if we discover their essential similarities, we no longer need to argue about who is 'right' or 'wrong'. Kabbalah allows us to have a living meaningful understanding of symbols, myths and dreams that are fluid in nature, and whose meaning may vary according to the direct, living experience of the person seeing the symbol.

Kabbalah is very useful to people who work with others in a therapeutic way, whether as psychotherapists, counsellors, healers, or in body therapies. Through its methods and practices, we can learn to understand the relationship between different energies. We are then in a position to foster what is sometimes called 'balance through inclusion'. This means, for instance, if someone has highly developed mental energies and much less developed emotional energies, we will create a balance through encouraging and 'elevating' the emotional energy until it reaches the same level as the mental energy. What we would not do is to bring the mental energy down to the level of the emotional. Through heightening the energy that is less developed, we grow through inclusion, always becoming more rather than less.

Kabbalah can also be applied to more direct spiritual development, whether it has a 'mystical' or 'magical' flavour. A 'mystic' sees the world, is unhappy with it in some way or another, so follows practices that attempt to 'rise above' or transcend the world. 'I don't like it here so I'll go somewhere else' is the catchphrase of the mystic. The magician, on the other hand, feels the same discontent with the world but rather than transcending it, attempts to bring more 'spiritual' energy into manifestation. 'I don't like it here so I'll do all I can to change it' is the catchphrase of the magician. Whether our inclination is to the mystical or magical path, we can use Kabbalah for both.

The sphere at the bottom of the Tree of Life (Malkuth) is related both to the body and the external physical world. This is most appropriate when we consider that in all Kabbalistic work we stress the importance of bringing our work back to ground. There is no point having great insights, making spiritual connections, balancing our inner energies or whatever, if this remains an abstract idea rather than a living reality. If we connect with harmony through our Kabbalistic work, for instance, the most important question would be: how can we express this harmony in our everyday life? If may only be a little thing – giving someone we know a hug, for example – but each time we ground or earth our experiences we make them real. Kabbalah has been described as 'a living temple of the spirit' – it is only a living temple when the spirit is brought alive through its use. This is always our ultimate aim.

THE TREE OF LIFE

When you first look at the Tree of Life it appears very complicated, but really it is easy to memorise and visualise. Basically it is composed of three triangles, with a circle or sphere (called a Sephirah) at each angle (diagram 2).

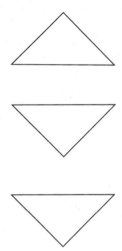

Diagram 2: Three triangles

The top triangle represents the Spirit that is within us and at the same time universal, common to everyone and everything else. The middle triangle represents the soul, the individual spark of the Universal Spirit that has, as it were, broken off to form the core of each living being. The bottom triangle represents the personality; the body, feelings and thoughts with which the soul has 'clothed' itself so that it may come into manifestation. The Tree of Life, therefore, is a complete map of consciousness. It is relevant to everything from the whole universe to each individual being. It represents, through its three basic triangles, the evolution of the individual, and through this, the evolution of the whole universe. Through recognising and owning everything that we are, we not only develop ourselves but we come to a greater understanding of the workings of our universe.

Being easy both to visualise and memorise, the Tree of Life serves as a useful and potent guide to the individual human being. It helps you to be exactly who you are right at this moment, and to understand more fully where you have come from and where you wish to go to. It is useful to look at where you have come from and to understand the experiences you have had so that you can learn from them. It is useful to know exactly where you are, which is always here and now. It is also helpful to feel a link with the future, not in the sense of a fortune teller with a crystal ball telling you that you are going to meet a tall dark stranger, but so that you can know in what direction you are heading and what are the most appropriate steps for you to take to move in that direction. When you fully comprehend the guidebook called Kabbalah you tune into the past, the present and the future, bringing harmony to your heart, health – in the sense of wholeness – to your whole being, and connection to everyone and everything else.

The Tree of Life is composed of eleven spheres, the nine that are at the points of the three triangles, and two further spheres positioned as shown in diagram 3:

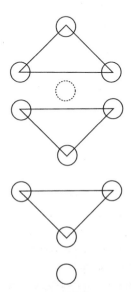

Diagram 3: Eleven spheres

The sphere at the bottom of the Tree, from where we always start Kabbalistic explorations, is called Malkuth. Representing our senses, and the planet Earth itself, it is the interface between our inner experience and what happens outside of us. Malkuth, literally 'the kingdom', is also sometimes called 'the gate'. Our senses are just that, the 'gate' through which we experience our world. If I look, for instance, at a painting and start interpreting it, I am looking at it in my own particular way and applying past knowledge and experience to it. I will have thoughts and feelings about what the picture depicts. None of this is Malkuth, which is the direct experience of sensing (in this case, seeing) without putting any interpretation or meaning into it.

You can explore this further in the exercise that follows. Part of the value of Kabbalah is that it allows us to analyse our personality functions and understand how each works separately. We can then 'reassemble' ourselves in a new way that includes more of ourselves and which makes us feel more whole.

PRACTICE

The practices in this book offer you the opportunity to connect with Kabbalah in a practical way. You may prefer to try some out immediately, or you may prefer to leave them until you are feeling more in the mood. Even if you do not intend to do an exercise, though, it is worth reading through as it will give you a flavour and deepen your understanding of the practical Kabbalah.

Appendix 1 (p. 203) gives you further details on how to approach the exercises, and includes the Kabbalistic Cross, the basics of which are well worth learning as it is an easy and powerful technique for centring, protecting and energising yourself all in one. I recommend before you read further you at least check out Appendix 1 as the suggestions there will deepen your experience and enjoyment of the exercises.

• The realisation of Malkuth

To start this exercise simply clap your hands together as hard and as loud as you can until you feeling tingling in your palms. Then hold your hands in the air and experience the tingling sensation.

Notice what you think about doing this, and any feelings it evokes. Perhaps you feel silly clapping your hands for no reason, perhaps you are wondering where this exercise is leading you. Any thoughts or feelings you are having are not the experience of Malkuth. Malkuth corresponds with the human body and the senses – any sensation, such as the tingling you have just been experiencing in your hands, is an experience of Malkuth. Once you do something with this – think about it, have an emotional reaction to it, anything at all – you are working with other spheres, not Malkuth.

Now clasp your two hands together in any way you wish, and notice the sensation of one hand against the other. You may have reactions again, such as perhaps thinking about prayer. Without rejecting these reactions or effects, pay no attention to them; they are not Malkuth. Simply experience the sense of touch, one hand against another. This, alone, is the pure experience of Malkuth.

Now look at any picture or photograph, perhaps a picture or poster on your wall, in a magazine, a newspaper, wherever. Once you start thinking about the subject of the picture, or having an emotional reaction to it, you are no longer experiencing Malkuth. You experience Malkuth by paying attention to what your eyes see and by not paying attention to the subject. It is not easy, but try doing this for a little while.

Finally, speak out loud any words and listen to your voice without
interpreting what it is you are saying. The sound of the words, totally devoid
of meaning, is an experience of Malkuth. Once you understand the words or
react to them, you are no longer just in Malkuth.

There is no implication intended here that there is anything wrong with
having thoughts, feelings, memories, emotional reactions and so on, or
that you should suppress them in any way. All of these things belong to
other spheres on the Tree of Life. The purpose of not paying attention
to them is to allow you to experience Malkuth on its own.

All the spheres on the Tree of Life have innumerable correspondences. Malkuth, for example, as well as corresponding to the Earth
and our senses, has animals, plants, minerals, gods and goddesses,
trees, elements, letters and numbers attributed to it. As this sphere is
about our primary experience, what we sense when we are 'grounded'
in our bodies, its correspondences will appropriately match this attribution. The animals associated with Malkuth include the dog and the
bull as very earthy creatures. You might like to think what other animals
you would attribute to the element of earth. The oak would be an
obvious tree to attribute here, for it represents strength and closeness
to the planet in a way no other tree does. Many correspondences will
vary, according to our personal connections and our cultural
background, although some correspondences do have a more universal
nature. Appendix 4 includes very detailed tables of correspondences
that you will explore and use in later chapters.

At the top of the Tree of Life is the sphere called Kether, which
represents the most central, or deepest, aspect of our spiritual being,
the place where our individuality blurs into union with all other
consciousness. The spheres between Kether and Malkuth, and the
complex array of paths that connect them, represent all the other
aspects of our being. All the spheres have correspondences like those
mentioned above, which we can directly experience, therefore adding
to our knowledge of the different parts of ourselves.

USING KABBALAH

The Tree of Life helps us to clarify our inner experiences. When we have
a clearer idea of what is inside us, of who we are, then we can more
easily find ways to express ourselves. This is particularly important for
our interpersonal relationships, because through the correspondences

of the Tree we can relate to the experience of other people, however apparently diverse they appear to be. For example, your basic values and mine might not appear to be the same, but once we understand the deeper connection behind the apparent differences, we are on a path towards mutual understanding.

Kabbalah helps us to understand symbols, whether experienced in myths, fantasies or dreams. If I have a dream, for instance, that involves driving down an endless dark tunnel at the end of which is a light I never can quite reach, I might understand this as representing a journey into my unconscious. The light at the end of the tunnel may be a glimpse of the sphere at the centre of the Tree, which is associated with inner harmony; I could then use the Tree to help me reach that light. This might be accomplished through any of a variety of techniques for this purpose: continuing the dream in a conscious visualisation, meditating on the corresponding symbols for that sphere, or simply through the increased awareness such a connection inevitably brings.

The spheres on the Tree of Life also correspond to the human body. Using Kabbalah, we can come to a greater understanding of our body energies and the relationship within us between physical, emotional and mental energies. For example, I might see the tension in my solar plexus as an expression of the relationship between the two spheres that correspond to that area of my body. These spheres also correspond to the thinking and feeling functions. By bringing about a stronger relationship between these two functions, perhaps by allowing my feelings more expression and not worrying about what I think I should do, I harmonise these two spheres on the Tree and the original tension is lessened.

The sphere that is at the centre of the Tree of Life is called Tiphareth and represents the sun in the solar system and the heart in the human system. Both the sun and the heart are at the centre, so Tiphareth also represents the centre of our psychological make-up, our own individual 'I', self or core identity. Whatever we may know about the solar system, and the fact that the earth goes round the sun and not vice versa, along with all our ancestors we experience the sun as being 'born' each morning, going through the day, then sinking and 'dying' at night, to be reborn again the next day. Our experience of human life is the same: we are born, we live and then we die and, if we believe this, we may be reborn sometime in the future.

If we could step from our terrestrial consciousness to a place on the sun, the view we have of the solar system is very different. Now the light is continuous and everything revolves around us at the centre or heart of the system. It is the same with our experience as living beings. We can step to our centre and live from there. Life is then continuous and, from this centre, we can harmoniously direct our lives. This harmony is the pure experience of Tiphareth. We can have ideas, concepts, feelings, emotions and sensations about this experience, but there is something beyond all these – the pure unattached quality of harmony. Using the Tree of Life can help us connect with this harmony.

The ultimate goal of Kabbalah is the full, living realisation of this harmonious connection. This not only aids in the development of the individual, but also furthers the cause of international and planetary peace. Given the unquestionable importance of these causes, Kabbalah is perhaps more relevant now than ever before.

PRACTICE

• The Kabbalistic Journal

If you have not done so already, look up Appendix 1, which guides you in how to use the exercises in this book.

Before starting this exercise, make yourself comfortable, close your eyes and take a few deep breaths. Be aware that you are a unique individual, choosing, at this very time, in this very space, to utilise your energies to enter into realms of magical consciousness.

Imagine you are standing in a field at the bottom of a hill. Look around you. Be aware of everything you can see. Take some time to build a clear picture of this field and your surroundings. Utilise your other senses: what can you smell? What can you hear? Perhaps the grass is long, maybe there are flowers blooming in your meadow. Perhaps you can see the sun shining on early morning dew. Let an image of this meadow clearly form around you.

Walk across the field to a path that slopes upwards towards a hill. Take your time to really feel your feet on the ground as you walk across the field. Be aware of what is around you.

Start walking along the path that gently slopes up the hill. Notice the terrain — what plants are there? How does the air smell? Take your time and enjoy your walk.

When you are about halfway up the slope, stop for a rest. Look back on the path you have travelled, and down to the fields below. Breathe in the air and feel refreshed and strong. Enjoy the sense of being alone in the beauty of nature.

Just as you are about to continue your journey, you notice something faintly glistening under a nearby rock. You go to investigate and, digging some earth and stones out from around it, you discover something wrapped in a golden cloth. Brush the dirt and dust off the wrapping, unfold it and see before you a book with a beautiful cover. Lift it up to the light. You feel excited and alive as you do this. This book is filled with energy. What colour is it? What shape is it? What designs may there be on the front? Let the image of this magical book become clear in your imagination.

Apprehensively you open the book and discover that the pages are pure white and completely blank. You now fully realise that this is a book for you in which you can keep a record of your Kabbalistic adventures and discoveries. You feel thrilled to be in possession of this, your magical journal.

When you feel ready, start walking to the top of the hill, carrying your new-found book with you. At the top you find a standing stone, about waist high. Place your book on top of this stone. Be aware that the energy of the sun, shining on your diary, charges it and lightens it. Be aware that the energy of the earth coming up through the stone, also charges and energises your diary. Allow your book to change size, colour or shape, to acquire new designs, or simply become radiant as it receives all this positive energy.

Pick up your journal and hold it in front of your heart. Affirm that in this book you will keep an honest record of your magical work. Let the energy of the book penetrate through your heart to the deepest, most secret depths of your being. Realise also that the energy from the secret depths of your being can also fill up the book with your own unique truth.

When you are ready, thank the sun and the stone, then walk briskly back down to the field where you started, bringing your Kabbalistic journal with you.

Back in the meadow, pay attention to feeling your feet on the solid ground. Open your eyes, bringing your imagined – and yet soon to be physically real! – journal into your everyday reality.

When you do any Kabbalistic or magical work, it is important that you keep a record of your journeying, your discoveries and insights, whether they are painful or joyous ones. This record can then help you to attune yourself to your life journey, affirm your commitment and strengthen your sense of purpose. With such a journal, your knowledge can become more accessible, and your understanding will increase. It is up to you to manifest this so far only imaginary diary into Malkuth. How can you do this?

HISTORY AND RELEVANCE

When we look into the history of Kabbalah, we find there are two quite distinct stories. Firstly, there is a 'mythical' history, which despite its fabulous nature, contains both important 'inner truths' and some incidents based on actual events. Secondly, there is a 'mundane' history, which, despite its basis in actual events, also contains fabulous elements. Let's start with a version of the mythical history that is based on the oral and written legends and myths of ancient Hebrews as well as more modern Jewish and non-Jewish Kabbalists.

THE MYTHICAL HISTORY

Originally, the Mother–Father of Creation taught the angels a special secret wisdom that forms the basis of what we now call Kabbalah. After the creation of humankind and the subsequent fall from grace, the angels decided to teach the Kabbalistic secrets to humans to help them regain their link with paradise, paradise being the result of unimpeded manifestation of divine energy on earth. Unfortunately, however, although a few individuals listened to this wisdom and applied it in their lives, the majority of early humans had no time for 'divine plans' and the like, being more interested in mundane affairs.

After many, many generations, the Mother–Father Deity ('God') made a pact or covenant with Abraham, part of which involved the revelation of the Kabbalistic wisdom. The central secret was the 'holy name' IHVH (Jehovah), which includes in its four simple letters the key to understanding the entire wisdom of Kabbalah. Abraham transmitted this wisdom to Isaac and Jacob, from whence it was transmitted to Joseph. Unfortunately, Joseph died before telling anyone else the secret, so the knowledge died with him. Abraham had, however, written down some of the more important elements in a book called 'Sepher Yetzirah', which was hidden in a cave.

The Mother–Father Deity decided that it would be appropriate to reveal the wisdom again only when an individual human reached a level of personal and spiritual development where they could ask for it to be revealed. Such a person was Moses. In captivity in Egypt, Moses managed to break the chains of slavery and ignorance through aligning his will and power with that of his highest Self. The Deity recognised his accomplishment and transmitted to him both an exoteric lore (the Ten Commandments) and the secret, inner, esoteric teachings of Kabbalah.

The Deity even gave Moses this new name (we no longer know

Moses' original name). The name Moses is composed of the three Hebrew letters Mem, Shin and Heh, representing water, fire and breath. There are many different ways of understanding this name Kabbalistically, perhaps the simplest being the most useful – that through conscious breathing techniques we are able to unite the fire and water (or male and female energies) within us. Moses was inspired to write down his understanding in a form that describes the mundane, exoteric teachings but which also describes through allusion, codes and symbolism, the secret inner teachings. These writings of Moses comprise the first four books of the Bible.

Some time after Moses, a group of learned and wise holy people came together, in secret, to create a 'mystery college' where the teachings could be taught, understood and, most importantly, practically applied to human affairs, both on an individual and collective level. As well as having a direct oral line of understanding of Kabbalah stemming from the original teachings given to Moses, they also rediscovered the teachings that Abraham had written down and hidden in a cave many centuries earlier. All our current knowledge of Kabbalah stems from this source, and this group of initiates has been known by various names throughout history – the Hidden Masters, Secret Chiefs, Invisible College, and so on.

There are, of course, many differing versions of the mythic history of Kabbalah, and this version brings together the elements of several different traditions to create a coherent, if fantastic, tale. Compare it now, if you will, with the more ordinary – and yet no less extraordinary – mundane history of Kabbalah.

THE MUNDANE HISTORY

The two central books of Kabbalistic wisdom and understanding are called 'Sepher Yetzirah' (Book of Formation) and 'Zohar' (Book of Splendour). These two books form the basis of all subsequent Kabbalistic teaching and development. No one really knows who wrote these books, or whether they were originated by the writers or simply the recording of a much older oral tradition.

The Sepher Yetzirah was written before the sixth century AD, possibly by Rabbi Akiba, an enlightened Jewish mystic, around AD 100. It is composed of less than two thousand words. Despite this brevity, however, it concerns itself with the origins of the universe and the central importance of humanity within the universe. It stresses the importance of the Hebrew alphabet as a key to understanding the universe. The Sepher Yetzirah is, at least potentially, so erudite and wise that many scholars believe that Akiba was definitely recording the findings of an ancient tradition rather than his own revelations alone.

The Zohar was possibly written by Rabbi Simon ben Jochai, a contemporary disciple of Akiba. Akiba was executed by the Romans and Rabbi Simon fled to the hills, hid in a cave and wrote the Zohar, basing his teachings on the wisdom of Moses. A central theme in the Zohar is that everything in the universe is connected to everything else and that every part of creation is in constant interaction and interplay with every other part. Underlying this 'cosmic dance' there is a hidden order and meaning. This hidden meaning can best be discovered through direct engagement with the things of the earth rather than through attempts to transcend the world.

Both the Zohar and the Sepher Yetzirah stress the importance of a female counterpart to 'God', thus the term I used earlier, the 'Mother–Father Deity'. The Zohar contains imagery of an erotic nature, and a direct link is made between sexual and spiritual union. Indeed, it is through the uniting of the male and female within ourselves that we can truly mirror the cosmic Deity, which is a complete synthesis of masculine and feminine energies.

Little more is heard of Kabbalah until a new explosion of interest in thirteenth-century Spain. One of the most influential early books in this period was called 'Sepher Bahir' (Book of Brilliance), which postulated a vast, unseen multi-layered cosmic reality beneath our more usual, everyday waking 'reality'. Then, in the early fourteenth century in Spain, a Rabbi called Moses de Leon published a version of the Zohar and these mysteries became available to many more mystics and scholars. Some people have suggested that Moses de Leon actually invented the Zohar, but even if that were true it would not change the great influence it had on the development of Jewish mysticism and subsequently the Western Mystery Tradition.

There was at that time enough of the teachings available for individuals to start applying them in the intended practical way. One of the greatest of these inner pioneers was born in Spain at the end of the thirteenth century. Abraham Abulafia had little or no formal training but at the age of thirty-one he gained spiritual enlightenment through Kabbalistic practices that involved the use of special body postures and breathing techniques. Abulafia became a well-known figure in his time and was disliked by both the Jewish and non-Jewish orthodoxy for his ability to use his clear insights and personal experience to cut through intellectual arguments and outmoded ritual. At one stage he was arrested and was to be burned by the papal authorities, only to be 'saved' when the Pope died during the night before the intended execution. For some reason they set Abulafia free after this, perhaps because they feared others might meet a similar fate as the Pope if they attempted to silence him!

During the Middle Ages, Kabbalah flourished throughout Europe but particularly in the Hebrew community of Safed in the Holy Land. By the end of the sixteenth century two 'schools' of Kabbalistic thought had established themselves, that of Moses Cordovero and that of Isaac Luria (who was also known as the 'Ari', which means 'lion'). The Kabbalistic teachings were seen as dangerous by orthodox Jewish authorities and were put out of bounds except as an intellectual study for more learned rabbis. The tradition continued to flourish underground, however.

The next great stage in Kabbalistic development happened in the eighteenth century. A great teacher, Israel ben Eliezer, arose, and became known as the Baal Shem Tov (which means 'bearer of the good name' and which is popularly shortened to 'the Besht'). The Besht is the founder of Hasidism (meaning 'devout ones' in Hebrew). The Besht was strongly influenced and affected by Kabbalistic theory and practice, and by the age of thirty-six showed deep spiritual mastery. He was a very charismatic individual who displayed great spiritual understanding, which he made available to ordinary people. He spoke of his teachings as a 'way of the heart' and stressed that as we are living in this world it is as important for us to enjoy the pleasures of our physical world as it is to pray and practise esoteric techniques.

Despite the fact that Hasidism flourished and is still very alive today, in the changing world of the eighteenth century, Jewish people, like many other people in the Western world at the time of the development of modern mechanistic and economic theories, lost interest in the more practical aspects of their spiritual roots. The orthodoxy prevailed, and it is not until very recent times, and after much Kabbalistic development in the Western Mystery Tradition, that there is renewed interest among Jewish people in the Jewish Kabbalah.

THE MYTHICAL VS MUNDANE HISTORY

Perhaps the two histories of Kabbalah are not really so distinct from each other as it appears when they are described in this way. Perhaps both are true in their own ways, and while the mundane history shows the 'outer' development of Kabbalah, the mythical, esoteric history has been running in parallel. Whatever is the truth of this, however, the most important thing is how relevant Kabbalah is to us in the modern world. From my experience, both working on myself and with many other individuals and groups, I know Kabbalah works extremely well as a way of personal, interpersonal and spiritual development. I believe this is what counts to us today, so although the history is of interest, whatever we choose to believe, we can experience the direct truth of Kabbalah in our own lives. Much of this work is possible through non-Jewish developments of Kabbalah within the last 150 years or so.

RECENT DEVELOPMENTS

During the middle to latter half of the nineteenth century, there was an explosion of interest in what we now call the Western Mystery Tradition. Eliphas Levi in France was one of the most influential figures, as were Wynn Westcott and MacGregor Mathers, both founders of the Golden Dawn Mystery School in England. Kabbalah was central to this revival of interest in the esoteric and occult, being the most comprehensive and practical map of human consciousness. All other esoteric lore, inner teachings, mystical approaches, occult practices and so on could be related to Kabbalah and brought into a coherent whole. A system of personal and spiritual growth was developed that could be applied without reference to Kabbalah and yet was rooted in the theories and practices of Kabbalah.

The interest in esoteric mysteries has continued until the present day, with many offshoots of the Golden Dawn and other 'secret societies' flourishing. Certain individuals have also been instrumental in popularising Kabbalah and its wisdom, notably Israel Regardie and Dion Fortune, both of whom were psychologists as well as Kabbalists and authors of highly influential books, and Aleister Crowley, the controversial occultist who, whatever else may be said about him, was a first-class Kabbalist. Rabbi Abraham Isaac Kook, who was chief rabbi during the founding of modern Israel, expressed interest in Jewish mysticism and Kabbalah and, particularly since the beginning of the 1960s, there has been a renewed interest in Jewish spiritual traditions. The name of Gershom Scholem immediately springs to mind as someone helping to establish a practical, modern-day, working version of Jewish Kabbalah.

In very recent times, some forms of Kabbalah have become popular among various celebrities. Kabbalah is not, nor ever has been, a cult, but of course as with all practices it is possible to adapt them to a variety of purposes. Just as with an individual it is vital to be able to distinguish between the behaviour of their personality and their innermost divine soul, the same applies to organisations.

It has been suggested that the different Kabbalistic threads can be given different transliterations of the Hebrew word QBLH to help distinguish them. Thus, 'Qabalah' refers to the Western Mystery Tradition version, 'Kabbalah' to the Jewish and 'Cabala' to the Christian version. While there is some value in such a distinction, particularly as the aims and methods of different schools of Kabbalah can vary considerably, this idea falls down on two main points. Firstly, writers and workers in the different schools often continue to use the three versions of QBLH without this distinction being made, and secondly – and more importantly – what really matters is the work done, not what it is called. Kabbalah, Qabbala, Qabalah, Kablah, Cabala . . . these are labels, and when we wish to tune into our own inner wisdom, what matters is whether the system works for us.

THE WESTERN MYSTERY TRADITION

The Western Mystery Tradition includes all the esoteric knowledge and teachings that come from 'the West' rather than those originating in 'the East' such as Yoga and Tantra. The disciplines of the Western Mystery Tradition include, therefore, alchemy, gnosticism, faery traditions, runes, tarot, various other occult sciences and arts, and Kabbalah. Indeed, Kabbalah has been described as the foundation of the Western Mystery Tradition, and it is true that it underpins much modern theory and practice. Some strands of the tradition are undoubtedly quite distinct and in no way originate from Kabbalah. One of the particularly useful – I would even say wonderful – aspects of Kabbalah, however, is its ability to include everything else through the system of correspondences. Not only differing aspects of the Western Mystery Tradition, but also all other systems of personal and spiritual development, whatever their origin, can be related back to the Tree of Life. In her work *The Mystical Qabalah*, Dion Fortune, one of the most important Kabbalists in the history of the Western Mystery Tradition, wrote: 'We see in the Tree of Life a glyph of the soul and the universe, and in the legends associated with it, the history of the evolution of the soul and the way of initiation.'

It is possible to describe the central, cohesive structure of any esoteric system as its 'Kabbalah', so sometimes we hear people talk of 'the Greek Kabbalah', 'the Chinese Kabbalah', 'the English Kabbalah' and so on. Sometimes such descriptions are based on a system of numerology where each letter of the language involved is given a numerical equivalent. Once this is achieved all the other correspondences will fit into the scheme. In the more strict sense, it is certainly dubious and even verging on the absurd to refer to a 'Chinese Kabbalah' or 'English Kabbalah'. On the other hand, if these systems work in a practical and meaningful way for those applying them to their own growth and initiation, all well and good. And as these systems will inevitably correspond with Kabbalah of the Western Mystery Tradition to which we refer here, they are perhaps not as outlandish as may at first appear. After all, if the aim of greater wisdom and understanding is achieved, does it really matter if the method is idiosyncratic?

Furthermore, if these other 'Kabbalahs' lead to delusion and glamour, perhaps this is chiefly related to the practitioners rather than their system – after all, our Kabbalah can also be misused by those who wish to bolster their own egos or acquire power over others. Working within a tradition does offer some level of safeguard against these pitfalls, for to progress fully with Kabbalistic initiation involves a transcendence of temporal ego and a surrender to the deeper forces within. Such a surrender almost automatically precludes the possibility of using the system for selfish gain.

KABBALAH AND MODERN SCIENCE

In this century, modern science, particularly physics, has moved away from the older mechanistic approach and now conceives the world in a more holistic fashion. It is believed, for instance, that even in the realm of subatomic particles, which can only be measured through complex and sophisticated equipment, the role of the experimenter plays a vital part. What the experimenter believes actually changes the results of the experiment! Everything (yes, literally everything!) is interconnected, all part of one organic unity. This is, of course, the view shared by many mystics of all persuasions through the ages, and Kabbalah is no different. The work of modern science makes discoveries and pronouncements that echo the words of spiritual masters. The so-called 'objectivity' of the traditional scientific method is seen for what it is – useful for experimentation that is definable within those terms, but unreal for work that explores the meaning and structure of our universe where all matter is alive with energy and potential.

We affect our universe: do not miss the importance of these simple words – we affect our universe. It is vital that we bring more consciousness into our actions, for if we affect our world then we are each responsible for the part we play. If I squirt an aerosol can that harms the atmosphere I can no longer say: oh well, what difference does my one little act make? Every act we perform does make a difference. Similarly, with our inner work, every act has an effect. This is the central message both of holistic sciences and of Kabbalah.

PRACTICE

• Creating a sacred space

A sacred space does not have to be a specific room or location, it is something you can create for yourself wherever you are. The following suggestions are intended to help you create your own sacred space. Truly the sacred space you create is inside you, the attitude, mind-set and feelings you bring to your Kabbalistic work. Your 'inner temple' or sacred space created in this way is perfectly safe and completely inviolable. It is important to feel comfortable both in your inner and outer world for a Kabbalistic practice of any kind to work most effectively.

To create an outer 'temple' or sacred space in which to work, the first act is to consecrate the room to your intention. You might like to do this through lighting candles and/or incense, sprinkling water, or through simply walking around the space voicing your intention for its use.

You are now ready to find your 'power spot' in the room where you are working. Focus in on your heart and start moving around the room with your eyes sufficiently open so as not to bump into anything but not so open that you can see objects and items in your room clearly. Don't try to work out where your power spot is, don't try to find it but instead let it find you. There is no way you can rationally discover a power spot, but if you follow this procedure you will find somewhere in your room where you feel better than you do elsewhere. Trust this feeling and choose this place as your power spot.

When you have located your power spot, you might like to do some expressive movement to claim it as yours. Find the kind of movement that feels most appropriate for you whether that is high-energy dance or simply twiddling your thumbs in the air. Animals have a natural tendency to do this – we have all seen dogs, for instance, turning round a few times before lying down. Your body has the same 'animal instincts' so when you choose to physically claim your sacred space, trust that your body knows what needs to be done.

Your movement or dance will be aided by the use of suitable music. If you can create your own, so much the better. Drumming, for instance, is always effective in such work. Alternatively you can choose suitable recorded music to play – something rhythmic and uplifting for dancing in your sacred space, for example. Personally I find instrumental music most effective, but whether you choose classical, rock, jazz, hip-hop or acid house music, the selection of suitable music can help you to focus your intention. It can also be great fun to devise musical accompaniment when you are dancing for a specific purpose. Try not to make this an intellectual pursuit, however – you can trust your body to tell you what music moves you most appropriately for any task!

To create an inner 'temple' or sacred space, centre yourself in any way you know, and pay attention to your breathing, initially keeping it deep and low but without forcing it in any way. You can then sanctify your sacred space through doing a simple 'warm up' dance, which expresses your intention. Use any movements or gestures that connect with your intention for creating a sacred space, and if any words or sounds come to you, let yourself express them freely.

Some people like to make prostrations to the earth that help support their creation of sacred space. You may not be in a suitable location to do this, but even then you could do it in your imagination. Don't fall for the trap of thinking your work will be any less effective if you do so, for so long as your intention is clear, the dedication of your sacred space can be accomplished in pretty much any circumstances.

So, remaining centred, focus on your heart once more and make a series of at least three ritual prostrations. Each time you prostrate yourself, give yourself permission to go right down to the floor, lying on your belly and feeling the ground beneath you. Your first prostration is to thank 'mother earth' for supporting you. Inwardly voice your thanks. Your second prostration is to affirm your awareness and choice in embarking upon whatever work you will do in this room you have sanctified. On the third (and any subsequent) prostration be aware of your specific intention for the work at hand. Be aware that in prostrating yourself to the earth you can affirm not only the sanctity of your work but also the sanctity of all life on our planet.

Finally, silently meditate in your power spot, aware of the sacred energies in both your inner and outer temples. The processes you have just undertaken will have affirmed your place in Malkuth. You are now ready to try the final practice in Chapter 1, which aims to connect you with the positive energy of your deepest soul. This, too, is of course a place of perfect safety and complete inviolability.

• The soul cloak

Between the lower spheres on the Tree of Life and the central sphere, Tiphareth, is a veil that is called the 'Veil of Paroketh'. This veil acts as a cloak so that until we make our own direct connection to soul energies we are not confused or dazzled by the energies that are then available to us. In the following chapters we will be looking at the journey of 'soul-making' using the Tree of Life, so this exercise is intended to prepare you for this work.

Before starting, sit comfortably, relax and focus for a while on your breathing. Do not force or change your breathing in any way, but simply allow your awareness to follow there as it enters your lungs then is released. If you are breathing in a very shallow way you may want to deepen your breathing a little but otherwise simply trust in your own breathing pattern. As you watch your breathing, become aware of any particular tensions in your body and choose to let go of these tensions with your out-breath.

Imagine you are wearing a dark, heavy, black cloak. The hood us up and is pulled right over your head, hiding your face. Spend a little while really imagining this cloak, feeling its presence all around your physical form.

This dark, hooded cloak is the cloak of your negativity, your fears and the negative emotions, thoughts and sensations you experience in your life. Really feel the heaviness of this cloak. Now become aware that this negative cloak is gradually lifting up and away from your body, taking with it all your negativity. Really feel this cloak loosening and lifting away from you.

Imagine the cloak slowly vanishing.

Once it is completely gone, you are free to clothe yourself in a new cloak of your choice, a cloak of love, joy, beauty, protection, or any other quality you choose. Choose the cloak you wish to wear right now.

Vividly imagine yourself wearing the new cloak you have chosen, this cloak of light and positive energy. See its colour and feel its strength and quality all around you.

Realise this new cloak is a symbol for your soul. Realise that as a soul you can wear whatever cloak you choose.

Realise you are a soul and choose wisely.

2

THE SPHERES
AND THE PATHS

*To those that understand themselves I will give to eat of the Tree of Life, which
is in the midst of paradise.*

Book of Revelations (adapted from 2:7)

Although the Tree of Life may look very complicated at first sight, it is actually quite simple, being composed of three triangles, one upright at the top and two upside down triangles beneath. There are nine spheres, one at each of the three points of the three triangles, plus two extra spheres, one between the top two triangles and one at the bottom, making a total of eleven spheres on the Tree of Life. The Hebrew word for these spheres is Sephira (plural Sephiroth), which means 'number' and each of the spheres is given a number, as shown in diagram 4.

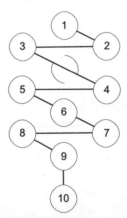

Diagram 4: The lightning flash

Note how the sphere between the two top triangles is not given a number; it is sometimes referred to as 'the sphere without a number'. The other ten spheres are numbered in the order shown by the lightning flash, which is said to be the order of creation – from number 1 (named Kether), which represents the highest or ultimate creator of the universe (and also the deepest, spiritual aspect of ourselves, the Self), to number 10, the sphere named Malkuth. You have already learnt that Malkuth represents the body and senses. It also represents the final result of the creation, the whole physical, manifest world and everything in it.

The lightning flash is described in the Sepher Yetzirah thus:

The ten sephiroth that appear out of nothing
have the appearance of a lightning flash.
Their origin is unseen and no end is perceptible.
The word is in them as they rise forth and as they return.

PRACTICE

• The lightning flash

After suitably preparing yourself, picture the Tree of Life as overlaying your body. Imagine a bolt of lightning manifest from nothingness and enter the top of your head at Kether. From there it quickly, without any deviation, travels through the remaining spheres (that is, to Chockmah on the left side of your head, to Binah on the right side of your head, Chesed left shoulder, Geburah right shoulder, Tiphareth at heart, Netzach at left belly and hip, Hod at right belly and hip, Yesod at genitals level, Malkuth at your feet).

 As you visualise this, make this flow of energy continuous, not so much a flash as a streaming of light. The energy pauses at each sphere to charge it up and to vitalise its essence. Then the energy flows on until it arrives at Malkuth. You can now feel the Tree complete, all the spheres lit with bright white lights. Realise yourself as connected to Malkuth and channel the energy that continuously flows through the Tree into Malkuth as now flowing into you. Accept this energy and take it into yourself. Allow it to fill you in whatever way feels right for you. (This is an excellent way of grounding energy.)

• The ascending serpent

After the primary ten lights were illuminated by the lightning flash, lesser lights sprang up between them, being the twenty-two letters of the Hebrew alphabet and the paths that join the spheres. The spheres can be reached through taking on (at least metaphorically) the form of a serpent, which is the archetypal model for climbing up the twenty-two lesser lights of the Tree of Life. By twisting and turning thought about on the Tree, a human mind can both reach the heights of spirit and choose to return to matter (see diagram 5).

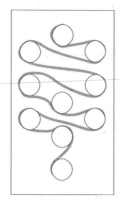

Diagram 5: The ascending serpent

The ascending serpent practice done on its own may lead to some level of dissociation whereas the lightning flash assures the energies are grounded. For this reason, the ascending serpent exercise should only ever be performed after the lightning flash exercise, and usually should be followed by a second lightning flash (that is, lightning flash, serpent ascending, lightning flash).

In this exercise the flow of energy follows the serpent's path up the Tree, travelling much more slowly than the lightning flash, and encircling each sphere as it passes it. (This is an excellent way of gently raising energy.)

• Flash, serpent, flash

Practise the previous two activities before continuing with the complete sequence: lightning flash, serpent ascending, lightning flash.

After preparation, perform this sequence, each lighting flash visualised as travelling down the front of the body with an out-breath, the serpent's path returning up the back of the body (with an in-breath).

[You can take more than one breath for each part, focusing your attention on the in or out part of the breath as appropriate.]

lightning flash	out-breath	fast as possible
serpent ascending	in-breath	slow as possible
lightning flash	out-breath	fast as possible

Repeat until you feel you have done enough. Don't force anything – this is not about forcing energy, more about finding how this flow is happening inside anyway. (This is an excellent way of circulating energy.)

The complete exercise can be used regularly at various times during the day, without attracting attention. It is worth remembering to do it at times of stress, subvocally hissing through your teeth on the out-breath.

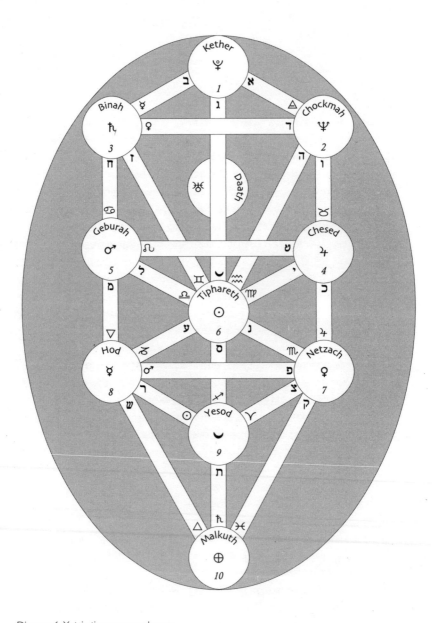

Diagram 6: Yetziratic correspondences

As always with such activities, ground yourself back into everyday reality afterwards. The point of Kabbalistic work of this kind is to bring you more fully into manifestation, a living embodiment of the divine spirit, not to leave you feeling ungrounded or disconnected from the 'real' world. Indeed, writing in your journal, having a cup of tea, relaxing with a friend, all such activities enable your body and feelings to relax after the moving energy work you have just undertaken.

In future, this exercise can be usefully performed before any specific Kabbalistic work. Once you are familiar with it you can perform it very quickly.

CORRESPONDENCES

As well as Hebrew names and numbers, each sphere on the Tree has numerous other correspondences associated with it, ranging from colours, symbols and images through to various gods, goddesses, tarot cards, animals, plants, minerals and so on. In fact, everything that exists (either in reality or in imagination) can be related to the Tree of Life. Diagram 6 shows the paths with some of their major correspondences. Each of the spheres also has a primary correspondence that relates it to different aspects of an individual person, and this is shown in diagram 7. Spend a little time now looking at these diagrams of the Tree of Life.

The ten spheres (excluding the eleventh one, Daath), are connected to one another by a complex array of twenty-two paths. These paths represent the subjective understanding and relationship possible when two particular spheres are connected. For instance, as Hod corresponds with thoughts and Netzach with feelings, the path that connects them represents the relationship between thoughts and feelings. In other words, if you feel as though you want to do something but you don't think it's a good idea, you are experiencing this particular path. Similarly, if you want to create a connection between your thinking and feeling functions, the correspondences associated with this particular path might help you to make such a link. We will look into these possibilities later in this book.

If we recall the three triangles from which the Tree is basically composed, and compare this with the information in diagram 7, we can see that the top triangle refers to the spiritual aspect of a person, that part of them that is connected to everyone and everything else. This is

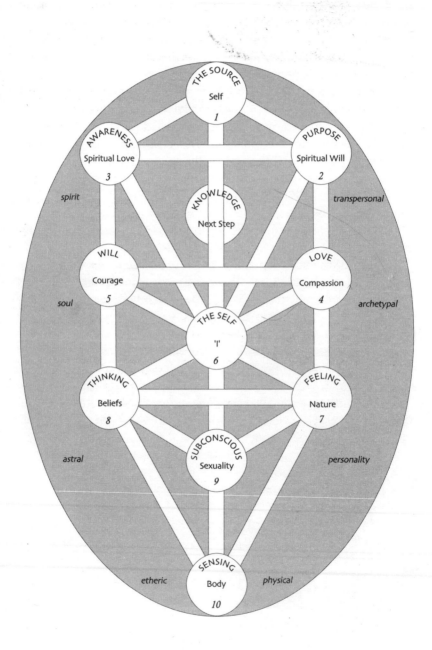

Diagram 7: The whole person

sometimes referred to as the Supernal Triad, and is the realm of the transpersonal. The middle triangle refers to the individual soul, that part of the total Spirit that has separated, as it were, into an individual spark of soul. The lower triangle refers to the personality, composed of thoughts, feelings, sensations and the subconscious realm.

There are numerous other ways of viewing the Tree of Life through its physical structure. Perhaps the most common division of the Tree is into three pillars. If you look at the Tree, you can see there is a 'left hand pillar' (with Binah at the top), a 'right hand pillar' (with Chockmah at the top) and a pillar between, which is called 'the middle pillar'. These three pillars correspond to the three energy channels said in Eastern mysticism to run through the body – the middle pillar relating to the spinal column. When we look at the Tree, we have to remember it is drawn as if we are looking at it overlaying an individual person. Thus in order to relate it to our own bodies, we have to imagine we turn around and back onto it. In other words, the left hand pillar corresponds to the right of your body, the right hand pillar to the left.

Just because there are 'left hand' and 'right hand' pillars on the Tree of Life, it does not mean that Kabbalistic system is in any way based on a patriarchal, polarised view of life. Some Kabbalistic writers have insisted on referring to the two pillars as 'male' and 'female', a dichotomy that is not part of the original map. Of course duality exists, but 'maleness' and 'femaleness' exist on both sides of the Tree. The Tree of Life is based on triangles. To see Hod and Netzach, for instance, as somehow opposed is incorrect. They form a continuum, which can only be truly realised and integrated when we introduce a third factor (or position) – in this case either Tiphareth or Yesod. To see Hod and

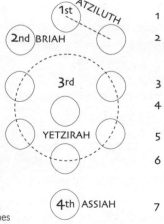

Diagram 8: Four worlds, seven planes

Netzach as somehow 'male' and 'female' is an even greater error – they are both 'male', 'female' and 'neither male nor female'. All Kabbalistic writings that suggest otherwise are predicated on a patriarchal world view that is at the very least outmoded and often directly harmful to the evolution of consciousness.

The Tree of Life has seven planes, which are roughly equivalent to the seven chakras or 'energy centres' of Eastern mysticism, although when we explore this in greater detail later in the book, you will see how the Kabbalistic version of these energy centres, while more complex than at first appears, adds a great deal to understanding their practical operation and meaning in our lives. The Tree is also divided into four separate 'worlds' whose names are indicated on diagram 8. We will also return to these Kabbalistic worlds later and explore how vitally important they are to a full understanding of the system.

If you look at the Tree of Life in detail you can see that, as well as the three triangles already discussed, there are very many more triangles. It is an interesting exercise to see just how many triangles you can spot on the Tree as the whole system is built upon a belief that everything manifests through trinities. When we start studying the physical structure of the Tree of Life, we also find hexagrams (six-pointed stars) and pentagrams (five-pointed stars), circles, crosses and other inter-esting shapes. The map has been developed over many centuries and it is not accident that all these shapes are included. Even if it was an accident, however, it would not change the value of the map, but would simply increase our wonder at its completeness and effectiveness as a map of consciousness.

It is important to remember that the map is not the territory. This may seem very obvious, but often when we start using maps of consciousness such as the Tree of Life we start confusing what the map shows us with our actual experience. Of primary importance is the experience, so the method with the Tree is to fit the map to your experience, not try and force your experience into the map. If you do the former, then the map can act as a guide to the territory of life, help you understand your consciousness and grow in the ways appropriate to your individual journey through life.

DEVELOPMENT OF THE SPHERES

To understand the whole Tree, composed as it is of eleven spheres and twenty-two connecting paths, we have to analyse the various aspects in detail. We will start with the spheres, because once you grasp the essential meaning of these, an understanding of the paths comes quite easily. It is important to remember, however, that when we analyse our consciousness in this way, it is essentially an artificial process. In reality, all the different aspects of us are part of one interconnected web of awareness. Our consciousness is then like a spider that moves around on this web, one minute in feelings, the next thinking about something, then lost in memories of the past, planning for the future, and so on.

The value in analysing our functions is twofold. Firstly, and most simply, it helps us to understand ourselves. Secondly, and perhaps more importantly, through analysing ourselves in this way, we move closer to the possibility of creating a harmonious synthesis of our various functions. When such a synthesis takes place, we become able to direct our lives with more clarity, and fulfil our creative and spiritual purpose.

As you read the following sections, look at the diagrams in this book to help you understand the description of the spheres.

THE REALM OF THE PERSONALITY

Malkuth: body and senses – increasing sensory awareness and connection, and realising the importance of the body and physical manifestation. Discovering the mysteries of the physical universe, the ability to discriminate, physical healing and overcoming inertia.

Yesod: subconscious – clearing out 'repressed' energies and the subsequent integration of these released energies into their correct sphere. Discovering the mysteries of the astral levels and lunar energies, to realise the workings of universal energies, and to connect with the divine plan.

Hod: thoughts, and Netzach: feelings – the balancing of thoughts and feelings, usually achieved through allowing the experience and expression of both. In Hod, discovering the mysteries of information systems and Mercurial energies, truthfulness, and greater ability to communicate clearly. In Netzach, discovering the mysteries of loving sexuality and Venusian energies, unselfishness, and increasing artistic creativity.

It is through Malkuth that you have your primary experience of the world. At any moment when you are aware of your environment, you are either seeing, hearing, smelling, tasting, touching or a combination of these. Life is not that simple, however, for when we use our senses to experience the world, or to express ourselves, we inevitably have thoughts and feelings about what is happening. Thoughts are attributed to Hod and feelings to Netzach. If we consider these three spheres on their own, we can say they are the spheres of the present time – all our 'here and now' awareness, wherever we are and whatever we are doing, is some combination of thinking, feeling and sensing.

All of our thinking, feeling and sensing is further affected and coloured by what has happened to us in the past. For instance, I may have had a friendly pet dog when I was a child whereas you were frequently chased and bitten by a savage dog that lived next door. Now when we are both confronted by a dog on the street, although it may be exactly the same dog, we will both see it differently, particularly in terms of our feelings about it. I might want to go up to it and stroke it, as I am seeing 'dog' as something kind and affectionate. You, however, might already be running away!

This example with a dog may seem rather trivial but is shows how we are affected by the past. It is as if we carry all our experiences from the past within us, and these experiences affect our current perceptions and awareness. If a woman was beaten by her father, it may well affect how she relates to adult men in later life, perhaps always being on guard for a potential attack. She may then be driven by an unconscious need for protection and be unable to make lasting and meaningful relationships with men. Similarly, if someone was over-mothered, perhaps she in turn unconsciously over-mothers her children. All of these incidents from the past that affect us, whether we are conscious of them or not, are attributed to Yesod on the Tree. Part of our work of growth and development in using the Tree of Life is to delve into our past and start releasing the energies that have been blocked there. We can then start to clarify and integrate our perception in the present moment, whatever we are doing.

As well as dealing with our 'stuff' from the past, as just described, the other main task of our work in this part of the Tree is to create a dynamic and living balance between our thinking, feeling and sensing functions. We relate to the world through these functions, so the clearer we are in understanding and using them, the more effective we become. Also, the more work we do to balance these spheres, the more able we are to receive energies coming from higher up the Tree (or deep inside ourselves).

There is no suggestion here that we have to be perfect in some way, or have to clear out all our old unconscious material. A true Kabbalist will welcome difficulties and problems, not try to transcend them, or gloss over them, but be willing to step right in and work with them, in so doing creating a reality in which they can be transformed into opportunities for growth and development. The first step in this process is almost always acceptance – when we truly accept what is, then we are in the right place to see what we may need to change.

THE REALM OF THE SOUL

Tiphareth: the centred self, 'the silent witness' – the building of a strong centre for the integration of our everyday relations with the world, and strengthening the connection to deeper, inner energies that may then manifest in our lives. Discovering the mysteries of beauty and harmony, solar energies, centred consciousness, and stimulating the energy of soul manifesting in life.

Geburah: the archetype of Will and Power, and Chesed: the archetype of Love and Awareness – the realisation of the central importance of the interplay of these archetypes in the unfolding of soul energy on earth. In Geburah discovering the mysteries of power and the use of Martian energies; purposeful change; awakening inner and outer strength. In Chesed discovering the mysteries of love and the use of Jupiterian energies; peace and love awakened; stimulating the forces of abundance.

The sphere at the centre of the Tree, Tiphareth, is the link between the lower personality spheres and the higher transpersonal spheres on the Tree. The soul, by analogy, can then said to be a similar link between the personality and the Spirit. Tiphareth is usually described as being the 'centre' or the 'I', the little self (with a small 's') that is our individual spark of the bigger Self (with a capital 'S') at the top of the Tree. From the point of view of the personality, Tiphareth is just this. As the 'I', Tiphareth can be understood to be that part of us that is *more than* body, feelings, thoughts or any combination of these.

If 'I' say that I have a feeling, I have a thought, I have a sensation, then the 'I' that has these things is Tiphareth. Instead of being a player in the drama of life, I can become the director. This is not to become remote and aloof, but rather to be a director who is willing to play a part, to connect with feelings and thoughts and really engage in the world. Kabbalistic work is not only about achieving deeper or higher states of consciousness in which we dis-attach from the mundane; it is equally about bringing this awareness to play in our everyday life.

When we become more centred in ourselves, we become more in control of our own destiny, and our own ability to stay in touch with the unfolding of the soul's individual purpose. We experience this through the archetypes of Love and Will as represented on the Tree by Chesed and Geburah. The interplay between these archetypes sets up issues and events in our lives through which we can realise our own inner divinity. We must not confuse these archetypes with the soul, but rather see them as the vehicles for its manifestation in the same way as the lower spheres on the Tree are seen as the vehicles of the personality.

THE BRIDGE BETWEEN SOUL AND SPIRIT

Daath: knowledge – discovering the mysteries of the shadow side of existence, the inner depths explored, leading to knowledge of the rainbow bridge. Shifting the centre of attention, speaking truth and walking in the way of Spirit within and between the worlds.

As no paths exist that cross the Abyss between the Spirit and Soul triangles on the Tree of Life, there are no attributions to the physical here, which suggests its existence is beyond the realm of human concern. There are certain conditions under which new paths connecting the surrounding spheres to Daath open up, however. One of the tasks facing practising Kabbalists today is the discovery of the attributions to correspond with these new paths. Currently, the only one of these paths that seems to have a fairly certain correspondence is the path from Daath to Binah, which is attributed to the asteroid Chiron, the Wounded Healer.

One thing we know about the mysterious 'non-existent' paths is that they all involve, in some way or another, crossing the Abyss. The pathless path from Binah to Chesed goes right across the Abyss. To understand what we mean by the Abyss, it is useful to consider some of the meanings for this word found in the *Oxford English Dictionary*. Etymologically, *abyss* comes from a Greek word meaning bottomless, or the deep. The primary two meanings then given are:

1. The great deep, the primal chaos; the bowels of the earth, the supposed cavity of the lower world; the infernal pit.

2. A bottomless gulf; any unfathomable or apparently unfathom-

able cavity or void space; a profound gulf, chasm, or void extending beneath.

From a Kabbalistic perspective, the most commonly used metaphor for the Abyss is a wasteland or desert. It is said, concerning this wasteland, that our only chance of passing through it is to learn to turn off our inner dialogue. Through turning off the six voices of the inner dialogue we are able to irrigate this desert through opening up and establishing the four new paths. You will discover how to practise this in a later chapter.

Turning off the inner dialogue does not mean to leave your body and the earth (although you do have that choice), it means *to be silent within* the body and the earth. This is what Carlos Castaneda, anthropologist and shaman's apprentice, calls stopping the world. In fact, there are many similarities between shamanic teachings and the more shamanic aspects of the practical Kabbalah, not least in the importance of achieving true inner silence. From our practical Kabbalistic viewpoint, there is no more important practice than this. Inner silence brings with it not just the potential of access to other realms of being but, perhaps most importantly while we are incarnated in our earthly form, the firm opening of the heart, the true centre of human consciousness.

PRACTICE

• Meditation for inner peace

This practice can help you to find inner peace and certainty, and to balance yourself, particularly at times of disturbance or low energy. It can also be used at any time as the first step – a tuning in, so to speak – to precede any other Kabbalistic or inner work you may be undertaking. Indeed, so powerful is this simple meditation, it cannot really be over-used and the benefits of performing it regularly cannot be overstated. It is a necessary step towards fully turning off your inner dialogue, which will be studied in a later chapter.

Find a comfortable posture in which you are relaxed but not so relaxed that you are liable to fall asleep. Pay attention to your breathing, not forcing it, simply watching the rhythmic flow in and out of your body at its natural pace.

After several minutes of simply sitting still and focusing your attention on your breathing, affirm silently to yourself: 'My body is at peace.'

Be aware of any sensations in your body – do not try to suppress them in any way, but do not become attached to them, either. Simply watch them pass through your consciousness. Then affirm silently: 'My emotions and feelings are at peace.' Again, do not try to suppress any emotions that arise, simply be aware of them and let them pass.

Then affirm silently: 'My thoughts are at peace.' Let any thoughts that arise be noted, but do not become attached to them. Spend a few minutes now watching sensations, emotions, feelings, thoughts, images, insights or anything else that comes into your consciousness. Observe these events without getting caught up or carried away by them.

Visualise your being as perfectly silent and at peace in a perfectly silent and peaceful world.

Affirm silently to yourself: 'I have sensations, emotions, feelings, thoughts, but I, as an individual spark of the Self, am eternally at peace and at one with the universal rhythm.'

Realise the truth of this statement.

THE REALM OF THE SPIRIT

Binah: Spiritual Love – discovering the mysteries of silence and secrecy, increasing understanding, and realising that all things are united.

Chockmah: Spiritual Purpose – discovering the mysteries of purpose and initiative, increasing wisdom, and realising the universal plan as manifest through the world.

Kether: the Divine Self – discovering the mysteries of unity and union, the inner quest and the amplification of spiritual energy and the revelation of divine inspiration.

The spheres above Geburah and Chesed are divided from the lower Tree by the Abyss, which represents the gulf between phenomenal reality and true spiritual connection. The spheres above the Abyss represent levels or states of awareness that some may only experience directly during the deepest, most meaningful moments in our life, sometimes called 'peak' experiences, when we feel at one with nature and all of life, when we feel Joy, Truth, Beauty and other qualities that can be attributed to the Spirit, or the deepest connection within us. Fortunately for us, however, we can also experience these qualities in our everyday world, for Tiphareth also acts as a channel so these energies 'come through' into our waking, ordinary reality.

Every time it feels good to be alive, every time you stop and hear a bird sing and feel wonder, or watch a child playing and feel moved, every time you experience clarity and insight where you know what is the 'right' thing for you to do, or those times when you become so immersed in movement, dance or physical activity that you seemingly lose all other awareness and simply tune into the physical world, all these times are direct experiences of the transpersonal realms represented by these spheres. We may not be in some pure, transcendent state where we experience unadulterated peace, for instance, but if we simply stop for a moment and experience peace in an everyday act it is no less real or meaningful. One of the main aims of all Kabbalistic work, as stressed throughout this book, is to manifest spiritual reality in the everyday world.

PATHS TO CONNECTION

As already described, many of the spheres are connected to others by paths. These paths represent the subjective understanding and relationship possible when a connection is made between two particular spheres. As an example, consider Malkuth and Netzach. Malkuth relates to the body and Netzach to the feelings, so the path between them shows the relationship between feelings and body. It is a commonly held psychological belief, borne out by the experience of therapists who work directly with body energies, that when we repress different emotions and feelings, aspects of their energy become held or deposited in the muscles and tissues of the body.

From this viewpoint, it is possible to deduce two ways to working to release these withheld feelings. We may find ways to access directly the memories associated with the feelings involved, then allow ourselves to re-experience them. This will then release some of the holding in the physical body. Alternatively, we may work directly on the body to release what is held there, thereby causing a release of the repressed feelings involved. The first way is working with this path from Netzach down through to Malkuth; the second way is working up the path from Malkuth towards Netzach.

Another way of working directly with the connections between the spheres is through what is often called 'pathworking'. We will look into this more deeply in Chapter 5. There are many ways of pathworking. One of the commonest is to imagine oneself passing through a door that leads to one of the paths, using the associated symbols, including the Hebrew letters, placed prominently on the door, to guide one into the appropriate imagery. We could plan a journey to Tiphareth, for instance, starting in Malkuth, travelling the path to Tiphareth from Hod. It is important when doing this work to return back to the ground (Malkuth) after each pathworking, partly so that the energy can be grounded, partly so the practitioner does not become 'spaced out'.

As with the spheres, all the paths have numerous correspondences associated with them – images, symbols and ideas of all kinds that help describe the energies involved with that path. One of the most commonly used symbol systems associated with the path is the Tarot cards, which you will also explore later in this book. As an example, among many other correspondences, the path between Netzach and Malkuth is associated with the Hebrew letter Qoph (meaning 'back of the head'), the moon, dogs howling at the moon, menstruation, the beetle, Pisces, and the dark night of the soul. Many of these symbols will be found on the Tarot card 'The Moon' that relates to this path. The Tarot cards therefore can be seen – and used – as compendiums of associated symbols for the paths. It is no coincidence that there are twenty-two trumps in the Tarot so they relate to the twenty-two connecting paths on the Tree.

The ten spheres on the Tree of Life (excluding Daath) are sometimes referred to as the first ten 'paths', then the other twenty-two paths that connect the spheres are called the eleventh to thirty-second paths. If you look at diagram 30 (page 209) you will see how these paths are numbered on the Tree. As well as being representations of the connections between the spheres, the connecting paths are also given a special name and correspondence, thus:

Path	Connecting spheres and meaning	
11th	1–2	scintillating path, facing the creator
12th	1–3	transparent path, seeing of visions
13th	1–6	uniting path, realising spiritual truth
14th	2–3	illuminating path, fundamental holiness
15th	2–6	constituting path, substance of creation
16th	2–4	eternal path, pleasure of paradise
17th	3–6	disposing path, foundation of faith
18th	3–5	influential path, understanding causality
19th	4–5	activating path, the experience of blessings
20th	4–6	intelligent path, knowledge of existence
21st	4–7	conciliatory path, transmitting divine influence

22nd	5–6	faithful path, increasing spiritual virtue
23rd	5–8	stable path, increasing consistency
24th	6–7	imaginative path, renewal and change
25th	6–9	tentative path, the alchemical processes
26th	6–8	renovating path, life force in action
27th	7–8	exciting path, the nature of existence
28th	7–9	admiral path, the formation of the body
29th	7–10	corporeal path, the formation of the body
30th	8–9	collecting path, celestial arts and astrology
31st	8–10	perpetual path, regulating the creation
32nd	9–10	administrative path, directing life energies

It is well worth comparing these brief, suggestive descriptions with the paths and the spheres they connect. They can greatly aid our understanding not only of the Tree of Life map, but also of the connections within ourselves between the differing states of consciousness attributed to the spheres.

PATHS FOR ALL USES

As the paths are representations of the subjective connections between the states of awareness shown in the spheres, whenever and however we use the Tree, we inevitably travel the paths. It is wise Kabbalistic practice to remember this, and to realise that there is nothing static suggested by the Tree, but that it is a diagrammatic representation of a constantly evolving and changing system. It is also worth guarding against the possibility of getting so caught up in travelling the paths that the point of the work is missed. Whenever we travel on the Tree, our goal is increased self-awareness, integration of the differing aspects of ourselves, and the full and clear manifestation of this work in the everyday, physical world. All paths, in true Kabbalistic practice, lead back to Malkuth, the world and the physical body.

Different Kabbalists, whether from different schools of practice or simply because they are individuals, use the Tree for different purposes. It is possible to work only with the bottom part of the Tree and use it as a guide to personal self-development. It is equally possible to work primarily with the deeper energies represented by the top part of the Tree, as a method towards spiritual enlightenment. Some people use the Tree to guide their rituals, ceremonies and group practices whereas other people avoid groups at all costs. It is truly wonderful that the Tree can be used in so many different ways and be personalised for individual uses. It is important also, however, to honour the tradition of the system that has been built up over many centuries of practice and experience. If you individualise your Tree so much that it no longer relates to other people's Trees, that is fine for you alone, but removes the possibility of relating your work to others. The Tree is designed so that we can relate our experiences. We do not live in isolation (except those of us reading this book who are hermits in inaccessible caves!). We live in a world where we are in constant relationship with all other beings, human and otherwise. Our life is enhanced when we use the Tree to aid rather than hinder this contact and relating.

All the different approaches and ways of working with the Tree of Life can enrich our lives through clearing out past conditioning, traumas and controls, dynamically balancing growth in the present, and through making a link to each individual's sense of purpose and meaning. The Tree of Life is a complete map of consciousness and it works best when it is used in its entirety. It is also a holistic model, however, and through using any part of it we are inevitably linked to the whole, for each part, each path and each sphere is not only connected into the whole scheme, but each part itself, while undeniably only a part, nevertheless includes the whole.

PRACTICAL CORRESPONDENCES

If you consider the correspondences to the spheres again, you can see that you have already met many different ones. For instance, you have learnt that Hod corresponds to the number eight, the thinking function, and is an aspect of the personality. We can now start connecting it to other 'universal' correspondences, for instance gods and goddesses primarily involved with the mind, thought and communication (for it is through words, which are in a sense spoken thoughts, that we primarily communicate). Such deities include Hermes (Greek), Thoth (Egyptian) and Mercury (Roman). A planet is associated with each sphere, so here we can fairly clearly attribute Mercury, the planet of communication. Spells, words of power and the element of air will correspond because of their association with the mind.

Many other items are traditionally attributed to each sphere, so in the case of Hod we find the colour orange, the vision of splendour, the precious stone opal, the perfume storax, the animal jackal, the herbs fennel and marjoram, the hazel tree and so on. See if you can work out why some of these items should be said to correspond to Hod. In doing this, you will actually be engaging Hod (thoughts) to do it! With all correspondences, the most important thing is to make your own connections. So, for instance, if in your experience the willow tree and a goldfish are more appropriate correspondences than the hazel tree and jackal, then these will be your personal correspondences for working in the sphere of the mind, Hod.

The whole point of using correspondences is to be able to relate your experience into the Tree, then see the relationship of this with the whole Tree. In this sense, any correspondence is appropriate so long as it works for you, but it is also useful to stretch yourself to see why certain correspondences have a more 'universal' application to the spheres. The opal is attributed to Hod, for instance, because it has the varied colours that correspond to Mercury, and the jackal because in the ancient world it was considered sacred to Mercury. In our modern world, however, we may not have much contact with jackals, and may think, for instance, that a dog is a better correspondence because of its mercurial nature.

By now you have probably explored Appendix 4 where there are detailed tables of correspondences for all the spheres and paths, The more correspondences we can connect to the Tree of Life, the more alive the system becomes and the more we are able to relate all our experiences of life – whatever they are and however they manifest – to our total body of knowledge and understanding. It is quite amazing how using the Tree of Life in this way appears to increase our ability to integrate the different aspects of our being.

Do not try to memorise any correspondences because they will lose their meaning. Much better to look at them with a spirit of inquiry, to try to understand why a certain idea, object, being, practice or whatever is attributed to that particular sphere or path. The more you do this the more the correspondences will come to life for you. If someone tells you, for instance, that a rabbit corresponds to Malkuth it is a very different experience than if you work it out for yourself. Incidentally, while a rabbit may correspond to Malkuth for many people, it will not be so for everyone. Another important aspect of not learning corre-spondences by rote, therefore, is that you can then start to find particular correspondences that work especially well for you. For some people, for instance, an earthworm is a much better Malkuth attribute than a rabbit.

That said, there are a few special correspondences that are worth, if not memorising, then at least becoming very familiar with. They will help you make connections between different spheres and paths and are:

- the Hebrew letters, their English equivalent and numerical value
- the physical structure and inner body components
- the celestial attributes
- the Tarot attributions.

3

WORLDS OF CREATION AND THE SACRED ALPHABET

Kabbalah is . . . the repository . . . of the mysteries hidden since the beginning of time. The diversity is only the expression of the infinite 'richness' of the one truth and in no way affects its transcendent and immutable unity.
Leo Schaya (*The Universal Meaning of the Kabbalah*)

The first sentence of Genesis in the Bible can be transliterated from Hebrew as 'Berashith Bera Elohim Ath Ha Shamain Va Ath Ha Aretz'. This can be very roughly translated as 'In the beginning God created the heaven and earth'. Once we start looking at these first words of Genesis from a Kabbalistic viewpoint, however, we find they contain a lot more than is apparent at first sight. As you learned in Chapter 1, the words in the first four books of the Bible are attributed to Moses, writing under divine inspiration, so it is not surprising to find much more hidden within these simple words. There are many different ways to 'read' these words Kabbalistically, one version being: 'Out of the universe the light of the sun brought the duality of existence into manifestation, expressing the Spirit through male and female principles. The Mother–Father Deity expressed itself through the cosmic principles represented by the first nine spheres of the Tree of Life and heaven and earth were created.'

If we look at this in more detail we can start to understand how Kabbalah sheds light on our understanding of this creation myth. The first word of the sentence in Hebrew is Berashith, 'In the beginning'. All Hebrew letters have a special meaning attributed to them, and a number. We will look at the numbers in more detail later, but for now let us consider the meaning of the letters in Berashith, or BRAShIT.

Beth	= a house or container (the universe)
Resh	= the sun
Aleph	= the beginning, duality – positive and negative
Shin	= Spirit
Yod	= male principle
Teth	= female principle

Put this together and we have: 'Out of the universe the light of the sun brought the duality of existence into manifestation, expressing the Spirit through the male and female principles.'

Of course, there are many other ways of putting these words together, creating different nuances of meaning. Other possibilities might include: 'the magician with the secret of the universe created the sun in the beginning to bring the Spirit of life through the secret gate of initiation into the manifest universe'; or 'the Spirit of God expressed the dual principle of life and death through cosmic manifestation; from this dual principle the first nine spheres of existence were created'. It is not that there is a right or wrong way to understand this word Berashith, more that each individual Kabbalist can come to his or her own understanding of the meaning, which also may well differ at different times.

If we now consider the word 'Elohim', usually translated as 'God', we find a very interesting mystery. The word ALHIM in Hebrew is composed of a feminine singular ALH with IM, which is a masculine plural, added. The word thus expresses the uniting of male and female principles. This is why I prefer to use the term 'the Mother–Father Deity', for in chapter 1 of Genesis, when the word 'Elohim' is used, this is closer to what is intended. It is only in chapter 2 of Genesis, after the creation is fully manifest, that IHVH, Jehovah, is used for 'God'. We will be looking in much more detail at this name of 'God' later.

Even the word ATh in Hebrew, composed as it is of two letters Aleph and Teth, and simply translated as 'the', contains a mystery. The letter Aleph is the first Hebrew letter, numbered 1, as is Kether, the first sphere on the Tree of Life. The letter Teth is the ninth Hebrew letter, numbered 9, as is Yesod, the ninth sphere on the Tree. Thus the simple word 'ATh' can be taken to represent the whole Tree minus the final manifestation in Malkuth, when the world itself is formed. This has led some scholars to believe that Genesis refers only to creation in potential. They say Exodus is concerned with the 'actual' manifestation, after Malkuth is created and when the Mother–Father Deity has formed itself into IHVH, Jehovah, a God with a special message for humankind.

So the creation of the universe as understood Kabbalistically is not about a single male God creating everything, but rather a complex unfolding of principles and energies originating from a source that includes both 'male' and 'female' energies. It is worth stressing that this interpretation is not the product of some strange, esoteric fantasy, but is very closely based on the original Hebrew text. Let us read it once more: 'Out of the universe the light of the sun brought the duality of existence into manifestation, expressing the Spirit through male and female principles. The Mother–Father Deity expressed itself through the cosmic principles represented by the first nine spheres of the Tree of Life and heaven and earth were created.'

To a Kabbalist, the Mother–Father Deity is seen as pure immanence, present in everything, manifest and unmanifest. When this Deity created the manifest universe, through the words 'let there be light', it was creating a duality – for if there is light then implicitly there is also dark, and it was through this duality that everything else could come into being. The Mother–Father Deity is present in both the light and the dark, in the unmanifest and the manifest, in everything at all times. The creation was an act of love, for the purpose of this original division was so that each part or polarity could realise itself as divine through recombining with the opposite polarity. All opposites are in harmonious balance with each other and whenever they unite they mirror the original creation of the universe.

Everything in Kabbalah is seen, however, in terms of trinities rather than dualities. The Mother–Father Deity is simultaneously Female and Male and the creation is the Child, thus creating a threesome. When Christians talk of the Father, Son and Holy Spirit they are referring to the same trinity, for the Hebrew word for 'holy spirit' is RUACH, which is a feminine noun. Thus the Trinity is Father, Child and Mother. This is also expressed in the Gnostic Deity name, IAO, where I is the male principle, O the female principle and A their offspring. The letters I and O are interestingly suggestive of male and female. In Kabbalah the female principle of the Deity is very important and is also known as Shekhinah, of which you will be learning more in a later chapter. Although the Jewish religion (and its Christian offshoot) may have become patriarchal in its current form, its secret inner teachings, as expressed through Kabbalah, are equally inclusive of both male and female.

THE SACRED ALPHABET

All alphabets are sacred to those who use them to communicate with other people. To me the English alphabet is very sacred – without it I could not write this book and share with you my understanding of Kabbalah. Without it I could not tell my loved ones how I feel about them. Beyond this 'mundane sacredness', however, certain alphabets have become known as particularly sacred because in their letters we find secret correspondences and meanings that add much to our understanding of ourselves and our universe. Sanskrit is an example of such a language from the East, Hebrew an example from the West. As we have already seen, to understand creation as described in Genesis we need a knowledge of the inner, 'secret' meaning of the Hebrew alphabet. Indeed, some Kabbalists believe that the books of the Old Testament written by Moses are all in code and cannot be interpreted unless this code is cracked.

Each Hebrew letter has a specific meaning and a number attributed to it. Each letter is a symbolic representation of a cosmic principle. The letter Aleph, the first letter of the Hebrew alphabet, is given – not surprisingly – the number 1. It is therefore a representation of the principle of Unity. Its specific meaning is 'ox'. At first sight this may seem peculiar, but the meanings are themselves suggestive rather than direct. Many ancient cultures believed that the universe originated from the belly of a cow or an ox-like creature. For example, in Egyptian mythology the goddess Ta-urt is represented by a hippopotamus and is the mother of all cycles of creation. She is, incidentally, the originator of the Tarot cards (Ta-urt = Tarot). So by giving the letter Aleph the meaning of 'ox', the suggestion is of the originator, that place from where all else comes. An ox may also suggest strength and purpose, other attributes relevant to the source of all creation.

It was believed by many ancient philosophers, Plato for instance, that the whole universe is based upon numbers. Modern physicists believe the same thing. A number can then be seen as a symbol that conveys an idea. By linking these numbers with the Hebrew alphabet, we have a compendium of understanding that can allow us to comprehend more clearly the universe and our place within it.

There are twenty-two letters in the Hebrew alphabet and they are related to the twenty-two paths on the Tree of Life. They represent the different states of consciousness that are created when the cosmic principles represented by the spheres are connected through human awareness. The letters then represent the essence or principle behind these connections. Beth, the second letter of the Hebrew alphabet, means 'house', but more than this it represents the archetype of all containers, all 'housings' from obvious physical dwellings through to the boundary of the whole of creation. This is why it is the first letter in the first word, Berashith, in the Bible, meaning, as we have learned, 'in the beginning'.

Three of the Hebrew letters correspond to the elements of air, water and fire – Aleph, Mem and Shin. They are known as the 'mother letters' and it is said all the other letters originate from them. Similarly, in esoteric teachings, it is said everything originates from various combinations of these three elements, air, water and fire. This includes, of course, the fourth element the earth. These three letters also correspond to the head (fire), chest (air) and belly (water) of a human being.

From these three mother letters arise seven 'double letters' representing the manifestation of duality. These letters (Beth, Gimel, Daleth, Kaph, Pe, Resh and Tau) also correspond to the seven directions (above, below, east, west, north, south and centre) and they have a relationship with the seven 'planets' of the ancients (Mercury, Moon, Venus, Jupiter, Mars, Sun and Saturn). In a human being they relate to the seven openings in the head – the two eyes, two ears, two nostrils and mouth. There are twelve remaining letters (He, Vau, Zain, Cheth, Teth, Yod, Lamed, Nun, Samekh, Ayin, Tzaddi and Qoph), which are called the single or simple letters. They correspond to the twelve signs of the zodiac. In the human being they correspond to sight, hearing, smell, speech, taste, sex, work, movement, anger, humour, imagination and sleep.

As we can now see, the twenty-two letters of the Hebrew alphabet are more than simple representations of sounds. T-H-E in English is simply a representation of the sounds that make up a word for the definite article. In Hebrew the two letters Aleph and Teth (that make up the Hebrew word for 'the', ATh) have correspondences that would lead to a deeper understanding of the word represented by these letters. This was described earlier, Aleph being the first letter and Teth the ninth, thus representing the nine archetypes of all existence that come into manifestation in 10, Malkuth. The number 10 in Hebrew is the letter Yod, which as well as 'hand' also means 'seed', the seed out of which all else grows.

Words of the same numerical value are considered to be explanatory of each other, and the art of understanding these relationships is called Gematria, the basis of Kabbalistic numerology. Appendix 2 shows the sacred Hebrew alphabet with its primary meaning and numerical equivalents. For instance, the Hebrew word for love is AHBH. A=1, H=5, B=2 and H=5, so the numerical value of this word is 13. The Hebrew word for Unity is AChD. A=1, Ch=8 and D=4, so the numerical value of this word is also 13. Therefore, through Gematria, we can say that Love and Unity are equivalent!

Another Hebrew word for unity is ALP: A=1, L=30 and P=80, a total of 111. The word APL also adds to 111 and means darkness, as does the word ASN (A=1, S=60, N=50), which means sudden death. At first sight it may seem difficult to relate unity, sudden death and darkness together, but the key to such understanding can always be found through meditation. There will be various ways of interpreting this relationship. The numerical identity between these three words may mean, for instance, that individual consciousness is annihilated in Unity and at the threshold of Unity there is darkness.

Gematria may seem like nonsense at first sight. If you think of Zen koans they may also initially seem like nonsense: silly stories about the sound of one hand clapping, for example. Their intention, however, is to transcend ordinary reality and create a mystical level of consciousness where insights about oneself and the universe can occur. The same is true of Gematria, and the excitement of making a personally meaningful connection between two or more apparently disconnected words or phrases has to be experienced to be understood.

GEMATRIA IN PRACTICE

Consider now some practical applications of Gematria that may bring it alive for you and suggest its deep value for your Kabbalistic practice. Gematria can be a complex business but the more you get into it, the more you find the underlying numerical structure of the universe reveals itself! A good way to get used to using Gematria is to learn the numerical value of the letters, then to be adding up things all over the place – the name of a road you walk down, someone you meet with a significance to you, the name of your breakfast cereal, and so on! This gives you practice and makes you familiar with the system.

The Kabbalistic way of using numerology is to find the numerical value of the name or word under investigation and then to factorise the numbers. You can find the numerical value of letters in the correspondence tables in Appendix 4. We do not do exoteric numerology where you add the numbers up and reduce them (where e.g. Will might be $6+10+30+30 = 76 = 13 = 4$). Factorisation means you break each number down to its factors: so, for example, Will is 76 which is 38×2, 19×4 (or $19 \times 2 \times 2$). When you get to a prime number (19 in this case) you cannot factorise it, so the prime numbers have particular significance, which you can really only learn through experience. Working with the numbers that you find through factorisation offers much deeper insight into the suggestive meaning of words and their numerical equivalents. The key is not to try to be 'scientifically accurate', whatever that might mean, but to allow your intuition to come into play and look for suggestive connections.

As an exercise, you might like to use Gematria to understand more about your own name. Using the techniques described above, find the numerical value of your name then, referring to the correspondence tables and your pre-existing knowledge of the Tree of Life and other esoteric subjects, see if you can understand something of the deeper meaning of this number. Don't worry if you do not get very far at this stage. Not only will your understanding of this number increase as your Kabbalistic knowledge increases, you'll find the meaning you divine from the number of your name will change in significance as you develop and grow in insight and initiation.

By way of example, I'll analyse the name 'Marilyn'. Marilyn (40+1+200+10+30+10+50) is 341, which factorises into two prime numbers, 31 and 11. Prime numbers, as mentioned, can be the most difficult to understand but in this instance before we get that far, we have an immediate connection. Thus 341 is the sum of the three mother letters, Aleph, Mem and Shin, which correspond to the head, chest and pelvis, or air, water and fire, so is a lovely balanced number inclusive of all levels (through manifesting into our world of earth). So we can immediately deduce that Marilyn 341 brings together the elements and manifests their deepest source.

Looking at the factors 31×11: 10 is the end of a cycle (10 spheres etc.) so 11 is the beginning of the next cycle, so 11 is considered to be the prime number of magic, energy tending to change. Then 31 is AL and LA , 'god' and 'not', the twin poles of the basic polarity of existence itself. AL is the infinitely small centre always expanding outwards to fill the circle; LA is the infinitely large circle always contracting inwards towards the centre, and the interplay of these two forces creates the physical universe as we experience it. So Marilyn (341) is the magic of the pulsing energy of existence!

Gematria, as this example shows, is about making all the connections you can from any source, then using these to creatively and intuitively reach your own meaning and understanding. There could be many others ways of analysing Marilyn, for instance.

THE GARDEN OF EDEN

One of the most fascinating myths in the Bible is that of the Garden of Eden, some wonderful place where, according to ordinary interpretation, something went wrong that led to the banishment of humankind from its splendours. In the patriarchal versions of this myth, the fault is placed at the feet of the woman involved – if only Eve had not eaten of that apple we would somehow all still be in this state of bliss. As you may have already guessed, this is not the Kabbalistic view.

Kabbalists believe that when the world was originally created, the Tree of Life and all that it represents was itself the Garden of Eden. This initial Tree, therefore, represented by the perfect existence in the garden, does not include within itself the knowledge of duality.

Everything is at one. The creatures who exist in this garden, represented by Adam and Eve, the son and the daughter, have not awakened to the realisation that something else exists beyond their perfect garden. They do not realise their separation and difference from one another. From the beginning, however, there was a shadow side to this Tree, represented by the Tree of Knowledge of Good and Evil.

One day, through the direct intervention of the Mother–Father Deity, Adam and Eve realised that they were different beings, clothed with a different form, one male, the other female. As soon as they realised this, duality was brought into the garden and the Tree of Knowledge of Good and Evil became part of their reality. Once they had awoken in this way, the Deity placed an Abyss between itself and its creation. This division was formed so that the created beings could experience being separate, existing in duality. In this separate existence they had the chance of reuniting, of bringing their two 'halves' together into union through an act of love, thus restoring or repairing the original unity. This way they could again realise their essential unity with the Deity and all of creation, transcending their separate existence in the world of duality. We all still have this opportunity, the chance of experiencing our own inner divinity. We can only bridge this Abyss and realise our true selves through love, for it is for the sake of love that we were divided in the first place.

This version of the 'fall' is very different from that often perpetuated, in which we all somehow carry an 'original sin' through which we are doomed unless saved by divine intervention. Rather than 'original sin', Kabbalists believe we have 'original grace' and it is through this grace we can come to know ourselves. We can experience this grace only in love, for it is through love that the Deity created the universe. When we experience true Love we are aligning ourselves with the Deity and realising our own innate divinity.

CREATION MYTHOLOGY

In the following Kabbalistic exegesis, I have followed the story as presented in Chapter 1 of the King James Version of the Bible, just updating some of the language and editing out the bits not relevant at the moment. Where it described the deity involved as 'God' I have replaced this with 'Deity' to become more neutral, and to be closer to the original. I am, of course, referring to the Mother–Father Deity as already discussed.

> *First Day of Creation: And Deity said, Let there be light: and there was light. And Deity saw the light, that it was good: and Deity divided the light from the darkness. And Deity called the light Day, and the darkness was called Night.*

The Supernal Triad, the Deity (Kether) creates Chockmah (light) and Binah (darkness).

> *Second Day of Creation: And Deity said, let there be a firmament in the midst of the waters, and let it divide the waters from the waters. And Deity made the firmament, and divided the waters which were under the firmament from the waters which were above the firmament.*

The firmament in the midst of the waters, the Abyss, dividing the Supernals from the next triangle on the Tree. The Second Triad is created.

> *Third Day of Creation: And Deity said, let the dry land appear. And Deity called the dry land Earth; and the gathering of the waters he called Seas. And Deity said, Let the earth bring forth grass, the herb yielding seed, and the fruit tree yielding fruit . . . each thing bringing forth its own seed.*

Creation of the 'earth', in this sense, the Third Triad, the manifest 'form' of the previous two triads.

> *Fourth Day of Creation: And Deity said, let there be lights in the firmament of the heaven to divide the day from the night; and let there be signs, and for seasons, and for days, and years. And Deity made two great lights; the greater light to rule the day, and the lesser light to rule the night; he made the stars also.*

The sun and the moon and the stars are created, bodies of 'fire' relating here to the first world of Atziluth (Fire).

> *Fifth Day of Creation: Deity said, Let the waters bring forth abundantly the moving creature that has life, and fowl that may fly above the earth. And Deity created great whales, and every living creature in the waters, and every winged fowl after his kind.*

Deity creates the second world of Briah (Water) (watery animal life) and the third world of Yetzirah (Air) (airy animal life).

Sixth Day of Creation: And Deity said, Let the earth bring forth cattle and creeping things, and the beasts of the earth.

The creation of the fourth world of Assiah (Earth), Malkuth and animals of the earth.

Still on the 'sixth day', now that the earth has been created, Deity continues:

Let us make humans in our image, after our likeness: and let them have dominion over the fishes of the sea, and over the birds of the air, and over the animals, and over all the earth, and over every thing that moves upon the earth.

Seventh Day of Creation: The whole Tree in the four worlds having been created, Deity has a day off!

PRACTICE

• Day of rest

We all need 'seventh days', days of rest, times when we devote a whole chunk of time and space to just do what we need to do to rest and recuperate from the demands of a life in the busy, modern world. Your task is to create a complete day of rest for yourself, doing just what you want for the day: for example, to visit a gallery, tend to the garden, read a book, relax in a spa, or simply lounge about doing nothing.

Reflect on and write in your Kabbalistic journal (if you are keeping one) how you got on with this activity, how well you managed it, and what kinds of resistance might have come up for you. Some people initially judge this exercise as too simple or even banal, but I assure you it has a greater depth than at first appears.

CREATING THE TREE OF LIFE

We have looked so far at a Kabbalistic theory of the creation of the world. There are other theories in Kabbalah, some similar, some quite different, apart from numerous creation theories in other esoteric systems. One of the most valuable aspects of Kabbalah, however, is that we do not have to 'believe' anything. Indeed, it is always stressed that our experience is of much more importance. Naturally we cannot have an experience of 'the creation' – if we were there we do not remember it! What we can do, however, is relate our experience of the world to the various theories and see what fits for us. Then, whatever theory we hold, it is based on our experience rather than something simply told to us. For me the above theory of creation feels good, but I do not 'believe' it is true. I am simply holding it as my current belief which, if my experience and understanding changes, I am quite happy to change. If this happens, however, I would not have to let go of Kabbalah, for all theories can be related to the Tree of Life, which is what makes it such a wonderfully universal system.

If we now consider the creation or formation of the actual Tree of Life itself, we find there is a description of this which, albeit still a theory, is based on numbers, so is a totally non-sectarian and non-biased approach. In following this description of the creation of the Tree of Life, based on the work of Aleister Crowley, we find we also come to a greater understanding of the actual creation of the universe.

The formation of the Tree of Life proceeds from Kether to Malkuth, following the path of the lightning flash. Above the Tree there are sometimes drawn three veils, which represent the absence of anything concrete. Kabbalists say this area above the Tree is veiled because this is as far as human knowledge and understanding can reach. It takes a long time to achieve a full understanding of this side of the veils, so we are advised to concentrate our efforts on understanding the manifest Tree, and not bother ourselves unduly about what may come after (or before, depending upon how you look at it). If we achieve a true experience and understanding of Kether we are united with the Mother–Father Deity. This is already an accomplishment so beyond our ordinary consciousness that to worry about what might come next seems rather foolish.

The first step in the formation of the Tree is the creation of Kether. A point appears that has neither parts nor magnitude, only position. It is positive, it exists, yet it is completely undefinable. It is the number 1, which is indivisible, and incapable of multiplication or division by itself.

It has a position but no other attributes. This does not mean much unless there is another position with which to compare it. This can only be created through the formation of a second point, which then forms (between the two points) a line. The only way the original 1 of Kether can become more is through duplication of itself (by reflection). The second point, Chockmah, is given the number 2 and corresponds to the will or purpose of the original point to duplicate itself.

All we have so far are two points at an indeterminable distance from each other. In order to discriminate between them there has to be a third point, Binah, the number 3. Three points can create a surface, a triangle. Now we are able to define any of these points in terms of its position relative to the other two. Thus an awareness (spiritual awareness) is born. Love is attributed to this third point, as being the agency of true awareness. We have now created the Supernal Triad, something that has a purpose and an awareness but is still completely unmanifest. There are three points but there is no idea of where any of them exist. Indeed, they are completely unmanifest. A fourth point (not in the plane of the triangle inscribed by the first three points) must arise, which formulates the idea of matter by creating a three-dimensional solid.

The original point in Kether can now be defined by three other co-ordinates. Something solid can exist, manifestation has taken place. The potential has become actual as from an original nothing, something has now emerged. This is Chesed on the Tree of Life. This initial 'matter' is exceedingly tenuous, however, for the only property of any given point is its position relative to the other three points. No change is possible, nothing can happen. A fifth point must be formed, and this is the concept of motion, called Geburah on the Tree. Only with motion (and the subsequent creation, through motion, of time) can events occur. Not only is the concrete idea of a point now possible, but the point can become self-conscious, because it can define itself in terms of time and motion – it has a past, present and future. This is Tiphareth, the number 6, the centre of the system, pure self-awareness capable of experience within the space–time continuum formed in Chesed and Geburah.

The remainder of the Tree then represents the vehicles that the self-conscious point in Tiphareth forms for its experience and expression. These are feeling (7, Netzach), thoughts (8, Hod), and sensations (10, Malkuth). These three vehicles carry within them their own knowledge and experience of the past represented by Yesod (9, the subconscious). In Malkuth, therefore, the original point's idea of itself is fulfilled and brought into complete manifestation.

This description of the creation of the Tree of Life is very neat in that it bypasses any need to believe in a particular religious or philosophical idea, being based as it is on pure number. Again, however, I would stress that the Tree of Life can be used as a practical, living map of consciousness, and agreement with this description is totally unnecessary. It cannot be over-emphasised that the Tree is what you make of it. It is initially useful, however, to use existing knowledge to make connections and help you build up the Tree until you have your own vibrantly alive Tree of Life in your consciousness. Then your own correspondences and understanding will blossom and the Tree will serve you in your growth and development.

DIFFERENT WORLDS

Our physical bodies are not just composed of cells, molecules, tissues, organs, skin, blood and the like. They are also composed of various different kinds of energy. For instance, there is the energy we use to stay alive, transforming our air and food intake into life energy. Then there is all the energy we use to interrelate with the world, whether in our work or play. We even use energy when we are resting and asleep; indeed, our lives are an ever-changing and never-ending interplay of energies.

Kabbalists believe, along with most others who investigate human energies, that there is another body, closely associated with and aligned to the physical body, called the etheric body. We normally only see our physical bodies, but if we could see all the energy being generated within us, as a separate entity, then we would be seeing our etheric 'double'. This etheric double corresponds to Malkuth as does the physical body. One simple way of experiencing your etheric double is to move a finger of one hand closer and closer to a finger of your other hand, until they are nearly but not quite touching. You can then sense the etheric double of each. This is something you can sense as quite distinct from, say, your body temperature or the pain from a skin abrasion, but it may take some practice to distinguish. It is best with such experiments to let go of your expectations and trust your own experience.

There are other energy bodies that correspond to the other spheres and planes on the Tree of Life. The energy body associated with the personality spheres on the Tree, and most particularly with Yesod, is the astral body. This too, while closely interwoven with the functioning of the personality through the thoughts, feelings and emotions, is clearly a body in its own right. Sometimes a distinction is made between the 'higher' astral (of Hod and Netzach) and the 'lower' (of

Yesod) but this distinction is one of quality rather than kind. The astral double is as real as our thoughts and feelings, albeit of a different order.

We can be aware of our astral double by simply allowing ourselves to relax and sink into an awake but disassociated reverie. Whenever we dream or daydream we are using astral energies. It is as if we are 'in another world', seeing what is happening there and having experiences that, on that imaginative level, are very real. We may be able to open our eyes and be back in the physical world at any moment, but that does not make the experience any less 'real'. And the deeper we allow ourselves to sink into the astral world, the more we start experiencing the kind of thinking and feeling associated with these energies.

Our physical, etheric and astral bodies are not really separate, but form a continuum from the physical outwards. They operate at different rates of vibration, but as with the different spheres on the Tree of Life, they are part of one continuous experience (just as the spheres are part of one Tree). This single Tree of Life can be usefully divided into different areas or 'worlds', however, so that we can come to a clearer understanding of how our different inner energies function.

THE FOUR WORLDS

If you look again at diagram 8 (page 56), you see that the Tree of Life can be divided into four 'worlds' or levels of energy. The first world, called Atziluth, is composed of Kether and Chockmah. Kether, in this sense, relates to the Mother–Father Creator and Chockmah to the Creator's will or purpose for coming to manifestation. It is said that the Creator and her/his will are inseparable, so it seems quite natural to include both of these spheres in the first world of energy. It is then referred to as the Creative World, the 'place' from where everything else originates.

The second world, called Briah, is composed of the third sphere alone. It is referred to as the Receptive World. If the Creator has a creative will, then this Creator, to be in balance, must also have a 'receptive' side. In the Kabbalistic tradition, all the spheres are both masculine and feminine in their energies so there is no correlation made between 'creative' and 'masculine' and 'receptive' and 'feminine' as in some other systems. Chockmah and Binah, both on the same plane on the Tree of Life, are equal and in dynamic balance with one another. One could not exist without the other.

The result of the interaction between these two worlds is the formation of a third world, Yetzirah, which is composed of all the remaining spheres except Malkuth. This third world is called the

Formative World, for it is in this world that all the different aspects that form the final physical manifestation are found. This includes the realm of archetypes (Chesed and Geburah), the soul or individual self (Tiphareth) and the vehicles for manifestation, or 'the personality spheres', represented by Netzach, Hod and Yesod.

The culmination of the process found in these first three worlds is the formation of a fourth, final world, called Assiah, which represents the actual physical manifestation, the world as we know it. For each of us as individual beings, it also represents the body as the physical substance through which we come into being. Sometimes these four worlds are represented by four separate Trees, one for each world, but for most practical purposes it usually makes more sense to stick with the one Tree of Life. As each individual sphere on the Tree is said to have a complete Tree within it we already have 11×11 spheres without multiplying this by a further 4!

At first you may wonder what is the value of splitting the Tree into four worlds. When you start relating these worlds to other maps and concepts of consciousness, however, it becomes clearer. We find in many different systems there is a division into four, such as the four 'elements of the wise' from alchemy: fire, water, air and earth. The first world relates to the creative fire, the second to the receptive water, the third to the formative air and the fourth to the material earth. Sometimes there is said to be a fifth element, Spirit, which is the breath of the Creator giving life to all the worlds.

If we look at the four worlds as progressive layers or veils that temper the light of the original creation, we can understand the underlying intention. For the physical world to exist and be populated by all the different beings, including humans, the original creative spark had to be kept aflame but veiled in such a way that it would not be too bright or blinding for the created beings. The first world is therefore seen as that of pure Spirit and, being associated with fire, can be seen clearly as something too powerful on its own to fulfil the function of creation. The second world of water is created to balance the fire. Once this is done it allows further creation to proceed, but for this formative energy to move into manifestation it has to be infused with the breath of the Creator. Air is the obvious medium for this. The fourth material world of the element of earth can then come into being.

It is said that the Creator wants us to experience the pure qualities of soul in the fullest sense. The Creator progressively veiled its energies so we could gradually but surely move back towards our source without being burnt up by too great an energy. Perhaps some of the people who in our society are deemed 'mad' or 'psychotic' have opened up to these energies too soon and have been 'burnt' by the creative fire. Whether this is the case or not, it certainly acts as a reminder to us to work at our own pace and, where necessary, to seek guidance from those who are already travelling the path.

You learned earlier how in Genesis, what is normally translated as 'God' in the original Hebrew is ELOHIM, the Mother–Father Creator. When the process reaches Exodus, where the actual physical mani-festation takes place, the word usually translated as 'God' is in Hebrew IHVH, Jehovah. It is sometimes said that this is the unspeakable name of 'God' and that if it is pronounced correctly the whole universe will cease to exist. For this reason, Jewish people often will not say Jehovah when they meet this word in the Bible but replace it with Adonai, a name for the personal 'god' within each of us. IHVH is seen by Kabbalists, however, as more than just an unpronounceable name of 'God'. It is seen as the key formula to understanding the whole of creation.

IHVH, sometimes called Tetragrammaton, is composed, as you can see, of four Hebrew letters, I-H-V-H, yod, heh, vau, heh. These four letters relate, in their given order, to the four worlds as discussed above. Through correspondences we then see that they also relate to the four elements. The four letters are also related to the four parts of a created being – I to the head, H to the shoulders and arms, V to the rest of the trunk and the final H to the legs. If you write these four Hebrew letters (הוהי) one directly under the other, you will even see that they pictorially represent a human body.

There are many more mysteries associated with IHVH; for instance, I relates to the 'father', H to the 'mother', V to the 'son' and the final H to the 'daughter'. These four are then said to represent force, pattern, activity and form. The force (will or energy) and the pattern (the blue-print or balance) come together, and two equally balanced creations result, the son and daughter. They represent the activity (doing) of the world and the form (or being) of the world. The more we delve into the mysteries of IHVH the more we find that it aids us in realising the beautiful cosmic pattern described in the Kabbalistic vision of creation.

THE REALM OF HUMAN CONCERN

Kabbalists consider the realm of human concern as a small part of a much longer string of worlds, possibly endless in number, most of which are beyond human consciousness. Each world is born from a previous world and then gives rise to a successive world (see diagram 9). As far

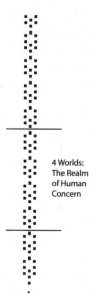

4 Worlds:
The Realm
of Human
Concern

Diagram 9: The human worlds

as we know, there is an infinite chain of such worlds, but from our human perspective there are only four worlds with which we need to concern ourselves. The first two worlds of fire and water are the basic building blocks of our universe, the Mother–Father Deity in its most abstract sense. This Mother–Father Deity is not to be confused with any concepts of god or goddess but is rather more analogous to the yin and yang principles of Taoism. Everything exists because of their interplay, but once we anthropomorphise them, once we give them any substance or meaning, if we believe in them or dismiss them, in fact once we do anything at all with them other than acknowledge their existence, we enter the realm of Yetzirah, the third or formative world.

All human knowledge, striving, faith, imagination, all human experience in fact, is rightly ascribed to Yetzirah with the (possible) exception of the basic experience of being physically alive, which is ascribed to Assiah, the fourth or material world. I say that is a possible exception only because it is so difficult for us, in the totality of our psychosomatic experience, to know what we are imagining and what is actually real. I believe I am embodied in this physical form, that I have a body and there is a physical world around me, but as modern science affirms, this may all be an illusion too. Indeed, some early Kabbalists claimed that the whole purpose of human existence was to learn how to come to earth in the fullest sense, something that we generally avoid through being seduced into believing the third world of Yetzirah is the real physical world. According to this theory, the world we imagine we live in has no more substance than that of our dreams. Of course, other Kabbalists, while agreeing with this, have also pointed out that if it is true, it might also conversely suggest that our so-called dreaming world is as real as the physical world.

Even though the realm of human concern contains four worlds, from an everyday perspective our attention is almost entirely engaged with the third and fourth worlds. It is in these two worlds that we expend most of our energy. As said, Kabbalists, considering that *everything* of which we are aware – all feelings, sensations, thoughts, intuitions, everything and anything else! – corresponds to the third world, then posit that the fourth, material world is normally experienced only through the process of thinking, feeling or sensing, all of which happen within the third world. Indeed, to 'come to earth' (the fourth world of Assiah), that is, to be fully grounded in our physical form, requires the grace and blessing bestowed by Shekhinah. Shekhinah, the indwelling spirit, is attributed to Malkuth in the fourth world, the most material part of the material realm. She is also ascribed to the final letter He of the divine name (and formula) IHVH, the four letters of which also correspond to the four worlds. Even more correctly, it is said she corresponds to the final tip of the final stroke of the last letter, thus identifying the fully created with the Creator, who corresponds more accurately to the first point of the first part of the letter Yod. This affirms the esoteric maxim: as above so below (but after another manner).

FOUR WORLDS OF COLOUR

Each of the four worlds has a particular colour scheme associated with it, but for all practical purposes, however, the traditional colours used are those of the second world as this is the world out of which all creation emerges. If you look at the Tree of Life coloured in the usual way, you will see that the spheres and paths follow this tradition. The colours of the first world are considered too rarified for practical use, and those of the third and fourth worlds too 'contaminated' to be of practical value. It has been found to be effective to use the colours of the second world both when we are learning to visualise the Tree and when we are using it for personal growth and healing.

The Supernal Triad of Kether, Chockmah and Binah, with regard to its colouring, indicates the nature of these spheres and the creative act. Kether, the 'divine spark', is white brilliance, white being the 'colour' that absorbs no other colours, but reflects them all out into its sur-roundings. Binah, the great sea of spiritual love, is black – black being the 'colour' that absorbs and includes all other colours. True spiritual love also absorbs and includes without rejection or judgement. Chockmah, sitting between these two, is then seen as silver grey, a mixture of white and black. Daath, incidentally, the 'sphere without a number', is also sometimes given no colour. In its manifestation, however, it is seen as a 'rainbow bridge' between the Supernals and the rest of the Tree and has thus been coloured accordingly.

It is interesting to observe that the three central spheres (those of 'soul') are coloured with the primary colours, that is, red (Geburah), blue (Chesed) and yellow (Tiphareth). The colours of the three personality spheres are combinations of the primary colours. Netzach is green (a mix of Chesed and Tiphareth, blue and yellow), Hod is orange (mixing the colours of Geburah and Tiphareth), while Yesod is purple (mixing the colours of Geburah and Chesed).

Malkuth was traditionally coloured with russet, citrine, olive and black to represent the four elements. As the elements are more usefully seen to correspond to different spheres and worlds on the Tree, this has been changed. Perhaps the most obvious colours for the earth might at first be thought to be green or brown, but when we work with Malkuth energies we find that a light, sky-blue colour is most effective. This is not surprising considering the high percentage of the earth's surface that is covered with water. Pictures from space missions confirm the beautiful blue colour of our planet. On a deeper level as well, the energy of our planet is seen as blue and was called 'orgone energy' by Wilhelm Reich, the controversial twentieth-century psychologist whose work focused on the healing of sexual energy.

If we look at the colours and relate them to the four worlds, we see that the first two worlds are involved with the creative and receptive aspects of creation and thus are shown either to reflect or absorb all colour. The third world, that of Yetzirah and formation, includes the three primary colours and the three colours created when these are mixed together. Assiah, the fourth world of the earth, is coloured in line with our perception of our planet, particularly as it is seen both energetically and from outer space. The coherence of this colouring for the Tree of Life is quite beautiful, and is a good example of the value in understanding Kabbalistic correspondences.

ENERGY CENTRES

The different energies we have within our bodies can be understood easily through the Tree of Life. As both Eastern and Western systems

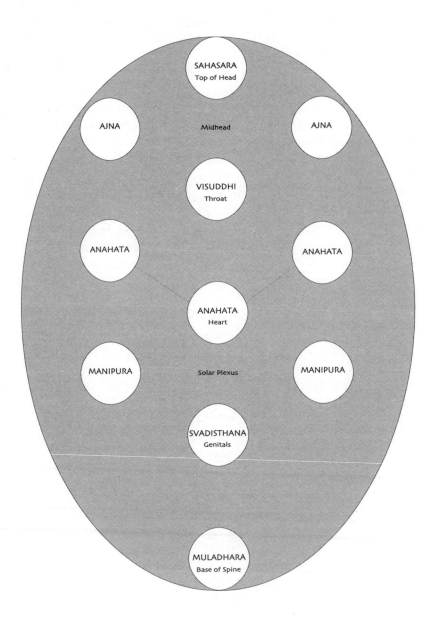

Diagram 10: Energy centres

attest, there are innumerable 'power points' within us. Eastern systems delineate seven major power points, which are called 'chakras' and these correspond to the Tree of Life. The unusual-looking names in diagram 10 are the original Sanskrit names of the chakras, each of which corresponds to a specific location within the body. When any of these major power points are opened, they give the individual powers of perception and creativity. That the Tree of Life fits onto the human body is vitally important to understanding Kabbalah, for it is through our bodies that we are able to bring anything into manifestation, and through which we can do healing, which we will explore in subsequent chapters. There would seem to be little point in accessing deep spiritual realms and having enlightening insights, for example, if we are unable to do something with this in our everyday world.

There are more power points in the body than the seven 'major' ones, and through closely considering our bodies with an imaginary Tree overlaid, we can quite easily find many of them. For example, the places where paths cross one another on the Tree, when related to the body, help us locate precise psycho-spiritual centres of great healing benefit. It is well worth looking at your own body to see if you can find the location of any of these other centres.

The major physical power points or chakras may be seen as 'rotating discs' of energy that, on the level of the energy bodies, are attached to

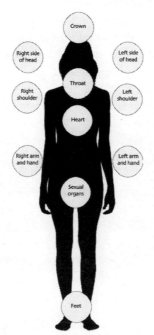

Diagram 11: The human body

the spine at seven specific points, from the base of the spine up to the very top. If we compare the chakra system to the Tree of Life (see diagram 10), we can see that some of the energy centres have more than one sphere corresponding to them. Some of the chakras are concerned with 'external duality', that is they are involved with outer balance, and these have a single sphere associated, the 'other half' of the polarity being outside the individual person. Those concerning 'internal duality' are involved with balance within the individual and have more than one sphere associated.

The solar plexus chakra, corresponding to Hod and Netzach, is dual in nature since the left and right hand sides of the individual have to be balanced for it to be effectively and fully open. In other words, if our thoughts (Hod) and our feelings (Netzach) are not balanced there will be issues to be worked through at this level of energy. The midhead chakra is also dual in nature, but on a deeper level as shown by its correspondence to Binah and Chockmah. It is concerned with the balance of spiritual Love and Will and when it is open gives the individual connection to deep spiritual insights.

We will be looking at the heart in relation to the Tree of Life in more depth in a later chapter. The heart chakra primarily relates to the central sphere on the Tree, Tiphareth. It is also associated with Geburah and Chesed, however, as it has a dual aspect that is concerned with the lessons the soul has to learn on its journey through life. A connected and subtly effective heart chooses to open or close as appropriate to the situation at hand, being able to heal itself and others but also able to protect its body, its means of expression. Tiphareth and the heart are associated with 'higher' feelings, values, love, service, altruism, and so on. Humanity as a whole is said to be moving in the current age from a primary focus on solar plexus issues towards a new connection and awakening of heart values.

The 'single' chakras, with regard to their position on the Tree of Life, are simpler to understand. Whereas with the other chakras the concern is with inner balance, these four chakras are concerned with outer balance. The base of spine chakra (Malkuth) – survival in the world; sacral chakra (Yesod) – interplay and interpersonal relationships, particularly sexually oriented ones; throat chakra (Daath) – expression and communication; and the crown chakra (Kether) – the realisation of unity within and without, and the connection to the Mother–Father Deity.

SOUL, PERSONALITY AND THE WORLD

Most of the time we are so involved with the everyday processes of physical survival, emotional reaction and intellectual fantasy that we have no time to consider anything that might be deemed 'spiritual'. Indeed, many people live their whole lives, albeit undoubtedly touched by the Spirit, without ever considering their deeper nature. If and when such moments arise, therefore, when we find ourselves face to face with our spiritual nature or our 'soul', they are often overpowering, or disturbing in some way. We may be frightened by the experience and choose to cut off, even deny its reality. Even if we enjoy the experience, it is likely that we will get caught up again in the everyday chores of life and lose sight of our connection.

When we consider these moments in our lives we tend to see them in terms of something we have had happen to us. Basically we act as if we are personalities who sometimes have spiritual experiences. We will say, in one way or another, that we 'have a soul'. One of the key concepts in Kabbalah is concerned with reversing this perception of our reality so that we become a soul who has a personality. We are not the lower part of the Tree with something deeper within us. We are encouraged to live our lives with the realisation that we are Tiphareth and the higher spheres, we are soul, and to come into manifestation we have clothed ourselves with the personality spheres (Netzach through to Malkuth). This is not just a concept, for we find if we start to believe this and, more importantly, act upon it, our world is transformed. What used to be problems that we were somehow forced to deal with are transformed into opportunities for our development and growth.

PRACTICE

• The holy chalice

In an earlier exercise, you connected to Malkuth (the senses), using the exercise to differentiate between what we were directly sensing (Malkuth) and what we thought about it (Hod) and what we felt about it (Netzach). When we think or feel something about what we are experiencing it was said to be 'not Malkuth'. As you may well be aware by now, when you had thoughts and feelings they were experiences of Hod and Netzach and the paths that connect these to Malkuth. In the following exercise you will be choosing to work directly with these two spheres, and then seeing how we can bring all three named spheres together in our work.

Firstly, therefore, I am going to ask you to connect with Hod. To do that, all you have to do is simply think about something, because once you are thinking you are using Hod. I am going to ask you to think specifically about the holy grail, a magical cup, or a chalice. If I could supply you with all the materials and skills you would need for this, what kind of chalice would you make? Spend some time now thinking about this – would it be a simple or elaborate cup, would it be made of metal of wood – which type? – would it be simple or encrusted with jewels . . .?

When you have thought about this chalice for a while, it is a good idea if you either draw a representation or write a description of it, to get a clear picture of what your chalice looks like. When you are ready, continue with the exercise.

Sit in a comfortable position, relax and close your eyes. Imagine you are in a wood, surrounded by light, young trees. Smell the fresh air around you, and allow yourself to really 'be' in this place. Feel your feet on the ground, imagine the sun shining through the trees and listen to the birdsong or other sounds of which you may be aware. Imagine you have your chalice with you.

As you tune into this place, imagine you can hear a spring bubbling up somewhere nearby and start to walk in that direction. Take your time, noticing what is around you, then come to a clearing or grove in the woods and see the spring. In your own time, walk up to the spring and fill your chalice with some of the crystal-clear, sparkling water that is gushing from it.

Drink from your chalice. How do you feel doing this? What does the water taste like? What effect does drinking this water from your magic cup have on you? How do you feel now you have imbibed it?

When you are ready, come back to your room, open your eyes and stay with how you are feeling. What was this experience like for you?

A chalice, grail or magic cup is a symbol usually associated with Netzach, which also corresponds to feelings and nature generally. In your imaginary journey to the spring you have travelled to this sphere. You started in Hod, thinking about your chalice, then you experienced drinking from this cup, having feelings associated with this, and perhaps some effects on your consciousness. In this exercise you have used both Hod (thoughts) and Netzach (feelings) and made a connection between them. As in all Kabbalistic work, it is now important for you to ground this experience in Malkuth, the body and external world. How can you express what you have connected with from this exercise in your everyday life?

4

REPARATION AND THE ARCHETYPES OF EXPERIENCE

The Tree of Life is fruit for those who follow heart-felt relations, and thus brings souls to wisdom.

King Solomon (Book of Proverbs 11:30)

One of the greatest and best-known esoteric maxims is: 'as above, so below', asserting as it does the essential identity between the Mother–Father Deity and the creation. We could say 'god' made man in his own image (and, of course, 'goddess' made woman in her own image). To a Kabbalist this is not acceptable, however, because it implies a dualism that denies our experiences when we connect with our inner world. It would be truer to say 'goddess-god' made 'woman-man' in its own image, then split this creation into two so that, through this division, the creation may experience love and realise its true essential identity with the Deity.

When we consider the triangles that make up the Tree of Life we see that, despite the flipping upside down of the second and third ones, the three triangles are reflections of each other. Kabbalists believe this is exactly the case, each triangle successfully clothing itself with denser matter until the world of Malkuth can be formed. Until Malkuth is created, the actual split into male and female does not occur. Despite the way the energy is made denser as it descends the Tree, the essence of the Deity is carried through all the spheres without being lessened or diluted at all. It is true to say, therefore, that the Deity is as equally in Malkuth as in Kether. Thus we return to the maxim: as above, so below.

A similar Kabbalistic maxim starts, 'Kether is in Malkuth and Malkuth is in Kether . . .' This clearly implies the same meaning. The macrocosm (represented by the top triangle) is perfectly reflected in the microcosm (represented by the bottom triangle). The Kabbalistic maxim continues, however, by saying '. . . but after another manner'. In other words, the Deity and the creation are the same except for a difference! This may sound like a contradiction until we understand what the difference is, namely the knowledge of existence. Once the creation achieves this self-knowledge, therefore, it becomes one with the Deity. This is exactly what the ancient oracle of Delphi meant when it stated, so simply and clearly, 'Know thyself.'

For a Kabbalist, this knowing of oneself has to be a direct experience, not simply a matter of faith. Without denying the importance of faith, it is clear that to have true self-knowledge we must have direct experience for ourselves. From this experience we may then have a living faith, based on our direct, experienced understanding, which is very different from a 'blind faith' based upon what someone else has told us to be the truth. For some people faith alone might be enough to sustain them and help them develop and grow closer to an understanding of their own inner nature, but Kabbalah stresses that if we are to truly know ourselves as one with the divine, we must experience this directly.

Everything that a Kabbalist experiences is seen as an opportunity for growth and movement towards self-realisation. Not least among these opportunities are those presented to us through our bodies. The body, represented by Malkuth, is seen as a living temple of the soul. It is through our bodies that we incarnate on this planet, and it is only through our bodies that we can interact with the dense matter of existence. It is vital, therefore, that we treat our bodies with all the respect that is due to such a precious temple.

Malkuth, as you know, also represents the external world and this too is seen as a temple, the outer temple in which we experience and express ourselves. We can thus make another connection, that between our inner temple (body) and outer temple (external world). It is important we treat our outer temple with as much respect as that we give our inner temple. When we abuse our planet, it reflects our abuse of ourselves. When we truly honour our bodies, we inevitably honour our outer temple too.

Whatever we know scientifically, from our planetary perspective we experience the sun as dying each evening and being reborn each morning. If we could stand on the sun, we would realise the light as continuous, at the centre of all activity, including the cycles of the Earth. Similarly, from our terrestrial perspective, we experience a similar cycle of life and death. As souls, however, we can realise our continuity, seeing that birth and death are transition points that bring us into and take us out of incarnation on the planet. If we experience this truth, we inevitably see that there is some purpose for coming into incarnation. For a Kabbalist this purpose is, in essence, to realise our true inner divinity and connection to the Deity.

For each of us, as individual souls, however, there is, in any incarnation, a particular purpose for being here. We have special lessons to learn, and until we truly experience and understand our lessons, we continue spiralling through an endless cycle of experiences (and incarnations even), with these lessons being presented to us in numerous different ways. Once a particular lesson is learnt, we can then move on to the next lesson. Each step in this unfolding process brings us nearer to the realisation of our purpose or 'true will', the reason why we are here. For one person the purpose might be to express love in some lofty, abstract sense, for another to express love in caring for sick or handicapped people. Perhaps for someone else it may be to stand against a particular injustice so more truth can be made manifest, for another it might simply be to act as a catalyst for someone else's progress. No individual's purpose is better or worse than another's. The key is to find our own purpose or true will and then to do it. When we achieve this we have truly aligned ourselves, as souls, with the Universal Spirit, and can actualise the identity between the microcosm and the macrocosm.

TIKKUN: REPAIRING THE PAST

Kabbalists believe that creation takes place through a process of fragmentation. In order to know itself, the Source or Creator, originally whole and beyond the negative veils, fragments into the Tree of Life. Our task, as living beings (and microcosms of the original Creator), is then to restore wholeness to ourselves and the universe. This process of restoring wholeness is called *tikkun,* which, translated into English, means restoration, restitution or reparation. This last word, reparation, is perhaps the most accurate as it suggests repair (of the broken vessels). For the individual Kabbalist, the aim of tikkun is to restore a sense of wholeness or perfection to the psyche. Perfection in this sense does not mean everything being perfected, but everything *as it is now* being seen and understood as perfect in itself.

You have already learned that the second triad on the Tree of Life represents, on an individual level, the soul. Each individual soul is a holographic replica of the total oneness of the Source. The breaking of the vessels implies the same, that each individual being has a piece of the broken vessels within. Through fragmentation, therefore, we each have an individual connection to the original Source. Tikkun is the process of refining and elevating the individual sparks of soul and reconnecting them to the spiritual level. This reparative process continues whether we co-operate with it or not, but as humans, our conscious intent can be to find ways to co-operate with and facilitate tikkun.

The original Kabbalistic myth includes three stages: tsimtsum (self-limitation), shevirath ha-kelim (fragmentation or breaking of the vessels) and tikkun (reparation). The Creator, in creating something, limits itself through tsimtsum. It is as if it contracts itself into a smaller space (just as each of us contract ourselves, as souls, into the smaller space of a body). The creation of each sphere on the Tree of Life then involves a progressive contraction then emanation. Each stage in this process involves a contraction as the energy arrives at (and creates) the sphere, followed by a breaking of the vessels so that the energy may emanate forth to the next sphere in the creative process.

PRACTICE

• Life restoration

Considering your life journey, what acts are you undertaking or could you undertake to co-operate and actively engage with the process of tikkun (reparation)?

Tikkun is truly the ground stone of Kabbalistic development, and to work at releasing blocked energies through Yesod, the sphere of the past, is the only way to truly become oneself, both in a spiritual and a material sense. Your birth, early development, family upbringing and education have all affected your abilities as you grow and develop, both individually and in relation to others. It is vital to explore your journey from the past, and consider ways to release energies for your personal and spiritual development.

THE JOURNEY FROM THE PAST

Kabbalists agree with the theorists of child development that it is useful to think of there being various stages we go through in our development into adulthood, psychologically as well as physically. What happens to us at these stages sets the scene for how we (neurotically or healthily) function on various levels in later life. Kabbalists believe that our basic source of energy is through Yesod, which if we were not to have any developmental issues, would give us access to a free-flowing, unlimited source of energy. Everyone, however, comes into life with issues to work on (and, sometimes, to work through – but not inevitably). What happens in our development is a result of soul transmitting these issues so we can have something to work with for our particular growth and development. These issues are 'deposited' as it were round Yesod, blocking the free flow of energy.

We carry the past within us in the form of all our memories and experiences, whether we remember them or not. Everything from the past makes us what we are in the present moment, and by reference to the past, we can obtain a clearer understanding of where we are in the here and now. This then helps us decide where we want to go and how to get there. Our personal past is more than just a store of memories, however, and also includes repressed complexes, long-forgotten memories, instincts and physical functions over which we (ordinarily) have no conscious control. It is primarily repressed material, often experienced in the form of unconscious controls upon us, phobias, obsessions, compulsive urges and so on, which we are most concerned in repairing. So long as these patterns or procedures from the past have a hold on us we cannot be truly free nor have all our energy available to us.

For instance, you might have had it instilled in you as a child that you must wash your hands every time after using the toilet. This in itself is sound advice, but you were conditioned into believing you have to do this or you are naughty. But travelling through a remoter country region, you cannot always do this and after every time you use the toilet you keep feeling a little sick. Of course it may be that you are being affected by some bacterium. It could equally be that, although you have forgotten it, you are really being affected by the parental voice that somewhere in your unconscious still tells you off when you don't do what you are told.

This is just one example of the many, many items that we carry within us from our past that may affect us at any moment. See if you can think of other such examples but do not be surprised if you find this difficult – after all, part of the power of such incidents from the past is that they are no longer remembered and thus exert that much stronger a hold on us. As we explore the past, it helps our growth because as we learn to integrate more of these 'older' or repressed aspects of ourselves, the more whole we become. When we release previously repressed energies, we feel healthier, have more energy available to us, and feel more freedom in our lives. In other words, we are making reparation.

All the discoveries you make from your past need to be integrated into your body to help release the body armour in your joints, tendons and muscles, which is where your body stores all the memories of pain, anxiety, and other sufferings from the past. The term body armour was coined by Wilhelm Reich to describe the way our bodies tense to help us deal with physical or emotional pain, but then become stuck in the tensed position after the trauma has passed. One of the greatest keys to understanding Kabbalah is to realise that spiritual connection, trans-personal insight, and all kinds of inner illumination, are accessed through your body. It is through your body that you can really transform who you are right now, because when you are fully in your body, you are completely here and now and no where or no time else.

Some early depictions of the Kabbalistic Tree of Life show the tree growing down into the earth with its roots reaching to heaven. The more we learn how to incarnate fully in our bodies, the more our roots reach up to heaven, the stronger our vessel for journeying into the deeper realms of the Tree. There's an old saying that it is dangerous to put your head in the clouds unless your feet are safely planted on the ground. This perfectly describes the Kabbalistic approach. Our task is not to 'trip out' but rather to 'come in', or as James Hillman, the psychologist, puts it, life is about 'growing down' rather than growing up. Kabbalah teaches that you are always right here and now in the reality you are creating, though you may have to work hard to live this reality.

Many of the memories from the past that spontaneously arise are in themselves of little significance. The easiest and most effective way of dealing with such memories is to just observe them and let them go. Not all memories are of such unimportance, though: connections and events from the past may have a serious effect on how free you are to live the life you want. These memories sometimes operate in subtle, unconscious ways that you hardly notice (but which nevertheless control you) or sometimes bring about devastating and life-shattering effects.

Conditioning and imprinting from the past that is currently controlling you tends to reveal itself in recognisable ways, if you put your mind to it. For instance, when a particular behaviour is inconsistent with the rest of your personality you can be fairly sure that something from the past is affecting you. When a part of you reacts in a way that is out of proportion, when you experience shame or guilt, or when you undertake persistent self-destructive behaviour, something from your past is controlling you. Through working with the present context of the past pattern, you can stop being a victim of the past and take charge of your life.

You have been collecting memories since you were born, or conceived, or perhaps before. Maybe you came into your earthly existence with memories from other lives. Whatever is true about that, however, it is undoubtedly true that whatever age you are, you have innumerable stored memories, many of them not immediately accessible to you. If we restrict ourselves to just the time since your birth, you've been through more than any human could possibly bear – and yet we do bear it. Right from your earliest relating with your parents or guardians, you soon learn there are people you can trust and others to mistrust in the world around you. Your very survival is at stake. If you learn that you cannot trust your environment you might decide to attempt to control it instead. In adult life you might become a 'control freak' or a manipulator of others' emotions.

To understand the significance that the birth experience and early childhood development has on your subsequent life is of profound importance. Childhood is a time of great exploration, and as you interacted with others, you learned to judge yourself as worthy or unworthy. How you relate in your early years also affects your self-confidence, and if things go badly you may be engulfed with feelings of shame and worthlessness that can adversely affect your later life. You may lack a true sense of individuality and self, and internally be always running yourself down. Perhaps you picked up your parents' fears and sense of worthlessness, conditions that may have been passed down through generations of family ancestors. When puberty comes, all this previous conditioning is thrown into the melting pot with your emerging sexuality. It is not surprising that for most people adolescence is a time of great upheaval and difficulty. The sexual energies that come to the fore during this period are the tip of the great storehouse of energy available to a Kabbalist. How we learn to deal with the sexual aspects of this energy sets the tone for our future Kabbalistic practice.

Students of Kabbalah often find it confusing at first that Yesod is attributed to both sexual energy and the subconscious, composed as it is of repressed material and so on, as we have just been discussing. If we consider sexual energy in its wider sense, however, when it might be more properly called 'life force', the attribution becomes clearer. Basically, what Kabbalah says is that if you had no past material that was blocking this energy, it would be completely freed up to use for your subsequent development. Yesod, in this sense, is rightly seen as the sphere of this sexual or life force and the 'subconscious' attribution more rightly understood as blockages to this energy, accrued around the sphere, as it were, that blocks its free flow and our free access to it. Of course, rather than looking at this negatively, we can reframe it in a most positive way because it is just these very 'blockages' that offer us the opportunity to grow and learn about ourselves in our incarnated state.

So sexual energy is the 'life force' itself and, while closely allied to sex, it may be engaged with and a relationship built with it, without the necessity of any particular or specific sexual activity. Indeed, some Kabbalists have used the absence of sexual activity as a pathway to contacting this energy. Most spiritual traditions, Western and Eastern, tell of a special power within your body, called the dragon power or kundalini. It is a power closely linked to your sexual energy and is sometimes described as a snake coiled at the base of the spine that uncoils and stretches up through the body as the energy is activated. It is also described as a dragon power that resides at the base of the clitoris or penis that similarly rises up through the body. It is considered dangerous to raise this power prematurely, but it is important that you start to build a relationship with it. We will explore this energy, and how to work with it, in a later chapter.

REFRAMING PAST INFLUENCES

As a child we are trained to view the concepts of the world, everything that is 'out there', as it were, in a specific way. We have to learn these concepts in order that we can communicate and interact with the rest of nature, and most particularly our fellow humans. Each concept in the child's mind is not formed instantly, but develops gradually, acquiring many different ramifications and connections before it is firmly lodged in the mind. For instance, to a child a tree is, at first, a circle with two parallel lines below. Only later, through observation based upon learning processes and inner development, does the tree appear as it does to the adult. This does not necessarily mean that there is nothing 'real' in the universe or that the tree does not really exist. A problem only arises when one particular set of concepts is taken as the only way of seeing the world and is believed to be the total reality of life. Kabbalistic development involves looking for a deeper reality behind all forms and concepts, to be able to recognise and ultimately manipulate the energy behind form. Kabbalah teaches that altering our perceptions regarding the reality behind all phenomena is the only effective way to change the phenomena themselves. It is obvious, yet it is easy to lose sight of the fact, that the way we view the world changes the way it is.

To retain and develop a sense of your true birthright, your innate worthiness as an individual spark of consciousness, is a tough task, a long, ongoing process that is the very stuff of life itself. If we believe a fundamental tenet of Kabbalah, that we are here so we can get to know ourselves, then all these events from our childhood are grist for the mill, offering us the opportunity to find out more about how we operate in the world. Underlying Kabbalistic philosophy is the idea that the whole point of incarnating (leaving a state of oneness) is, through the resultant separation, to find ways to experience the energy of oneness again. If you were always in a state of oneness, no such experience would be possible. A succinct phrase from Aleister Crowley is often quoted in occult circles: we are divided for the sake of love and for the chance of union. This stresses the theme of oneness and separation, and it is through understanding how this polarity operates within you that you can bring your will into alignment with universal will.

The key to being able to change your relationship with the past so you can release energy for your development now is to learn to be able to change your connections to your early conditioning and imprinting, and to learn to reprogramme yourself. Conditioning includes all the behaviour patterns and ideas that you've taken on board from your parents, teachers, and all the other well-meaning (or not) people you met in your formative years. Your conditioning was mostly finished by the onset of the teenage years, but is constantly being affected and altered, for example, through the media, political manipulations, advertising and so on. Therein lies an important clue: if *they* can affect changes to your conditioning, so can you. This is the aim of consciousness-raising techniques; whether the aim is magical: to raise energy to enter the astral realm, for instance; political: to change conditioning around racism, fascism, or other social ills, for instance; or therapeutic: to clear a life-restricting pattern, for instance. Many different techniques focus on changing the negative aspects of basic conditioning, whether through body work, emotional release, mental understanding or spiritual insight. A wise Kabbalist will recognise when aspects of his or her process require the support or assistance of another and act accordingly.

If you compare yourself to a computer, your conditioning is like a program that is always on when you are conscious. Such programs affect the way you operate, and unless they are updated in some way, or removed, will continue to affect you in the same way. You will keep repeating the pattern produced from this influence. Something that, for example, affects your preference for margarine or butter may be of little or no real consequence. But if you have a conditioned pattern that leads you to undervalue yourself, it is vital you find ways to release your energy for your Kabbalistic progress. Luckily there are lots of ways of working on these issues and freeing yourself from past conditioning. Many books and courses tackle such issues effectively.

There are many different activities you can undertake to free yourself (at least to a partial degree) from past conditioning, some of which have already been discussed. Mostly this is work you can do yourself, but when deep-seated complexes are involved it is good Kabbalistic practice to find a healer to assist you. This healer might operate in a variety of different ways from psychic healing, through counselling and coaching to hands-on manipulations. The key to finding someone suitable to assist you in this work is to trust your own judgement as to whether a particular healer seems suitable for you and your needs. Perhaps surprisingly, sometimes a practitioner who seems mundane and non-magical may be more effective than someone advertising themselves as working in more esoteric ways. Choose wisely.

Your imprinting is another matter altogether. In the computer analogy your imprinting is like the fixed operating system, burned permanently into the hardware. Imprinting is partly genetic, partly happens in the womb, and is partly achieved through very early, pre-conceptual experiences. If you want to change your imprinting, you have to accept it is so deeply rooted within you that you will only achieve meaningful and permanent changes through long, hard work that might include much pain and difficulty. The corollary to this is that great energy will be released from this work. Gurdjieff, the enigmatic Armenian occultist, called it 'intentional suffering', to undertake such hard work and to use the energy released to strengthen your centre and increase your personal power. Christian magicians call it growing a soul. It may seem strange to read of Christian magicians, but Christianity has always had an esoteric or magical branch (as most other religions do). The followers of the esoteric branches of religions usually believe their practices are more in line with the earlier (and therefore more 'pure') forms of the original teachings. There are several books written from a Christian perspective that describe Jesus as a magician or even specifically as a Kabbalist.

The American philosopher Jacob Needleman talks about the lost doctrine of the soul in Christianity in his book *Lost Christianity*, and says: 'the soul is not a fixed entity . . . it is an actual energy, but one that is only at some beginning stage of its development and action'. While every day the individual may experience the appearance of this energy in an embryonic form, it is almost always dispersed and comes to nothing. Early Christian mystics considered it vital that we work to build or catch a soul through our life activities. Indeed, the belief was that it was the only way to ensure continued existence after life. The practices of esoteric Christianity suggest you need to struggle against the attempts of the personality to divert you from your efforts at moving towards soul. In our everyday state we think about life and give ourselves explanations, we react emotionally or physically to cover our inner suffering, and our ego tries everything to avoid the question 'what are you here for?' Only through persistent effort can you hold to the inner quest and keep your attention focused on your true inner desire to find meaning and purpose in life. This is another effective way of working on clearing past conditioning.

The very same theme was taken up from a different perspective by the shaman Don Juan, who said that doing such work is the only way to 'slip past the eagle' who devours all consciousness at the moment of death. Death is always with you, maybe death is waiting just behind your left shoulder, waiting to tap you, so when it does and you look round, you will be facing your death. It is vital for a Kabbalist to find ways to acknowledge the presence of death and start to build a relationship with it, then you will be ready for your last dance. The notion is that death will wait for you to finish your last dance, but the danger is you will be taken before you can even start performing it. Thus it is a good idea to treat your whole life as your last dance.

Of course, for all you really know, even on the level of your deepest imprinting, it is possible that you may have already chosen everything that happens to you in your life even before you were born! Can you even be sure you really exist or that you have a past or future? One certain truth is that, as the person you consider yourself to be right now, you are going to die. Even if I have a soul, go to heaven, reincarnate or whatever, 'Will Parfitt' as an individual character will pass away. The same is true for all of us. So perhaps too much time delving into the past and working on clearing ancient blocks to your freedom may divert you from your two main tasks as a Kabbalist, the living of life in the here and now and preparing yourself for your encounter with death.

PRACTICE

• Reframing an image

Images and symbols are the language of the unconscious. Therefore, one excellent method for working with a negative memory involves the use of imagery. First, think back to an incident that still has the power to make you feel unhappy, ill at ease or uncomfortable whenever you recall it. As you recall this negative memory, try not to become caught up in any emotions that may resurface, but concentrate instead on how your body feels in response to it.

After spending some time with the image, and what you feel it represents, you change the image until it becomes less threatening, more pleasing, totally different, whatever is appropriate to the situation. Remember that you are in control of this image, it is not in control of you. When you have changed it, you imagine the image in front of you as large and bright as you can, then draw its energy into your body, letting this new, positive energy fill you with its life-enhancing qualities.

BEYOND INDIVIDUAL PAST

We all are DNA getting to know itself. Each cell division, from the very first that follows the moment of conception, through to those taking place in your body right now, is operated by your genetic code held on the chromosomes in your cells. Kabbalists who can see into the cellular and genetic levels of energy say they see energy replicating itself with consciousness. The work of Jeremy Narby, the Swiss anthropologist who spent time living with Amazonian shamans, suggests that consciousness is universal. Perhaps you are your own ancestor, constantly replicating yourself but in different forms. At heart, if that is true, every event in your life is the result of the DNA dividing itself, continuously pleasuring itself in the energy released.

Then there are your family ancestors, your parents, grandparents, back and back, your greatest, greatest grandparents somewhere in some distant past, the 'you' that existed back then (and the 'them' who exist now because of you). Honour them as you honour yourself, they brought you here through a chain of replication, and you live within them as much as they live within you.

Earth ancestors, the energies of the earth itself, all these physical ancestors are worth contact. Look at the rocks where some cliff face has split open, layer upon layer of ancestors, each rock a part of an unfolding whole. I can show you a rock where King Arthur still resides, and will continue to reside until the rain and wind turn his form into someone or something else. Fix a cloud in your sight and watch the charioteer change to a wizened face then a couple embracing. *The image changes but the energy remains.*

You don't really have to look out for your ancestors, because they're always looking out for you. It's good to give them some time, though. All the different levels of ancestors can be contacted through the use of will and imagination. The simplest method is to state your intent clearly (e.g. 'I will make space for the wisdom of the ancestors in my life') and then to find practical ways of implementing this intent in your everyday life. Often just to remember your intent and watch for manifestations of its effect is enough, particularly in the case of personal ancestors who often seem to be most available for contact, perhaps not surprisingly considering the personal connection.

As well as ancestors in our own line, when we consider our past beyond our personal life, we also have to consider the cultural field within which we live. From the perspective of ego, if that was all we were, then perhaps it might be true to consider ourselves as really nothing more than the product of our culture. From a deeper spiritual perspective, however, we may think that the culture within which we find ourselves has little if anything to do with our 'true nature'. The Kabbalistic view is is to hold both possibilities, to let both polarities in any such debate be present. Then it's not a matter of whether you are a product of your culture or not. Then you can truthfully say: I am a product of my culture *and* I am more than that. Such a position enables you to make clearer and more effective choices than you can if you position yourself on one side or the other of such a debate.

In our dual world, built as it is on polarity, whatever you believe (thesis) must imply also its opposite (antithesis). If you try to include both by moving yourself to somewhere between the two, you end up in a place that is neither one nor the other. On the other hand, if you move to a new position that *includes* both polarities, then you have a new perspective (synthesis) from where you can make clearer choices about your actions. This is essential to a full understanding of how Kabbalistic magic operates and can be applied not just to culture but in any situation in which you find yourself prey to the forces of polarity. Much of our Kabbalistic work is about finding how to build a strong centre from whence the work of synthesis can proceed.

WORKING WITH PAST ENERGIES

We usually act as if the past has a hold on us, as if we are victims to circumstances, childhood development, bad school teachers, society and so on. If only I had been born to millionaire parents what a better upbringing I would have had – and so, consequently what a better life

I'd be able to lead now. If only I can shake off the hold of that sexual abuse from my childhood, I could realise my full potential. The key is to let go of the past. It won't let go of you, however much you struggle. Truth is, you have lived the past you've lived, it is done, written in the books, finished, and there is not a damn thing you can do about that. On a deeper level you can come to realise that there is no past to have had, that right now you experience what you experience. Either way you look at it, the choice is in your hands. Are you going to let the past keep control of you or are you going to make the choice to have your past rather than letting it have you?

A good way of working with a difficult situation from the past is to remind yourself that although you may not be able to forget these difficulties, you can forgive those involved. That is not to say it is okay that you were misused or abused, far from it. Rather it is about re-owning the energy that is caught up in your memories of these incidents, particularly those aspects of the energy that are held in your body and block the free flow of your life force. Whatever you remember from your past, good or bad, acknowledge that it happened, but let it go now, be here in this moment. You are then filled with memories of the events you have experienced throughout your life so far, but they do not consume you.

Don't let memories of past events eat you up, and don't let people from the past, however abusive their behaviour, have a hold on you now. Forgiveness is a great key for making this shift in consciousness, not just a verbal acknowledgement of forgiveness but a heartfelt release. Don't be misled here, forgiveness isn't always that easy to access, and has to be reached through a process, not just from one verbal acknowledgement. Then forgiveness removes any lack of wholeness, bringing love both to the person forgiven and to the forgiver. You can never have enough forgiveness.

A victim is powerless; you are not. As a Kabbalist, you take responsibility for who you are and realise that, whatever situation you are in, you created it just that way to develop your spiritual practice. A major premise of Kabbalah is that *whatever you do it is the best you can do at that time*. This is also always true of others, including your parents, your partners, everyone with whom you interact. Realising this brings acceptance, and true acceptance brings clarity to your personal and spiritual development.

PRACTICE

• **Blessings**

Bless your parents or guardians for doing the best they could.

Bless your best friend or partner for doing the best he or she is able.

Bless yourself for doing the best you can.

Through this approach, all your memories, all your past experiences, instead of eating you up, become food for you, giving you energy as you release their hold. That way, your personal power is increased not decreased by your past.

And if something from the past is too big, too deep, too horrible, too fixating to let you make a clear choice in this way, get help. Choose one of the many different therapies that are designed to help you do that. In one way or another, most forms of psychotherapy deal with clearing past blockages that restrict your functioning in life. If you need to get help from a therapist or healer, of whatever persuasion, don't see it as a failure in any way. On the contrary, it shows your commitment to your development, and the benefits to a Kabbalist from working on releasing past blockages are enormous.

POSSIBLE PAST LIVES

You may have memories that appear to show that you have lived before, often as a human being on this planet, but sometimes on other planets, in other places, on other planes, and even occasionally as other types of beings. Whatever the truth or not of such experiences, whether they are genuine memories or not, they can be relevant to your Kabbalistic development. We don't need to enter into discussions about the possibilities of reincarnation because if the memory is meaningful to your life and you can integrate what you learn from such a memory, all well and good. If it merely titillates you, or inflates your ego, you had better watch out!

When such memories do arise, you can take the opportunity to reflect on them and learn what message about yourself they are offering you. It may be that you have lived many lives before, trans-incarnating over and over until you finally have integrated all the lessons your soul originally came into being to learn. It may be this is your only life and all such memories are fantasies. In either case, if the message is there, it is worth considering if it is relevant and how you can put it to use in a grounded, magical way.

Many people, of course, have no such memories even after hypnosis. Perhaps they disbelieve that such things are possible, or fear that the memories that may be evoked will be too painful to face, or fear that they will become inflated after realising they were Jesus Christ or some other well-known character from history. These fears are well founded, and such dangers do exist, which is why it is vital to treat even the most elevated of messages with great caution. Indeed, it is such messages that it is especially important to treat with caution. Pragmatic Kabbalistic philosophy asks: how useful is this information? Its worth and value are dependent upon a strongly affirmative response. That is not to say, however, that for any particular individual the belief that an inner voice is that of some famous person, or a past life was lived as Cleopatra, is wrong. The key then is to simply check if this spirit or memory serves you, and how you can put it to life-affirming use in your life now.

Most techniques for remembering past lives work through inducing a light trance in the person, who then visualises backwards. Such methods also work best when there is a witness to the process. Some physical pressure techniques are sometimes used, as are special energy points in the body, but Kabbalists generally find such procedures are not necessary. Once relaxed and in a light trance, all you have to do is allow your consciousness to drift backwards, and simply watch as you enter the spaces and memories that relate to previous lives. Don't censor or judge, just see what images and ideas appear. It doesn't matter if they are 'real' or not, because you are choosing to connect with whatever will have relevance to you. Both so-called good and bad memories have equal importance as everything you can possibly imagine is part of your path towards full knowledge and understanding of who you are.

At the end of any such journey into your past, it is important to come forward to the present day, here and now in the place where you are and do something mundane to ground your consciousness. I cannot stress enough that a mystical experience that separates you from your mundane, earthly existence and, in a state of bliss, leads you to temporarily forget all outer reality is wonderful. To become attached to such experiences, however, is to fall into a mystical trap. Kabbalah stresses the importance of avoiding this through always paying attention to bringing all transpersonal energies back to ground and finding a way of expressing them in the ordinary world.

All of us unconsciously re-enact the same events, from past lives or earlier in this life, in an attempt to meet needs that have not yet been met, or learn lessons that have not yet been integrated in our development. Working on your early life experiences, and the work of past life recall, gives you the opportunity to discover more about yourself, and manifest your real purpose for being incarnated on this planet at this time. You may become aware of your awareness excitedly dancing from one experience to another, yet always present, never ending and never changing.

PRACTICE

• Recapitulation

Recapitulation is a term invented by Carlos Castaneda to describe techniques for re-owning energy that you have tied up with people from your past. Such practices have been used by Kabbalists for many years, sometimes under the title of the 'magical memory', but Castaneda's version of such practice is particularly effective.

The first step is to make a recapitulation list that should include the name of every single person with whom you've had contact in your life, from your parents to people with whom you've only had minimal contact. As you make such a list, you find that you remember very many more people than you would have believed possible. This can include people who have played significant parts in your life but whom you've apparently forgotten. It sounds really daunting, even impossible, to make a list of everyone you have ever had contact with, but a major part of the technique is overcoming such self-imposed limitations and working hard at remembering.

Once the list is completed (or as complete as you can make it), you then take each person on the list in turn and consider all your interactions with this person in as full a detail as possible. An essential part of the process is to feel the emotional charge associated for you with that person as fully as you can. Then, using your will and imagination, the two most powerful forces in your Kabbalistic armoury, you let go of all the positive *and* negative connections with this person. A charge of previously unavailable energy is released, which you can then draw back into yourself.

It might take you a lifetime to complete it, but using your intent to start and to maintain such a project is the essence of good Kabbalistic practice, and essential training on your journey from the past. Any energy that you have released from your work on the past is now available to you to assist in releasing yourself from the restrictions imposed by empty expectations and wishes, and you can learn how connecting with your real inner purpose unlocks a vast storehouse of potential energy.

ARCHETYPES OF EXPERIENCE

The two primary archetypes that mould our experience are 'Love' and 'Will'. These are represented on the Tree of Life by Chesed and Geburah, the two spheres that, together with Tiphareth, form the soul triangle. This is not to say that Love and Will are the same as soul, but through an understanding of correspondences, we can say that the purpose for the soul's incarnation is expressed, in each individual, through their relationship with these two archetypes.

The archetypes of Love and Will manifest in our personalities in a variety of ways. Very simply, we can say that most people tend to be more developed in their connection to one of these archetypes and relatively underdeveloped in their connection to the other. Someone who has developed their Geburah, for instance, will tend to be self-determined, have focused awareness and be strong enough to assert themselves appropriately. If the development of Geburah has been at the expense of Chesed (the archetype of Love), they may tend to be manipulative, selfish and ambitious, and have an underlying fear of becoming impotent and powerless. On the other hand, someone who has a well-developed connection to Chesed will tend to be co-operative, sensitive, caring and receptive. If the development of Chesed has been at the expense of Geburah (the archetype of Will), however, they will tend towards attachment, dependency, conformity, and have an underlying fear of loneliness or of being totally bereft of love.

In either case, whether the imbalance is on the side of Geburah or Chesed, we need to re-balance through bringing the level of the less developed archetype up to the level of the more developed one. This way we create a dynamic balance through inclusion. The archetype that has been developed more will also need work done on it, but rather than depressing it, a Kabbalist will work actively to refine its distortions. As well as this 'psychological' work, a Kabbalist will also work 'magically' through finding ways of aligning his or her personal connection to Will and Love (as expressed through Geburah and Chesed) to Spiritual Will and Love, which are represented by Chockmah and Binah, the second and third spheres on the Tree of Life.

We can see that personal will is on the left hand column of the Tree of Life under Spiritual Love, and personal love is on the right hand column under Spiritual Will (Purpose). If we see these two planes on the Tree as the bases of the top two triangles, to align the triangles so their correspondences match, we would need not only to invert one of them, we would also have to spiral it round. This spiralling effect shown on the Tree of Life indicates how the connection between the Supernal Triad of the Spirit and the second triangle of soul is not made through simple reflection of the energy, but involves an active spiralling process. We are reminded of the DNA spiral as being a similar key, on another level, to the understanding of the meaning of life.

In our personalities, we find a correlation between Love and Will and 'female' and 'male'. Firstly, it must be stressed that all men and all women have both 'female' and 'male' inside them. A soul that manifests as a man usually manifests a deeper soul connection to the 'feminine' and vice versa. However this may be, we all tend to manifest our connection to Geburah and Chesed through how we learn to relate to our own male and female qualities. We learn much of this from our parents. Generally speaking, a baby views its mother as a living embodiment of Love, its father as a living representation of Will. From the interaction between our parents and between them and us, we start to learn how we are going to manifest our understanding of Love and Will in our current incarnation.

From the Mother–Father Deity right through to the most earthly manifest 'maleness' or 'femaleness', Kabbalah stresses the absolute equality of male and female. If we apply the maxim 'as above, so below' to this, we can see that another aspect of the work for a female Kabbalist is to elevate the 'inner male' and to refine the 'outer female'. Correspondingly, for a male Kabbalist the work is to elevate the 'inner female' and refine the 'outer male'. This work ensures balance and the subsequent alignment with the soul. It also, of course, aids the work of the soul in its journey towards alignment and integration with the Spiritual Triad. A Kabbalist will maintain that this is just one example of how the most mundane, everyday work we perform on our growth and development is no less important than work that appears deeper or loftier. Indeed, just as the 'god name' for Kether, the Spiritual Self, is Eheieh, meaning 'I Am That I Am', a Kabbalist affirms in his or her work an essential connection to the

Divine and will also say, in moments of true connection and ecstasy, 'I am that I am.'

When we actively participate in the mysteries of the Tree of Life, we are aligning our human imagination with the Divine Imagination. It was this Divine Imagination that the Deity used to create the cosmos. By using our human imagination to work with the Tree, we start to comprehend the Divine Imagination. You may now wonder why we have not yet met an attribution for 'imagination' on the Tree of Life. Quite simply, it is because human imagination and Divine Imagination are always inseparable, and the whole Tree of Life, and all it represents, is the product of this imagination. This is not to say the world is unreal in some way. On the contrary, it is a positive affirmation of the Absolute Reality of all creation.

A MULTIPLICITY OF UNITY

We are all divine, not in some abstract sense, but in our everyday lives. Whatever we do, we are never disconnected from our essential nature. The myths of gods and goddesses often show us that even divine beings may stray from their purpose and misdirect their energies. We humans are no different! To realise and, more importantly, to manifest our essential divinity, we have to work at it. This is a life-long process and extreme caution is advised when we meet those who would tell us of their 'great initiations', 'spiritual attainment', 'understanding of the true Kabbalah' and so forth. Part of the work of Kabbalah, in showing us our own true nature, is to help us re-own our power from all the 'masters', 'secret chiefs', gurus, shamen and the like. To a Kabbalist, everyone met on the path is at least an equal, and always possibly just the person we need to teach us a particular lesson.

As well as being surrounded by this endless multiplicity of other 'divine beings' masquerading as humans, all other entities in all the universes, whether imagined or 'real', are truly aspects of the Divine. A Kabbalist is on the look-out, therefore, for messages, teachings, understanding, not only from other humans or from some direct spiritual inspiration, but also from archangels, angels, demons, animals, plants and rocks! If this sounds fantastic, consider what it means to view the world this way. Whatever we may believe (consciously), our unconscious carries endless possibilities. If we can connect to this realm of the unconscious, we can liberate energies that can enrich our understanding of ourselves and all our potential. Without choice, we tap into the unconscious every night in our dreams. Kabbalah says how much better to tap into the unconscious as often as possible. Or, indeed, how wonderful to realise that everything in our lives is a manifestation from the unconscious. From this viewpoint it is no less strange or fantastic to talk to an archangel than it is to dream of a goldfish.

The danger with this work is that the practitioner will get carried away in her or his own personal imagination to a degree that becomes dangerously ungrounded. This is why we constantly stress for all Kabbalistic work the importance of grounding. All work starts in Malkuth and ends there. If we do not follow this advice we do so at our own peril and can easily fall prey to the glamours of self-delusion and 'self-importance', which lead only to 'self-destruction'. This is often described Kabbalistically as building a castle on the sands of the Abyss (between the Supernal Triad and the rest of the Tree). However strong a castle it may be, it has lost its connection to the Spirit and, having no grounds in Malkuth, its foundations shift with the sands of the Abyss and are doomed to dissolution.

It is also important with all Kabbalistic work – and for that matter for all work of self-development whatever the system – to remember the sacredness of all life. Everything has its 'angel', its 'divine breath', from each individual cell through to the planet Earth and the whole universe. Everything is interconnected, nothing in our universe is separate (however temporarily separate it may sometimes appear). To be truly divine ourselves, we cannot deny the divinity of any other being, for to do so would deny our own divinity. Kabbalists believe that every being is a spark of the divine. As such we all have the right to do what we will, and no one has the right to interfere with another being's will. If what we think is our will does interfere with someone else, then we are not doing our true will.

During the last couple of centuries, it was believed that science would lead us from a magical philosophy to one where we would fully understand and harness the inorganic substance of the universe. Modern science, however, has led us to realise that the two central truths of magical philosophy are accurate. The first is that that there is a lot more out there in the universe than we are aware of, and the second is that our involvement makes a difference. It is generally accepted nowadays in scientific circles (as it always has been in magical ones) that each and every action creates an effect. Simply by observing something you affect the outcome (as in, for instance, the participation of an observer to subatomic particle experiments chang-ing the way the particles behave). We are not remote and ineffective pieces of the universe but rather the universe exists because of us and each little act can make a difference. It has become rather a cliché to assert that a butterfly beating its wings in, say, China can cause a storm in, for example, Holland, but it is scientifically and magically true.

On an everyday basis, however, each of us has a collective responsibility to the totality of life. Every time we do anything that is thoughtless, uncaring or 'off-mark' in some way, we lessen the total amount of connection and consciousness on our planet. Conversely, every time we do something with care, whenever we act from our true selves, we add to the pool of positive consciousness on our planet. We are all individually responsible, and each act we perform does make a difference. The Tree of Life can aid us in aligning ourselves with the purpose and intention of the Deity, and in becoming true and clear receptacles for the inflow of spiritual and psychic energies. Through the work we do on ourselves, it offers us a connection to our common work of collective responsibility.

MANIFESTING THE SOUL

In a later chapter we will discuss in detail the central importance of the heart in all Kabbalist work. The heart is represented on the Tree of Life by Tiphareth, the sphere in the centre of the diagram numbered six. Tiphareth means 'Beauty' and 'Harmony'. The beauty referred to is that created when everything in our being is synthesised into a complete whole, the harmony is that which results from living from a clearly defined centre. The experience of Tiphareth, of having a distinct self-consciousness that we can clearly define and separate from the contents of our consciousness, is what distinguishes us from most other living beings.

We do not usually experience pure self-consciousness, however, but instead experience it mixed with and veiled by everything we are sensing, feeling and thinking at any time. We usually live our lives identified with or attached to our personalities. To make our self-consciousness an explicit, experienced fact we need to be able to disattach ourselves from the 'contents' of consciousness. We need to make the 'flip over' referred to earlier where we become a soul with a personality rather than a personality with a soul.

Through deliberate dis-identification from the personality and identification with the soul, we gain freedom and the power of choice to be identified with or dis-identified from any aspect of our personality according to what is appropriate for any given situation. Thus we may learn to utilise our whole personality in an inclusive and harmonious way. When we do this, we are manifesting our soul energy, not in some exclusive 'pure' way, as if it is something 'out there', but directly through being exactly who are at any given moment.

We have already seen how Kabbalists stress the importance of 'grounding', of bringing all insights, experiences, spiritual connections, soul energies, inspiration and so on into manifestation. We continually return to two questions: what is the point of coming into incarnation if we are going to spend our time here attempting to separate from or 'transcend' the earth in some way? And what is the point of having a spiritual insight or connection if it remains ungrounded, unconnected to the everyday flow of energy on our planet?

If we believe, as Kabbalists do, that the purpose of incarnation is to further the realisation of soul in everything that is made manifest, and to further the work of tikkun, we do this effectively only through engaging ourselves with the world of matter as represented by Malkuth. In other words, we have to connect Tiphareth to the earth. To do this effectively, there are four steps:

- banish all other ideas apart from the matter at hand, be one-pointed in Hod (representing our thinking function)
- purify our feelings, be clear and connected in Netzach (representing our feeling function)
- consecrate ourselves to the work of incarnation, dedicating ourselves to the single purpose of manifesting Tiphareth (in this sense representing our experience of soul through our intuitive function)
- ground ourselves in direct relationship to the earth, bringing our inner connections into clear manifestation in Malkuth (representing our sensing function, our bodies as a whole, and the physical world).

Sometimes we cannot achieve these aims, perhaps because we lack the will to do it, we become distracted, we devalue our own importance, or we inflate our importance out of all proportion. Fear can also get in the way of clearly manifesting soul energies – fear of the responsibility involved, of losing our individuality, or misusing power, of inadequacy, loneliness, of being rejected, of being 'wrong' in some way, and so on. By thoroughly connecting ourselves to the Tree of Life and continuously grounding our work in Malkuth, however, we may achieve our aims in a centred and grounded way. The following exercise offers us the opportunity of receiving a 'gift' from the soul and then finding ways of using this gift in the world.

PRACTICE

• A gift to ground

Make yourself comfortable, relax and take a few deep breaths. As you breathe out, let go of any nagging tensions in your body, and as you breathe in, be aware that you are breathing in life-giving energy.

Close your eyes and imagine you are standing on a windswept moor. Take some time to imagine this place as clearly as you can. Fill in as much detail as possible – what can you see around you? What can you smell, hear, taste on the wind? Is it raining lightly or with wind-swept gushes of rain that beat against your body? How do you feel? What are you wearing? Really allow yourself to get a sense of being alone on this windswept moor.

As you look around you, see in the near distance a solitary standing stone. Start walking in the direction of this stone, staying connected to the feeling of being alone on the windy moor.

Just as you reach the stone, there is an opening in the clouds above and a ray of light shines onto the stone, illuminating it clearly. Lying atop the stone is a small object, a gift left here for you by an angel. Don't try and work out what this gift may be, but without judgement or censorship see what the gift actually is. In your own time, pick up the gift, hold it tightly in your hands, then thank the angel for leaving it for you.

Return to your everyday consciousness, back in the room where you started, bringing the gift with you. You may like to spend a little while now writing about this experience and describing the gift, or drawing a picture of it. Consider your gift in detail – what is it? What does it mean to you? You may not know what the gift is, or what it is for, but trust it was the right gift for you to receive at this time. If you stay attached to it, and remain conscious of it, its meaning will become clearer.

Whether you understand the meaning of your gift or not, the most important action for you now is to find some way to manifest this gift in Malkuth. Maybe there is some action you can take to ground this gift symbolically. For instance, if your gift was a red heart, to ground it you may need to express your love to someone. Perhaps you received a precious jewel and you need to acquire such a jewel in 'real life', that is, get hold of a real ruby or manifest something equally precious to you in your life. Maybe all you need to do to ground your gift is to remain aware of it and let its energy infuse your actions. You have to find your own way of grounding your gift, for in so doing you will bring some soul energy into manifestation on the earth. You are then participating in the most important work for a Kabbalist, making a direct link between Tiphareth and Malkuth.

5

THE JOURNEY, PATHWORKING AND THE TAROT

Blessed are they that follow the commandments, for they have access to the Tree of Life and may enter through the gates of matter.

Book of Revelations (adapted from 22:14)

We can see the whole of life as a journey. We are born out of a state of undifferentiated unity then we walk the path of life, becoming more and more differentiated, more individually ourselves. As we learn to integrate our experiences and realise our potential, we move towards a new unity, more of a chosen union. Finally, we reach the end of our journey and step into death, consciously or unconsciously, willingly or unwillingly. Just as we tread the path of our life journey towards our death, so we can similarly see different parts and areas of our life as little journeys within the larger life journey. For example, adolescence can be seen as a journey from childhood towards adulthood; education is a journey towards greater knowledge; marriage a shared journey of discovery, and so on. A single day in our life can be viewed as a journey, from awakening back to sleep, and within any single day we will make many even smaller journeys. Even in reading this book you make numerous journeys from one paragraph to the next.

Whether our journeys are internal or external ones, whether they are long and complicated or short and simple, whether they are pursued singly or whether we are travelling many journeys at once, we are always stepping along pathways from somewhere to somewhere else. Looked at this way we can say that each step on every path is as significant as every other step. Further, the most important step is always the next step, for without making the next step we do not journey forwards. This may sound very obvious, but we often live without this awareness. We look forward to our goal, missing many individual steps on the way, sometimes even stepping onto a completely different path than we intended. We look backwards, congratulating ourselves or worrying over some steps we have already made, perhaps wishing we could change them. We generally find it very difficult to focus on our current path and the next step we have to make to carry us forwards.

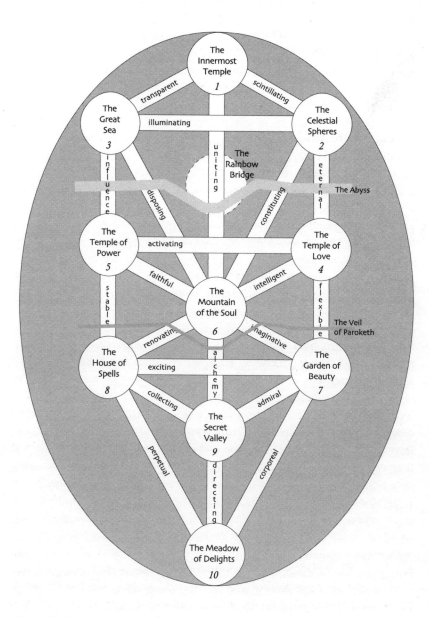

Diagram 12: Pathworking

If we apply this understanding to our work with the Tree of Life we can see two clear principles emerging. Firstly, that we are travelling on the paths of the Tree at all times, even though we may not always be aware of where we are on the Tree. Secondly, the most important step for us to take is the next, so we are well advised to concentrate on that step before worrying about others we may need to take later. In this book we have already spoken of the twenty-two paths that connect the ten spheres on the Tree of Life. Traditionally the spheres are also called 'paths', so in this context it is said there are thirty-two paths on the Tree. As the Tree of Life is a map of our consciousness, the more clearly we become aware of where we are on the Tree (that is, in our lives), the more effectively we can experience the world and express ourselves appropriately (see diagram 12).

'Pathworking' is a term used quite frequently these days to describe any kind of 'guided fantasy' or 'directed daydreaming', whether it involves Kabbalah or not. For a Kabbalist the term refers to making a connection with one or more of the 'thirty-two paths' on the Tree of Life. Beyond that, it can be applied to any method for making such connections, from formal rituals through to simple realisations of the need to make psychological connections. For instance, if I knew that I needed to balance my feeling and thinking functions, I would do work with the path that connects Hod and Netzach, for this is the path relating to the relationship between these two functions.

More often than not, when people speak of pathworking with the Tree of Life they are referring to the setting up of complex 'stories' that can be used to direct the imagination of the aspirant through the required paths to a particular goal. We might decide, for instance, to travel up the Middle Pillar to Tiphareth, passing through the path connecting Malkuth to Yesod, Yesod itself, then the path from Yesod to Tiphareth. Our 'guiding fantasy' would incorporate symbols and images that correspond to these paths. You are (hopefully) already familiar with the complex tables of correspondences in Appendix 4. Using appropriately selected correspondences you could create a story of a journey that incorporates some of these images and ideas, which would then direct your consciousness into the appropriate sphere. For instance, for a pathworking from Malkuth to Yesod, you might travel initially to a dark wood where lots of nightshade grows and imagine that a strange being with a crocodile-like face gives you a potion of rue to drink; then you may travel on past a purple-hued pool where watercress grows in abundance and have a magical encounter with a hare; and so on.

If you wish to create your own pathworking in this way, the first step is to write the story of the journey as suggested in the last paragraph but with imagery relevant to the path you wish to travel. Include as much detail as you can, and write clearly in the present tense. To then perform the pathworking you have written, centre yourself, close your eyes and let the story guide you into these other realms of consciousness. You might like to tape the pathworking, reading the story slowly and with suitable gaps, and use this to guide you. Alternatively, you could share with a friend, each taking a turn at travelling the path involved. Many of the exercises you have already met in this book are simple forms of pathworking and may give you some good pointers on how to effectively perform a pathworking. Later in this chapter you will explore more sophisticated pathworking.

Many people use pathworking simply in this way, although generally it is considered more effective to do some preliminary work, which will 'raise energy', which simply means to do some activity that shifts your attention away from your everyday concerns. This might entail imagining you are in a magical circle that separates you from the 'outside' world; dancing vigorously to raise consciousness; performing the Kabbalistic Cross; invoking protecting archangels, and so forth. The essence of the work, however, is to achieve a state where you are receptive to the suggestions that the pathworking makes to you. If you are successful you will have an experience of the path that you are travelling, including relevant insights and understanding. The two most important factors are that the work should be done appropriately, not just for amusement or curiosity, and that, as has already been stressed, you re-ground yourself in Malkuth. The most effective way to do this is to engage in some everyday activity. Some people, for instance, find having a cup of tea and a few biscuits, taking a walk, or even socialising with friends, is effective for this. No pathworking is complete – or truly Kabbalistic – unless it brings the traveller back to the earth.

Another way of pathworking is simply to imagine the Hebrew letters (or other appropriate symbols) on a door through which you then project your consciousness. If you wanted to travel the path from Malkuth to Netzach, for instance, you would imagine a suitable door with the letter 'Qoph' brightly emblazoned upon it, then imagine that you open the door and pass into the world behind. Whatever you imagine is then your experience of that path. You would finish this work by coming back out of the door and closing it firmly shut. This type of pathworking is much less structured than those where all the symbols are prearranged. This way is often more effective, for each individual makes connections with his or her own inner world of symbols rather than trying to impose symbols that may not have that much relevance. For example, if you don't relate at all to crocodiles and, for you, a bull is a better animal to attribute to the path from Malkuth to Yesod, then it is better for you to be honest to your own inner world of symbols than try to fit yourself into something to which you do not relate.

Magic has been defined as the 'science and art of causing willed change to occur'. In other words, whenever we do anything from choice and it causes a change, we are doing magic. If we want a certain book, go to a shop and exchange a token (money) for this book, then we have performed an act of magic. If we do a pathworking and understand a little more about ourselves, we have similarly performed an act of magic. The Kabbalistic way is a way of magic and, as with all true magic, it has the ultimate aim of manifesting more love and understanding in the universe. When we use our Kabbalistic knowledge and understanding wisely, we perform many magical acts and, through these, partake of the greatest magical act of all, the work of tikkun, the aim of which is the complete re-manifestation of Eden on earth in which all women and men freely and equally partake of the richness and splendour of life.

THE ELEVENTH PATH

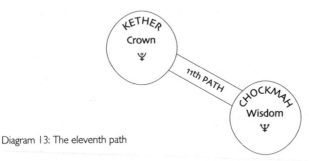

Diagram 13: The eleventh path

There are many different ways to connect with the paths on the Tree of Life and to understand how the four worlds operate within the realm of human concern. The techniques discussed next can be applied in principle to any path, but the obvious place to start is the first path associated with the lightning flash, known as the eleventh path, connecting Kether and Chockmah (see diagram 13).

You can immediately make a connection with this path simply through considering what you understand about Kether and Chockmah. As Kether is attributed to the Source (or Self) and Chockmah is the sphere of spiritual will, we might, for instance, infer that this path represents the connection between the spheres, or the force manifesting from the will of the original creative energy. But what does that mean in practical terms? To answer this question, it is necessary to explore the attributes of this path further.

Each of the thirty-two paths on the Tree of Life is given a suggestive name in the Sepher Yetzirah. The eleventh path is known as the scintillating path (from the noun scintillation). The *Oxford English Dictionary* suggests some connections where scintillation is described, among other things, as:

- the action of scintillating; emission of sparks or spark-like flashes of light
- the twinkling or tremulous motion of the light of the fixed stars
- the flashing of the eyes
- a flash, a brilliant display (of wit, of thought).

These definitions, and those you may find for the Sepher Yetzirah's descriptive terms for the other paths, are a good place to start for useful correspondences. Of course, in the case of the first and second worlds of Atziluth and Briah, which are beyond all ordinary human understanding, none of the correspondences apply. For these two worlds, our exploratory work needs to be receptive and reflective, turning attention inside to find our deepest connections. The following meditation may be useful in this context.

PRACTICE

• The eleventh path

Silently meditate upon the eleventh path. Don't do anything, don't try to make anything happen, just hold the idea of this path in mind. What comes to mind?

Make notes, then consider that all the information, all the ideas, and all the connections you have made rightly belong to the third or fourth worlds. If you let go of all these and return to meditation on this path, what comes now?

Remember that Yetzirah (the third, formative world) contains all the correspondences, all connections, associations, ideas, indeed everything we can think or feel or imagine about this (or any) path. It is as if Yetzirah sits between the totally abstract and as yet unmanifest worlds of Spirit (Atziluth and Briah) and the fully concrete and manifest world of matter (Assiah). Yetzirah, in this sense, is like a large circle that encompasses absolutely everything of which we can be aware in normal states of consciousness, so much so that if anything could exist outside this circle it would immediately expand to include it. The eleventh path can be understood as the highest manifestation of a personal connection to deity, but only in the context of realising this is a description, not the experience itself.

First and foremost, we will consider the corresponding letter from the sacred Hebrew alphabet, which in this case is the letter Aleph. Aleph is the first of the mother letters, and is attributed to the number one, the sound of *a* and the element of air. As well as ox, which is the usual meaning ascribed to Aleph, this letter (in Hebrew) can also mean a familiar animal, a friend, a gentle thing, a captain or duke, a governor, or guide. Aleph is usually described as meaning an ox, however, and interestingly the shape of the letter suggests the shape of a yoke. The main underlying idea to this attribute seems to be that of ploughing. As the Zohar describes Aleph as the beginning of all including the beginning of the substance of god, it is worth reflecting also on the etymological connection between yoking and yoga, which has the same root. As yoga is usually translated as union with god, the connection is very apparent.

PRACTICE

• Exploring the eleventh path through Aleph

Diagram 14: Aleph

This activity is in three parts, and it is preferable to do each part as a discrete exercise.

1. Write out or draw the letter Aleph on an A4 size sheet of paper,

colouring the letter with light grey (or silver).

In a dimly lit or dark room, place a candle flame in front of and to one side of the grey letter Aleph then, after preparation, sit and meditate upon the image.

Allow your inner dialogue to slow or stop and keep returning your attention to silent contemplation of the letter. Keep this up for at least twenty minutes.

Note any results.

2. Sitting or lying comfortably with a dim light in your room (candlelight is ideal), close your eyes and breathe deeply.

Imagine a door before you, any type of door you care to imagine, with the letter Aleph clearly visible on its surface in clear bright white light.

For now do not go through the door but open it and see what is on the other side. Allow whatever images emerge to appear before you. Do not judge or censor them.

If it feels right for you, you may go through the door and step into the world you see there. If you decide to do this, only go a little way into this world. You can always return at another time if you wish.

Whether you go into the world behind the door or not, when you have finished and returned, firmly and willfully close the door shut.

Note any results.

3. Try making and holding the shape of the letter with your body, moving your limbs to mirror the strokes of the letter.

What feelings, thoughts, sensations, or any other responses do you have when holding this shape?

• Pathworking the eleventh path

The following list shows some correspondences to the eleventh path. Collect together some of these objects or representations of them (pictures will do if nothing else is available).

oil:	melissa
herb:	hyssop and/or eyebright
flower:	daisy
tree:	spruce (e.g. a leaf, a piece of bark, etc.)
magical instruments:	dagger, fan, stick
animal:	tiger

(You might like to look up other correspondences in Appendix 4.)

Create, write and perform a pathworking for the eleventh path in which, as well as using some of the symbols listed above, you include meeting with a sylph, the legendary being attributed to this path. Sylphs are usually depicted as diaphanous and beguiling creatures, rather like the fairies of fairy tales, who are a form of sylph. On the dark side they can also be obsessive and drain your energy. In his book *Nightside of Eden*, Kenneth Grant, the accomplished British magician, says that negative encounters with sylphs are the origin of myths concerning magicians being imprisoned in a non-physical form, that they have got this way because sylphs draw more and more vital energy from an unwary intruder on this path. Grant suggests that sylphs are very dangerous beings that have been whitewashed through fairy tales.

On your pathworking, therefore, once you have established a safe place or circle in which to work, your first task is to find out if the sylph you meet is friendly or dangerous. The simplest and most effective way of doing this is to project (or strongly imagine) the shape of an upright pentagram blazing on the body of the creature. If the sylph crumples up, disappears, or otherwise reacts badly to your pentagram, say the Kabbalistic Cross and ask a friendly sylph to appear. If you do not meet a friendly sylph by no later than your third attempt, return to your normal consciousness and very clearly close your circle of working through removing any objects you may have placed in or around the circle, stamping your feet on the floor a few times and stating out loud very clearly your intent to close the circle. Attempt the exercise again at another time.

THE ELEVENTH PATH IN THE FOURTH WORLD

The fourth world is the realm of specific physical body correspondences. You might like to review these connections through paying particular attention to the physical structure and inner body components columns in the correspondence tables.

One of the main physical correspondences to this path is the pituitary gland. This gland is about the size of a pea and lies in a space at the base of the skull. The pituitary gland consists of three lobes, the two main ones being the anterior and posterior lobes, which are more specifically attributed to the paths connecting Chockmah to Chesed and Binah to Geburah. The anterior lobe secretes hormones associated with growth, controlling the bones and muscles, and with gender and sexuality. The posterior lobe contains hormones that are involved in sexual functioning in women and the functioning of the kidneys in both men and women. The third lobe, known as the intermediate lobe, is described in anatomy books as having little known significance to the human system and is the part of the gland most closely associated with the eleventh path. It is almost certainly intimately linked to feeling factors; modern research shows, for instance, that a child not receiving enough tactile stimuli can develop physical abnormalities that directly relate to the depression of pituitary functioning.

The pituitary gland is often associated in books on esoteric anatomy with the ajna chakra (or third eye, as it is more commonly known), especially when it develops, expands and links with the pineal gland (corresponding to the twelfth path) to form the activated third eye. The pituitary gland is also considered to be the master gland of the endocrine system, which influences all metabolic processes. This makes clear its attribution to the eleventh path, connecting, as it does, the spheres associated with our deepest spiritual connection (Kether) and our Purpose or True Will (Chockmah).

PRACTICE

• Healing with the eleventh path

Now consider the physical disorders corresponding to this path: optical defects, ear disorders (both on left side), hearing, balance, seeing.

Decide on a healing regime for any of the eleventh path disorders that apply to yourself or someone else on whose healing you can work. This may involve, for instance, the laying on of hands with a healing intent, the use of the appropriately corresponding oils or herbs, calling forth the presence of healing angels, or any other relevant healing techniques known to you. We will be exploring healing techniques in more details in Chapter 7, but before then it is good practice for you to try to devise your own healing methods. (If you do this work involving another person you must explain what you intend and obtain their full agreement, even if the healing is in absence. An exception to this might be if you choose to do a healing of your relationship with a person who is either dead or no longer accessible to you.)

TAROT AND THE TREE OF LIFE

Tarot cards are pictorial, symbolic representations of the cycles of time, and the processes we go through in connecting and interacting with these cycles of time. The Tarot can help us understand our own essential nature, how we live in cycles within cycles, and how to understand our relationships with other beings, indeed with all life. No one really knows the origins of the Tarot. There are many different theories as to where Tarot originates, ranging from ancient Egypt through the Gypsies in the Dark Ages to Italian card makers in the late fourteenth century. In the most pragmatic sense, it doesn't really matter where they come from, what is important is if they work for us today. Most people's experience is that they do.

The Tarot is a sophisticated tool, not for showing us what will be, but for reflecting on what is and revealing the possibilities of what *might* be. Using the Tarot for divination involves a process of self-transformation – we are offered the opportunity to discover more of who we are. We can then make informed and life-affirming decisions about who we want to become and where we wish to go. When we use the Tarot for divination we find our lives are not predetermined by outside forces, but that we really can make choices.

The origins of the Tarot cards and Kabbalah seem strangely interwoven, certainly in 'mythical history' if not in the mundane. The seventy-eight cards of the Tarot may be assigned to the spheres and paths on the Tree in a very straightforward and easy to understand manner. Thus they become very useful 'compendiums' of symbols for pathworking on the Tree of Life. There are seventy-eight cards in a full Tarot pack, four suits of ten each, called the minor Arcana, sixteen 'court cards' and twenty-two 'Major Arcana', 'Atus' or 'trumps'. Diagram 15 shows the attribution of the Tarot onto the Tree of Life. I recommend you study this diagram while reading this section.

Different Tarot designs will more or less agree with the Kabbalistic correspondences, but all Tarot cards, of whatever design, can be related to the Tree. Some Tarot packs, however, are more appropriate because they have been deliberately designed with the Tree of Life in mind. The Thoth Tarot Cards display a deep understanding of Kabbalah and also happen to be among the most beautifully designed cards. Because of this, they can act as very suitable images for pathworking. We might, for instance, instead of imagining a door with a Hebrew letter, imagine a curtain with the Tarot symbol emblazoned on it, or simply project ourselves into the world depicted in the design.

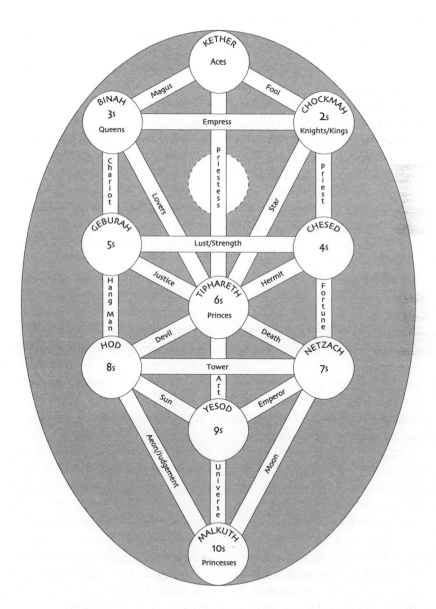

Diagram 15: The Tarot

Whether Tarot originated in Egypt or not, there is an interesting connection between the word Tarot and the Egyptian goddess Ta-urt. This goddess, often represented by a hippopotamus, is called 'the mother of revolutions and cycles of time'. The twenty-two major arcana can take you into, out of and even beyond the wheel of time, offering a perspective on life that enables you to function better. They also show connections between different states of awareness, for instance, the card called 'the tower' represents how a person may experience the relationship between thinking and feeling within their psyche. The major arcana are said to be under the direction of Ta-urt's son who is named Thoth. He corresponds to the Greek and Roman god Mercury, a god of communication. Sometimes the whole Tarot is called 'the Book of Thoth', emphasising how the value of the cards is in what they communicate to us and how they teach us to communicate with others.

The sixteen court cards show how different types of people interact with the wheel of life. We have all the different types represented by the court cards within us, but certain ones will predominate for different people at different times. The forty minor cards represent the energy of the wheel of life itself, analysed into forty component parts, ten in each of four suits. These suits correspond to the four elements of fire, water, air and earth, and to the suits in an ordinary deck of cards. The ten cards in each suit are numbered from one to ten; the one or ace represents the purest form of the element, through to the ten, which represents the element its most material manifestation.

The different correspondences of the Tarot cards to the Tree of Life make divination simpler and more accurate. The analysis of the energy or wheel of life into its component parts helps us understand these energies and recognise our unique part in the play of life. Using the Tarot for divination offers us more choice about how we want our life to be, so we may be in control of our own fate rather than feeling like a victim to the blind whim of fate.

The ace of each suit, corresponding to Kether, is the pure form of that energy, so, for example, the ace of wands is pure creative energy. Each card then represents a progressive degradation of this energy until the ten, which is its most material form, is reached. The ten of wands represents the complete manifestation of creativity. This journey, from the ace to the ten in each suit, is a move from 'potential' energy to 'kinetic' energy. The six represents energy in its 'ideal' balanced form, and the ten, as well as representing its complete manifestation, also includes the seed of decay into the next suit.

The perfection of the attribution of the Tarot cards to the Tree of Life is quite astounding. Consider the four '4's in a Tarot pack. Because they are numbered four they relate to Chesed, love. The four of wands corresponds to the first world and therefore the element of fire; the four of cups to the second world and the element of water; the four of swords to the third world and the element of air; and the four of discs to the fourth world and the element of earth. The four of wands is therefore the fiery, creative part of Love; the four of cups the watery, receptive part of Love; the four of swords the airy, formative part of Love; the four of discs the earthly, material part of Love.

WHAT IS DIVINATION?

Divination works on the principle that everything is connected to everything else. Through investigating one thing we can glean information about something else. Divination takes a divination tool – the Tarot cards, stones, sticks, patterns in tealeaves, and so on – and relates the information revealed through its use to the life of the querant (the person for whom the divination is done). The idea that pictures on cards or patterns of stones, for instance, might reveal information about someone's life is strange to the Newtonian linear world view that has so influenced Western science for centuries. That world view is changing, however, as ideas from the New Science become popularised. It is a central theme of modern Quantum theories that we do not nor cannot understand what happens with our linear thought. Not even the scientists who make up the theories can do that, but the theories nevertheless describe things that do happen. As Fritzjof Capra says in his book *The Tao of Physics*: 'Particles are not isolated grains of matter, but are probability patterns, interconnections in an inseparable cosmic web.' This statement forms the basis of the theory of how divination works, it is just usually described in more esoteric language.

To be able to understand the message received through divination, the diviner has to change her or his consciousness in some way. Following a particular practice, usually shamanic in nature, the diviner receives messages from spirits from another world. Such messages are interpreted by the diviner in a way that helps the querant deal more effectively with their future life. Sometimes this information takes the form of foreknowledge and prediction, but usually it is more ambiguous and unspecific – warnings, suggestions, images, portents, possibilities and so on. In divinatory systems such as the Tarot, a dialogue between the diviner and the querant often adds more information, fleshing out the message from the Tarot, thus enabling the revelations to be more specifically applied. In other systems of divination, such as from oracles, the messages are usually more ambiguous and open to a wide variety of interpretations. Sometimes they are non-verbal messages, definitely aimed at affecting the unconscious mind of the querant. Part of the individual seeker's work is then to use this knowledge to guide him or her in subsequent life events.

There are many practices undertaken by diviners to put them in the right state to receive inspiration. Most if not all aim in some way to still and empty the mind of the practitioner. Through 'turning off the inner dialogue' we open ourselves to other realms of being and understanding from whence we can return with the new divinatory knowledge. While we all innately have this ability, some people are more skilled at achieving this stillness and openness. Everyone can undertake a divination, however, because the work is not about having psychic abilities per se, but more about being able to put one's own concerns and interests aside for a few brief moments and concentrate on another person's life journey. While sometimes it is difficult to do this, even the most basic counselling course shows how easily people can learn to be willing to listen to others.

The second major skill for a diviner, after being able to still the mind, is not to be attached to psychic powers but to let them come and go as needed. When individuals become attached to psychic powers it can lead to all kinds of delusion, glamour and dishonesty. There is an old joke about a psychic who says, 'I see nothing', but such honesty is a refreshing aspect of a true psychic. There is nothing wrong with developing psychic abilities, or in making oneself a suitable receptacle for psychic powers if they come. The point is, however, that we become good diviners not through developing powers but through developing ourselves. We are then ready when such powers emerge, which they will do, to use an effective divination tool such as the Tarot.

Each Tarot card combines pictures with words and symbols to represent a natural energy. As we are all part of nature, these energies are constantly within us, affecting our journey through life. The Tarot is one way of framing, articulating and evoking these energies into conscious recognition, showing us aspects of our experience to help us understand ourselves better. This is particularly true with regard to time, repetition, cyclical return, periodic law, and the sense that everything in life is part of a cycle, and we live within cycles which themselves are parts of larger cycles.

The Tarot combines all these ideas and experiences. If we believe that everything happens in cycles then we can say the Tarot is concerned with the essential nature of life, which is cyclical. In this sense the Tarot of something is its essence, its innermost nature or principle. To connect with the wheel of Tarot is to understand more of the wheels of nature and fate, the wheels of wisdom and folly that define our life journey.

Each Tarot card represents a facet of who you are. For example, the first two cards in a Tarot deck are the Fool and the Magus. On the surface the Fool is stupid, often depicted as blindly stepping over a cliff. Similarly the Magus is wise, conjuring the world into existence through magical arts. On a deeper level, however, we find the Fool is not as first appears; letting go into the world, surrendering to a larger wisdom, he or she lives life to the full. As William Blake indicated, the fool who persists in folly becomes wise. And the Magus is not so wise when he or she becomes fixated with ideas and techniques and misses the natural flow of energies, trying to make things happen that will happen anyway in their own good time. Using the wisdom of the Tarot to inform your divination, you can learn to trust your inner processes both when you feel 'wise' and when you feel 'foolish'. Through accepting ourselves as we are, we recognise where we are in life and can creatively and joyously divine our future.

The best way to understand the Tarot cards is to treat them as living beings. You can imagine them as seventy-eight people with whom you are acquainted, some you know well, some a little and some hardly if at all. As you work with the cards you build your relationship with each of these 'living beings' and observe their changing relationships with one another. Seventy-eight people is quite a large group, so you don't have to feel it is necessary to get to know them well all at once. It might take a lifetime to build a relationship with a particular card, and some cards you might never really like. You are almost certainly bound to have favourites, ones you prefer to hang out with and enjoy. In this way, the different cards really are just like people.

You can get to know these 'people' better through different card awareness techniques such as visualisation, through grounding the insights they bring, and through the process of divination itself. As with 'real' people, though, the best way is through spending time with them and getting to know their nature and how you interact with them. If you want to tell someone about a group of people you know, you are likely to tell stories about them that communicate their nature and how they behave. It is the same with divination using the Tarot. The diviner 'tells a story' to the querant, which enables the querant to understand more about the cards and why the particular ones that have emerged in the spread are relevant at this particular time. We all like hearing stories, and the better you become as a story teller, the better you will be able to communicate the insights from a Tarot reading to your subject.

When the cards are not being used they should be kept in a safe place that you treat as sacred – that simply means, not using the cards for other purposes, but treating them with respect. One way to do this is through using your will and imagination and keeping the cards in a temple of the Tarot. You create this temple through a visualisation. Then whenever you pick up the cards, you imagine you are taking them up from the altar in the temple of the Tarot. Similarly, whenever you finish using the cards you place them, in imagination, back into their sacred space in the temple.

THE TAROT JOURNEY

Tarot cards can be clearly and meaningfully interpreted as representing indicators of the stages on the journey of life, and the following suggestions develop this theme. While reading about the cards here, it is worth having a Tree of Life showing the Tarot attributions at hand (as diagram 15).

THE FOOL
The first Tarot card, an archetypal image of undifferentiated unity, from where we start, the divine spirit in physical incarnation, the pre-ego, purity and innocence.

THE MAGUS (OR MAGICIAN)
Birth itself, the emergence of ego, the beginning of the life journey and process of differentiation. Ego often has a bad press, but it is equally important to be able to build a strong ego as it is to be able to let go of ego. The ego acts as a container for our psychic energies, and without a strong enough ego we can be prone to psychological disorders that may throw us off balance. Also, a well-developed ego can offer us enough strength to experience the deepest spiritual connections without becoming inflated.

THE PRIESTESS, THE EMPRESS, THE EMPEROR, THE HIEROPHANT (OR PRIEST)
The four functions of intuition (Priestess), feeling (Empress), thinking (Emperor), and sensing (Hierophant), learning the lessons of incarn-ation, connecting to our purpose for being here, the search for and

discovery of self. All these four cards include a polarity between moving forwards to life or backwards to the womb, and thus represent the duality at the basis of all existence.

THE LOVERS, THE CHARIOT, STRENGTH (OR LUST), THE HERMIT

These four cards represent further stages of our development, particularly relating to adolescence: the outer journey and relating to others (the Lovers), a sense of purpose and relationship to ourselves (the Chariot), the desire for life, relating outwards (extraverted), the life force itself (Strength), and the inner journey, relating inwards (introverted), the process of self-examination (the Hermit).

FORTUNE (OR THE WHEEL)

This card, halfway through the major arcana, is the key turning point on the journey of individuation. Change is afoot, bringing your intentions and wishes closer to fruition, along with a willingness to go with the flow. There is awakening, a sensing of the wheel of life turning, transition, and crisis (e.g. adolescence, midlife etc.).

ADJUSTMENT (OR JUSTICE), THE HANGED MAN

After the awakening, the crisis, there needs to be adjustment to the new life, balance being created between the conscious and unconscious processes. The individual is willing to fight for his or her own values and feelings. This involves also being willing to sacrifice for the sake of others and endure the pain that is sometimes needed to go forward. The sacrifice of the old values, the reversal of intent, brings initiation.

DEATH, TEMPERANCE (ALCHEMY OR ART), DEVIL

Death necessitates stepping into the unknown and offering a hand of friendship even to those who appear as enemies. Energy is released from the death of the old self, the ego is transcended and the path moves towards maturation. The Devil energy now comes into its own, embracing life with gusto, engaging for the love of it with your particular interests and directions. The battle is to stay on course, between submitting or absorbing and transmuting into higher form, as the new is emerging. The Temperance (or Alchemy) card balances these two energies through including both, the true alchemy that now begins. It involves finding a better way to do things through putting things together in a new way, using creative thought to bring new innovations to light. The bringer forth of light is awakened.

TOWER, STAR
These cards represent the material reorientation that follows spiritual reorientation as light irradiates the personality, with the attendant shattering of earthly illusion; on a practical level, working on creating a character that can usefully relate and negotiate in the modern world. This involves trusting your inner guidance and the central sense of one's own worth, leading to true self-actualisation, becoming oneself, a guide in darkness.

MOON, SUN
In the return, the dark night of soul is encountered, the real test of faith built on experience, and learning to truly trust in one's own perceptions. This brings reconciliation, the dawning of the golden light, the marriage of the alchemical brother and sister. In the world, dancing in the light with a bright step, being optimistic and sharing good feelings with others, playing together.

JUDGEMENT (OR AEON), UNIVERSE (OR WORLD)
The rebirth of the integrated self (the mystical rebirth), the true awakening to new beginnings, built on the foundation of the old, the spirit of the primal fire. Wholeness and fulfilment, the return to the world where everyone you look upon is enlightened. Enjoying the unfolding of life, the child in the womb awaiting birth of the next cycle.

The imagery in Tarot cards, as already mentioned, is very useful for pathworking as it offers rich and evocative imagery to guide your inner vision. Coupled with a knowledge of how the major arcana relate to the journey of an individual through life, the Tarot is an astonishingly powerful tool to aid a Kabbalist on the journey of self-discovery. In the next section on ritual dance, you will learn more of how to tune your consciousness to a suitable state for deeply connecting with the imagery that may emerge during your explorations with the Tarot.

KABBALISTIC RITUAL

Through ritual we can by-pass our everyday states of consciousness and bring ourselves closer to Tiphareth where we co-operate with rather than resist the unfolding of our life journey. Our habitual inner dialogue of unfocused chatter in Hod and our emotional reactions from Netzach and Yesod can be turned off. No longer controlled by our personality spheres, we are open to enter the realm of soul. When we dance or move in this way, we are using our abilities to focus and move to enter altered states of consciousness. We can then release energies from Yesod, and use these energies to clear our current consciousness. From the realm of soul we can gain a knowledge and understanding of our potential – in other words, we can divine our future possibilities.

Ritual dance is one of the oldest forms of dance, yet how easy it is to miss the relevance of ritual when we see it as something obscure, strange or even frightening. We all perform rituals every day in our lives – from the rituals of rising in the morning through to the rituals of going to bed at night. If we make our rituals conscious then we empower ourselves. We give ourselves the opportunity to change and restructure our daily life rituals so they serve rather than hinder us. Performing our own rituals through which we connect to our body offers us such an opportunity. We can become connected to our soul energy and root this directly onto the earth, Malkuth.

To create Kabbalistic ritual dances is not difficult; they do not require the learning of any particular dance or life skills. Indeed, such dancing may not involve any dancing as such at all, and even those of you who really don't like dancing, or feel you are unable, can find a way of doing this kind of 'dance'. So long as you have the ability to move some parts of your body as you choose, you can do a Kabbalistic dance. The key is to choose to bring consciousness into your movement, and in this to connect with various Kabbalistic correspondences. For instance, we can create a simple Kabbalistic ritual dance through the correspondences of the four elements of fire, water, air and earth onto the Tree of Life. People used to believe that everything is composed of these four elements in different combinations. So, for instance, a cloud is fiery in its ability to become a storm, water in its composition and when it rains, airy in its movement, and earth when it clings to mountains or becomes a low mist.

There are various different ways to attribute the elements onto the Tree of Life. Perhaps the simplest, and most useful to us here, is shown in the accompanying table, which also shows how we can apply the four elements to some aspects of the human being.

Fire	Water	Air	Earth
Netzach	Yesod	Hod	Malkuth
feelings	emotions	thoughts	senses
sight	taste	smell	touch
heart/	belly/	head/	feet/arms/
solar plexus	abdomen	shoulders	legs/feet

As can be seen from the table, the correspondences give us the basis for creating a dance, one in which we pay attention to our feelings, emotions, thoughts and senses. Through connecting with different aspects of all the elements, you can balance your inner world. The sense of hearing is not in the table for it is connected to what is sometimes called 'the fifth element' – that of Spirit. So when you use your ears to attune yourself to any music you choose for your rituals, you are invoking Spirit! That said, it makes sense, then, to choose music that you like and which strongly suggests to you the element in question.

If we create a ritual dance that incorporates the four elements, taking us through the four lower spheres on the Tree, our aim is twofold. The first aim, as stated, is to create a state of inner balance. We may, for instance, do four separate dances, using earth, air, water and fire to connect us symbolically to these elements. As we do our 'dance of the four elements' it is important to be aware of our sensory world, to stay tuned in and really pay attention to what we are sensing.

The second aim is to lead us towards Tiphareth, where we can connect with our soul energies. After balancing ourselves with the four elements, therefore, we can then create a dance that helps us transcend our attachment with these lower spheres, and reach Tiphareth or centred consciousness. The best way to do this is to 'dance until we drop', holding our intention clearly as we do this. If we dance as long and as hard as we can, we can break through the veil of Paroketh, which separates Tiphareth from the lower spheres on the Tree of Life. When we cannot dance any more, we allow ourselves to drop to the floor, at least figuratively. Breathing deeply, we can then focus on how we feel and our expectation of being reborn in Tiphareth. When we have recovered our breath, we rise to our feet and do a 'dance of awakening', expressing our joy at having entered the realm of the soul. If we have successfully transcended our everyday consciousness, we will find ourselves connected to Tiphareth.

When we connect to our centre in this way, we can really let ourselves express our link with all the different qualities we may express through our souls – joy, love, beauty, truth, honesty, trust, intuition, and so on. As we move and dance, we can become aware of the 'cup of receptivity' within ourselves. Doing this, we gain insights and understanding about our purpose or 'true will' for being incarnated on the planet at this time. Finally, as with all Kabbalistic working, we will do a last dance to express this connection and bring us back to Malkuth. All work ends with grounding.

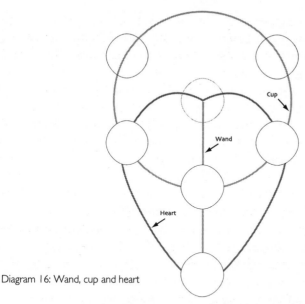

Diagram 16: Wand, cup and heart

Diagram 16 shows how our Kabbalistic ritual dance fits onto the Tree of Life. The single line represents our dancing of the four elements through the four lower spheres. It depicts the wand of intention. The circle represents our consciousness, centred in Tiphareth and radiating soul energies into our being. As a circle it depicts the cup of receptivity. It also passes through Chesed, Geburah, Netzach and Hod, thus symbolically linking the archetypes of Love and Will to our feeling and thinking functions. The heart then represents our reconnection with the ground, bringing the heart energy from Tiphareth into our everyday lives. As a heart it depicts the essential element of all Kabbalistic work, that of bringing more love into manifestation. We will develop this theme in the last chapter of this book. The heart (in diagram 16) starts in Tiphareth, passes through Netzach and Hod, then ends in Malkuth. This symbolically indicates how we can use our mind, feelings and body to ground our work.

When we dance the 'wand of intention', 'cup of receptivity' and 'heart of connection' in this way, we connect to a basic yet vital Kabbalistic trinity, which helps us bring a balance of Will (intention) and Love (receptivity) into our world.

CREATING A LAMEN

A lamen is a 'power object' created by a Kabbalist to declare the nature of his or her 'Great Work'. This Great Work is your personal

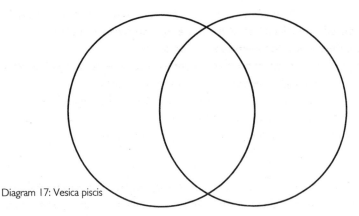

Diagram 17: Vesica piscis

development and spiritual growth as your Soul manifests through your life. The 'vesica piscis' shape is usually used for a lamen because it is created through the overlapping of two circles – so it represents the interlocking of the spiritual and mundane worlds (see diagram 17). Your lamen can be any other shape that 'speaks' to you.

At all times the essential aspect of everyone's Great Work is to make contact with Tiphareth and express this contact. For this reason the lamen is usually attributed to Tiphareth. Each individual lamen contains symbols and images that represent the Kabbalist and his or her own 'keys to power' ('power with', not 'power over') and his or her 'keys to love' (not sentimental attraction but the love that underpins everything). Of course, your lamen will undoubtedly change as your knowledge and understanding of the Tree of Life increases. As you create new lamens to replace old ones, then you are also creating a record of your Kabbalistic development.

PRACTICE

• The lamen ritual

Before commencing the work, perform the Kabbalistic Cross (or your equivalent).

Start by facing north (earth). Close your eyes, focus on the circle around you and focus on a point in the north at the periphery of your vision.

Shift your focus to a point on your right . . . then behind . . . then to the left . . . then return to focus ahead of you.

Which point felt faintest, which direction were you least connected to?

Physically face that direction and bring up or strengthen the energy there:

take up an appropriate posture (for example, this may be defensive, excited, open, closed, worshipful, etc. What is the right posture for you?)

Make the sounds that seem appropriate to you.

Let go of any preconceptions you might have about what is 'right' or what you 'should be doing' or what the 'four directions' mean.

Go to each of the other directions and follow the same procedure.

Find the centre of your circle, the centre of your 'power spot', sit and quietly meditate on the energies to which you have connected.

You are now going to create a lamen. You can construct your lamen by including any symbols that you know/feel you connect with as aspects of you and your Great Work. Remember that symbols include numbers – are there any important numbers you might like to include? Names of deities? Images? Other important symbols with which you particularly connect? Is it going to be linear, representational or abstract, black and white or colour, simple or complex, etc.?

There is no right or wrong way of creating a lamen – you put into your lamen whatever you wish. It might be enough to simply visualise your lamen, though I would strongly recommend you make one physically if at all possible. It is traditionally worn as a 'breast plate' so make the size accordingly. Construct it of whatever material you like – paper will do, but if so you will need to paste it onto card so it is 'solid' enough to be worn. Its final appearance will reflect your magical intention, so construct it with care.

Do not feel you have to complete it at once, or that once it is constructed you have to live with it forever more. You may find as your work progresses you want to alter it, or even re-create it anew to express new knowledge, understanding and connections.

6

WAYS OF STILLNESS AND PATHWAYS TO INNER PEACE

The crucial notion is that through calming the whirl of thoughts that is our ordinary mind, we open a door that leads to an exalted awareness of the wonder of the entire cosmos.

Edward Hoffman (*Opening The Inner Gates*)

The last chapter focused on ways of action that use pathworking and dance, for instance, to connect with the Tree of Life and utilise its guidance in our lives. In this chapter we are concentrating on 'ways of stillness', particularly meditation, contemplation and prayer. The aim of both ways of action and stillness is to connect with the deeper or higher aspects of ourselves and find ways of manifesting this energy and understanding in our everyday lives. In Kabbalistic work we do not wish to simply 'bliss out', to transcend the mundane and leave the material world behind. On the contrary, our aim is always to clarify our union with spiritual realms and then express this in our lives.

Of course, sometimes just touching the deeper aspects of our nature can in itself be enough. For some people prayer or contemplation is so nourishing and spiritually enriching in itself they feel no need to express their connection. But even when this is the case, it is still true that the link made with these energies may bring better human relations into manifestation, for if we are connecting to spiritual energies, we radiate these out to other people and the planet in general. It is inevitable that if we, as individuals, transform ourselves in some way, that transformation will affect those with whom we come into contact.

Many different meanings are given to the word meditation, and there are many different types of meditation and meditative techniques. The word is often used interchangeably with contemplation, which is then sometimes used as an alternative word for prayer. Meditation is not the same as prayer, however, although there are many similarities. We will look at prayer and contemplation later in this chapter, but let us first examine in more depth the subject of meditation.

At the simplest level, if we concentrate on something – anything at all – we are meditating. The more we learn to control our 'personality functions' as represented by Hod, Netzach and Malkuth and stop them from intruding upon our concentration, the more deeply we enter the meditative state. In fact, many spiritual disciplines – Kabbalah among them – consider this work to be of primary importance.

It is often believed that meditation is primarily an abstract activity, involved with turning inwards and somehow transcending the 'ordinary world' of Malkuth. Meditation does involve concentration, reflection, understanding and being receptive. It also includes, however, ways of bringing these connections into outer expression and it is therefore also a very active and outer-directed technique. In this sense, meditation could be defined as the conscious and deliberate use of inner powers and energies to fulfil a specific purpose.

The first action in most types of meditation is to still ourselves in some way. To achieve this physically, to still our Malkuth connection in other words, we might sit in a particular posture and slow down our breathing. Although in Yoga there are many postures, all with different meanings and purposes, for simple meditation the key is to find a posture that suits you and stick to it. Then in order to calm our thoughts and feelings – our Hod and Netzach connections – we have to shift our attention from its normal outer orientation towards the stillness of our inner world. To do this effectively we have to enter a state of emotional peace and direct our thoughts either to stop or be one-pointed.

In essence, whatever methods or techniques we choose to use, the aim is to 'turn off the inner dialogue'. This inner dialogue is what is occurring naturally all the time within our consciousness. I feel something and then I think something about it; I hurt my arm and I feel pain; I react to your unkind words then I plot my revenge . . . and so on. It is as if we have little 'sub-personalities' within us that are composed of various combinations of our Hod, Netzach and Malkuth functions, and these sub-personalities are all affected by what we carry from our past in Yesod. For instance, one sub-personality might be primarily rooted in Hod and will therefore process any experience in terms of the intellect. It will tend to think things through, be rational, make decisions based on 'sensible solutions', and so on. Another sub-personality might be rooted primarily in Netzach, process experiences in terms of what it feels about them, react non-rationally and make decisions based on 'what feels right'.

These sub-personalities need not be in conflict – either because at their own level they come to some kind of agreement, or because we learn to view them from a separate, deeper perspective. This perspective is attained in Tiphareth, from where we can witness and direct our actions more clearly. But because most of the time, whether in conflict or not, our sub-personalities keep up a constant chatter inside us, they block our access to inner silence. We have to reach this inner silence, in order to make our prayers and meditation effective, and to be connected to our soul energies, represented on the Tree of Life by the central triangle of spheres. Thus the importance of 'turning off the inner dialogue'. Later in the chapter we will explore ways to reduce the volume and eventually turn off the inner chatter.

The Tree of Life is a map of our awareness that, once we learn to use it, can aid us in silencing the 'chattering' voices of our sub-personalities so that we come to a deep connection with aspects of our inner nature. Beyond this, it also offers us a map of our spiritual nature, which, once we have reached a place of silence, we can then use to understand our subsequent experiences. After turning off our inner dialogue, we see ourselves and our world in a new light. We have entered the realms of the Spirit and soul as represented on the Tree of Life by Tiphareth and above.

A major purpose of all personal and spiritual growth is to connect with our soul, and this is clearly the central aim of Kabbalah. Meditation, prayer and contemplation offer us a way towards this goal. However we choose to meditate or pray, it is important that we remember this central aim and do not become distracted by side-issues that can lead us away from our path. The ways of stillness – like the ways of action – are techniques that aid us on our journey, not goals in themselves.

PRAYER AND KABBALAH

Kabbalists believe that one of the simplest and quickest ways to connect with the deeper levels of our being is through prayer. Kabbalistic prayer, like meditation, however, is not simply a passive process, but involves active participation. To reach the deep states of connection that are possible through prayer it is important that we engage our whole being, not suppressing any aspect of ourselves. For this reason, during the opening stages of prayer, Kabbalists may move their bodies, often in a swaying motion, and willingly speak out any passing emotions or thoughts. The idea of this is to activate the energy of the whole being during the opening stages of the contemplation. Of course there are times when it is appropriate to sit perfectly still and to remain silent, but is important to stress that this is not the only way to pray, and if we do not let out the thoughts, feelings and sensations that intrude at the beginning of our prayer, they are very likely to intrude upon us at a later stage.

Once we have engaged our whole personality in the process of prayer, we are then able to proceed to the next step where we go deeper into ourselves. Now we will sit still and not allow any thoughts or feelings to impinge upon our silent concentration. We act as if only the Mother–Father Deity and ourselves exist, and that during this time, while we are communing with the Deity on a totally personal level, nothing can disturb or distract us.

Prayer is commonly seen as a way of asking for something. We tell 'god' that 'he' is great in some way, we 'confess our sins', 'ask forgiveness', then get down to the real function of saying what we want to happen! Even if what we want to happen is totally altruistic and unselfish, however, Kabbalists strongly believe that this is most definitely not the function of prayer. Rather it is to connect us with the deeper or higher aspects of our being and then express this connection in our daily lives. In the process of making this connection we might ask for divine guidance, forgiveness and understanding, but we always remember that this guidance can only come from inside ourselves. If we are inspired this is something inside us. Whether it originates from some abstract, separate 'god' or whether it originates at some deep level of our being ultimately makes no difference. What matters is that we still ourselves so we can hear the message from within, then, most importantly, that we live our lives in accord with this.

The Christian Lord's Prayer is a good example of how a simple prayer, intended to make a deep and satisfying connection with inner wisdom and understanding, can be used in many different ways and for many different aims. However it is used, it is a powerfully invocative prayer, but when we learn the meaning of the original Aramaic words, we find a simplicity and beauty that is missing from the usual translations. A translation of the Aramaic original follows, and this clearly shows how it is related to the Tree of Life. The usual translation is appended to each line for comparison purposes only.

As you read the Kabbalistic Lord's Prayer, consider the Tree of Life. Initially a link is made with the Supernal Triad of Kether, Chockmah and Binah. The creative process instigated in this Spiritual realm is then expressed through the third world of Yetzirah, then grounded in the fourth world of Assiah (Malkuth) with the words 'Grant our daily need for bread and insight'. The second half of the prayer then ascends the Middle Pillar of the Tree of Life, making a clear connection between the earth and the Spiritual Deity represented by Kether. A final statement closes the prayer and affirms the relevance of this work to our whole being, not just as an abstract or disconnected piece of supplication.

There are different movements and gestures that can be associated with this Kabbalistic Lord's Prayer, but for now I would recommend that you simply use this prayer as a guide to your Kabbalistic studies and as a way of connecting yourself with the energies of the Tree of Life. If you follow the advice regarding contemplation, engage your whole being, then stand upright and voice this prayer, being aware of its relationship to the Tree, you will find it is a very powerful aid to your spiritual development.

As you know, Kabbalists often use another technique called 'The Kabbalistic Cross'. This takes the last phrase of the 'standard' Lord's Prayer, 'For thine is the kingdom, the power and the glory, for ever and ever, amen' and uses it as a way of focusing consciousness. It is a very powerful technique and is described in detail in Appendix 1. The Kabbalistic Lord's Prayer described next is, however, a more complete contemplative device and can be used to make a deeper connection not only with the form of the Tree of Life but with the force that informs it.

THE KABBALISTIC LORD'S PRAYER

Kether:	*Mother–Father of the cosmos,* *Your eternal presence is within us all.* *(Our father which art in heaven)*
Chockmah:	*Focus your light within us.* *(hallowed be thy name)*
Binah:	*Create the conditions for unity now,* *through our willing hearts and hands.* *(Thy kingdom come, thy will be done)*
Chesed–Yesod:	*Your one will then acts with ours,* *as in all light, so in all forms.* *(in earth as it is in heaven)*
Malkuth:	*Grant our daily need for bread and insight.* *(Give us each day our daily bread)*

Malkuth–Yesod:	*Loose the binds of mistakes around us,*
	as we release the ties we hold on others.
	(Forgive us our trespasses as we forgive . . .)

Yesod–Tiphareth:	*Heaven and earth are united, fulfilling*
	true purpose.
	(For thine is the kingdom)

Tiphareth–Kether:	*The power and the love, always becoming.*
	(the power and the glory, for ever and ever)

Affirmation:	*Sealed in trust and faith,*
	we affirm this with our whole being.
	Amen.

This version of the Aramaic Lord's Prayer is based on several versions, some of which may be found on the Internet. If you are interested in studying it further, I highly recommend the book by Neil Douglas-Klotz listed in the Bibliography.

PRACTICE

• The Temple of Inner Silence

Imagine or create a circle around yourself and stand at its centre, then imagine a strong cord coming from the middle of your body and going right down into the centre of the earth. It roots you firmly to your spot.

Imagine there is a hook or anchor on the end of the cord, and feel it attach to the earth very firmly.

Look round your temple: imagine, sense and feel the presence of the guardians and angels of your place of working; imagine, sense and feel the presence of the guardians and angels of this place where you are on the planet. Welcome their presence now.

Close your eyes, and expand your awareness to the immediate environment and nearby countryside. Silently ask the good spirits of this countryside to be present for you and your work, and to assist you in your Great Work.

Return to full awareness of your physical body. Tune into your heart, and be aware of the energy in your heart. Breathe into your heart centre now, feeling energy building up. Let your heart centre open as much as is appropriate for you right now.

Make yourself physically comfortable and follow the visualisation carefully:

Imagine you are in a meadow on a beautiful sunny day . . . Become aware of your environment. Look around you – what do you see on this beautiful, sunny day? Can you hear birds singing? Feel a cool, refreshing breeze caress your cheeks.

Notice how you are dressed. What are you wearing on your feet? . . . Feel your feel on the ground, start walking a little, really feeling what it is like to be in this meadow on this sunny day.

As you look around you, notice what you can see in each direction – there may be trees, distant mountains, hills. Build up a strong sense of being wherever you are.

Notice in one direction, some little distance from you, that you can see the Temple of Inner Silence, its structure glistening in the sunlight . . . Start walking in the direction of this Temple, really being conscious of what you feel as you are walking in that direction.

Feel the contact of your feet on the ground – is it level, rising, dipping? . . . As you travel towards the Temple, look about you at the trees, the bushes, the grass and flowers.

Use all your senses to fully appreciate where you are. Be aware of the scenery, the warmth of the sun on your skin, the scents in the air . . . Also be aware of your anticipation, excitement, whatever you feel as you walk towards the Temple of Inner Silence.

You are now approaching your Temple. What does it look like? . . . See your Temple, in whatever form it has appeared to you, as bathed in clear, vibrant light.

You will soon enter the Temple of Inner Silence, but before you do, be aware that when you do so you will be safely enveloped by complete and total inner silence.

Walk up to the entrance of the Temple of Inner Silence and step inside. You feel the atmosphere around you, the peace and silence, the vibrant splendour of this temple. Give yourself over to the experience as fully as you are able.

When you feel ready, leave the temple and, feeling the impact of the beautiful day in your meadow, allow yourself to be filled with the joy of what you have just experienced. In your own time, but with a brisk and engaged walk, cross the meadow to where you started and bring your attention back to your 'everyday' reality. Make sure you ground yourself fully back into your body before continuing.

PATHWAYS TO INNER SILENCE

As you know, if you stop what you are doing for a few moments and simply listen to what is happening inside, you discover that a lot of the time you are having an inner dialogue with yourself. 'Should I do what he suggests now, or should I do it later . . . what's for tea anyway . . . look, listen, concentrate on this, it's important . . . I wonder if Mike will phone? . . .' and so on.

We create our own reality by keeping a dialogue going with ourselves about our world and what we perceive or imagine is happening. This is not necessarily a bad thing because it helps keep us grounded and able to relate to other people and the world in general. The problem is when we get caught up with this inner dialogue and forget there is anything else. If we learn to turn off the inner dialogue we can reach a place of silence, Tiphareth, in which we contact our real inner power and purpose. We reach the real world behind images, thoughts, fantasies, feelings, sensations and so on.

There are many ways of doing this, and it appears as the central theme in most practical teachings. For example, in the works of Carlos Castaneda, the shaman Don Juan frequently tells Carlos, his apprentice, that turning off the inner dialogue is the most important goal in sorcery, for when it is achieved everything else becomes possible. In the Western Mystery Tradition, a similar aim is described as one-pointedness. It is claimed that any thought that is held in this state of silence becomes a definite command since there are no other thoughts to compete with it.

In Yoga, there are various practices that also lead to the same goal. Firstly there is asana, controlling the body through various postures, then yama and niyama for controlling emotional reactions, then dharana for controlling the mind. These techniques have the single aim of achieving dhyana – which is turning off the inner dialogue and reaching a still, silent place within. Dhyana is the original root of the word Zen, and the main aim of Zen meditation is the same – to stop the rational mind and reach states beyond the incessant questioning, thinking and reasoning that holds us back from our inner peace and true identity.

In Taoism the aim is again the same: in the *Tao Te Ching* we are told that the Tao resembles the emptiness of space; to employ it we must avoid creating an inner dialogue, which we can do through 'making our sharpness blunt'.

Many of us have been brought up to believe that we have a soul that somehow, irrespective of what we do, remains constant and unchanged. From this position, it can appear strange to learn, when we delve into the teachings of Kabbalah and most other systems of spiritual development, that this may not be the case. We find that the soul has to be 'caught' or, at the very least, 'developed' and cannot just be taken for granted. Looked at this way, it can be said the primary aim of the inner quest is to find a soul and then to work at connecting with it. Ouspensky, a major figure in twentieth-century esotericism and pupil of the Armenian mystic Gurdjieff sums this up well when, describing the teachings of Gurdjieff in *In Search of the Miraculous*, he says: 'man as we know him is not a complete being . . . nature develops him only up to a certain point and then leaves him, either to develop further, by his own efforts and devices, or to live and die such as he was born'.

Even in methods where non-action is stressed, such as Taoism, nothing can be taken for granted. For instance, in the *Tao Te Ching*, Lao-Tzu says: 'He who attains the Tao is everlasting. Though his body may decay he never perishes.' In other words, it is possible not to attain the Tao and, by implication, perish along with the body. With a few exceptions where it is stressed that there is nothing to attain and, more significantly, there is nothing to be done, everywhere else we find a division between the person who has and the person who has not attained.

There are two threads running through most teachings about the meaning of life. On an outer level we are told that all we have to do is have faith in some teacher or teaching and we are doing enough. Once we start questioning, however, and commence our inner quest, we find there is an inner level where we are told we have to achieve something or we are lost. In Hinduism, for instance, on an outer level we are led to believe that the soul is innately and indivisibly one with God or the Absolute. Then we are told that, for this to be realised in an individual, specific practices have to be undertaken. Similarly in Buddhism, it is said that everything in life is an illusion and in a state of suffering because of the desire inherent in duality. The only truth or reality is total emptiness or 'the Void'. To experience this emptiness, however, an individual has to live by certain 'right' actions. Unless this is achieved he or she is bound to an endless cycle of meaningless bondage on the wheel of death and rebirth.

So if we need to 'catch a soul' how can be go about this? As we have already seen, an essential component in the process is to turn off the inner dialogue and find that inner state of total and undiluted silence. But to do this is not easy and involves effort, persistence, sacrifice and even suffering. It is this very effort and suffering that enables us to catch a soul. Similarly, the goal of 'absolute vacuity' recommended in the *Tao Te Ching* is not achieved without effort (though, of course, the enigmatic approach of Taoism tells us that if we make it an effort we are equally doomed to failure!).

The practices of Kabbalah suggest we need to struggle against the attempts of the personality to divert us from our efforts at moving towards soul. In our everyday state we think about life and give ourselves explanations, we react emotionally or physically to cover our inner suffering, and our ego tries everything to avoid the question 'what are we here for?' Only through persistent effort can we hold to the inner quest and keep our attention focused on our true inner desire to find meaning and purpose in our lives.

Anyone who visualises a simple image such as a blue circle or a white cross and tries, even for just one minute, to hold this image steady and unchanged in consciousness, finds out just how difficult it is to concentrate one-pointedly. Similarly, when we start to practise meditation, yoga, or any other similar techniques, we find our resistances are triggered. Most people, if they are asked to meditate for just ten minutes each day for just one month, will find that before the month is out they will have found all sorts of reasons to miss a day here, shorten the time there, or even stop altogether. To embark upon the inner quest may not be difficult, but to maintain our work does involve effort and suffering. Perhaps if we keep in mind that without this effort and suffering we are not guaranteed to even have a soul, let alone be able to develop our connection to it, we can be spurred into more persistent action.

If we focus on what is often termed 'heart energy' we may more easily achieve our aim of 'turning off the internal dialogue'. A 'by-product' almost of focusing on heart energy is that we are then achieving our aim without exploiting or manipulating other people or our environment. We are truly stepping forward on a 'path with heart'. It is well worth keeping this focus in mind when practising Kabbalah. Certainly it will aid your discovery of your personal connection to Tiphareth.

PRACTICE

• Inner silence meditation

Relax and centre yourself.

Think about Inner Silence. Hold the concept of Inner Silence in your mind and reflect upon it. Ask yourself questions about this quality: what is it? what is its nature? what is its meaning? and so on. (If you keep a journal it is a good idea to record your ideas, and any images that emerge.)

Now let go of your reflection and let your attention focus instead on your breathing, not changing it in any way, but just its natural rhythm.

Be still and receptive; what does inner silence mean to you now? Consider the value of Inner Silence, its purpose, its use in your life and on the planet as a whole. What differences would there be if Inner Silence was in abundance?

Desire Inner Silence.

Allow Inner Silence to be in your body. Assume a posture that expresses this quality. Relax all your tensions, let them drift away. Breathe slowly. Allow Inner Silence to express itself on your face. Visualise yourself with that expression.

Invoke the quality of Inner Silence. Imagine you are in a place where you feel Inner Silence – a quiet beach, with a loved one, in a Temple of Inner Silence, wherever you choose. Try to really feel it.

Repeat silently to yourself the words Inner Silence several times. Let the quality permeate you, to the point of identification if possible. Allow yourself to be Inner Silence.

Resolve to remain infused with Inner Silence, to be the living embodiment of Inner Silence, to radiate Inner Silence.

Let an image emerge that symbolises for you your connection to Inner Silence . . . Trust what comes and allow it to develop, to change, to become stronger, whatever the imagery does . . . Look at it closely, consider its colour, depth, light – any specific features of this symbol. Affirm to yourself that you will remember this symbol and be able to use it as an aid to connecting again to Inner Silence whenever you will.

Now gently bring yourself back to your everyday consciousness and do something to ground your energy.

For instance, you could draw on a piece of paper or card your symbol for Inner Silence, then place this sign where you can see it daily, or at least frequently. You could make several such signs and place them strategically around your home. Whenever you notice a sign, recall within yourself the feeling of Inner Silence.

NOT DOING

Don Juan Matus was the (probably mythical) shaman and teacher of Carlos Castaneda, who wrote many books about his relationship with this magical figure. It may seem strange to bring the teachings of a Mexican shaman into a book on Kabbalah, but when these teachings describe a very practical approach to attaining true inner silence, the reason becomes clearer. Indeed, there is a scene described in one of Castaneda's books where Don Juan scratches a figure in the ground to illustrate the energetic composition of a human being and the surrounding world. While it might not have been exactly the Tree of Life we use, its similarities are truly remarkable. Of course, one of the most wonderful aspects of Kabbalah is the ability to create correspondences with any other system of attainment (or anything else for that matter!). This is true, but there are very precise correlations between Castaneda's work and Kabbalah that are very helpful in understanding the practices of the living, practical Kabbalah.

Carlos Castaneda was an anthropologist of Peruvian origins who has influenced the spiritual and magical practices of most modern occultists (whether they are aware of this or not). There is a mass of evidence (much of it available via the Internet) that Castaneda fabricated the encounters with Don Juan that he describes in his books. For all practical magical purposes, however, it doesn't matter at all whether these teachings are made up or not. The system presented by Castaneda is coherent and, most significantly, it works. Indeed, if he did invent Don Juan and concoct the whole system, it makes Castaneda an even more remarkable magician.

The basic premise of magic (or naugalism as Castaneda calls it) is that the so-called 'reality' of our ordinary world is only a description, and in fact only one of many possible descriptions. Rather than simply looking at the one 'reality' presented to us by our standard conditioning, we have to *see* the world as it really is. To do this involves the key concept of the whole system, which Castaneda calls 'stopping the world'. To stop the world we have to 'turn off the internal dialogue', an activity of central importance in all magical systems. In Castaneda's sorcery, there is a series of distinct steps a magician has to undertake in order to achieve this goal, which are: eradicating personal history, losing self-importance, using death as an adviser, assuming responsibility for your acts, living life as a warrior, disrupting life routines, and making yourself inaccessible to the everyday while becoming accessible to power. You will realise how we have already been exploring many of these themes from a Kabbalistic perspective.

The last task for a sorcerer to perform is called *not doing*, which Don Juan defines as 'to not do what you know how to do'. One way to practise this is through consciously shifting your gaze while regarding common objects; for instance, seeing the shadows and patterns between the leaves and branches of a tree rather than looking at the leaves and branches themselves; or looking at the shadow cast by a rock and seeing this as solid rather than the rock.

These sorts of practices are preliminary to the ultimate not-doing, which involves shifting your attention from the ego towards a deeper connection to the source of all energy. Castaneda has Don Juan explain that when these activities are successfully completed, 'the magician feels he has entered a new plane of existence. His entire range of perceptions has altered. He finds himself in a dimension which will alter and transform itself according to his will.' This is, of course, the aim of Kabbalistic magic (and healing), thus asserting a deep connection between Kabbalah and shamanism.

THE SIX PATHS OF THE INNER DIALOGUE

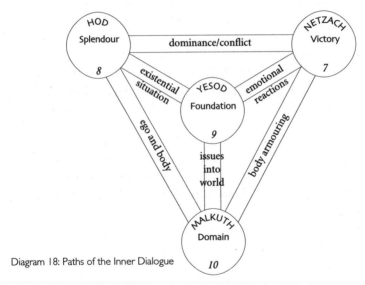

Diagram 18: Paths of the Inner Dialogue

Consider the following descriptions of the types of inner dialogue associated with each of the six paths (as in diagram 18). To achieve full inner silence, a Kabbalist needs to be able to turn off all these voices, including those – the most difficult – that arise from Yesod, all the voices from the past that try to control the individual in the present.

Path connecting spheres 7 and 8: the dialogue between feelings and thoughts: the inner dialogue par excellence. Either thinking or feeling is very dominant, or they may be in conflict with each other (the range of experience from total disregard of each other, through constant bickering to all-out war!).

Path connecting spheres 7 and 9: the dialogue between feelings and the past. This is the path of emotions and emotional reactions (particularly in the sense of emotions being feelings controlled by past events and turned from responses to reactions).

Path connecting spheres 7 and 10: the dialogue between feelings and the body. This path is closely connected to unexpressed and unacknowledged feelings, which are deposited in the physical realm as body armouring.

Path connecting spheres 8 and 9: the dialogue between thinking and the past. The existential situation, including all the major life questions – what is the meaning of life, etc. An associated experience is the illusion of being free but still imprisoned. Slothfulness and cynicism are responses to this.

Path connecting spheres 8 and 10: the dialogue between thinking and the body. Shows how the ego treats the body and interacts with the physical world. Similar to the path from 7 to 10 but a mental version.

Path connecting spheres 9 and 10: the dialogue between the past and the body. Includes both the parts of you that feel able to 'dance' through life and those that do not. How able are you to move as appropriate to your current existential situation? Indicates how you respond and react to blockages.

PRACTICE

• Inner voices

Reflect on how you relate these six paths to the experience of your inner dialogue, and which paths you find most difficult to still and silence.

Turning off the six voices of the inner dialogue gives you access to other realms of existence, other realities. Be careful not to become obsessed with these other realities. While they can be useful and it is important to access these realms, our ultimate aim is to cross the Abyss and achieve freedom. This again parallels the teachings of Don Juan, Castaneda's teacher. He stresses the importance of not getting caught up in engaging with what they call the inorganic realms and losing sight of the ultimate aim of freedom.

Accessing these paths means travelling through the Abyss and entering the realms of knowledge. Knowledge can be dangerous if it is misapplied; the serpent is said to rear his head to Daath and be ready to devour the unworthy, as the eagle devours those who do not make the crossing in Castaneda. Working in this realm is like building castles on sand. However strong the edifice may seem, it is built on illusion. Knowledge without Understanding (Binah), that is without having crossed the Abyss, can devour us.

The safest and truthfully the only real way to cross the Abyss is through the path of the priestess, straight from the heart at Tiphareth. Even the letter attributed to that path gives us a clue. Gimel is the camel, the carrier of the necessary provisions for such a crossing. Camels are noted for carrying water, the basic – and final – requirement for survival. Without water we die. We cannot take this path with anything else other than water.

Crowley reminds us of the importance of being in a good state physically to undertake any such work. In *Eight Lectures on Yoga* he says: 'It is therefore necessary, if we wish to make the universal and final union (Yoga) with the absolute, to master every element of our being, to protect it against all civil and external war (to turn off the inner dialogue), to intensify every faculty to the utmost, to train ourselves in knowledge and power to the utmost; so that at the proper moment we may be in perfect condition to fling ourselves up into the furnace of ecstasy that flames from the abyss of annihilation.'

In the light of what has already been explored, consider this quote from Krishnamurti, one of the pre-eminent mystics of the twentieth century, writing in *Meditations*: 'Man, in order to escape his conflicts, has invented many forms of meditation. These have been based on desire, will and the urge for achievement and imply conflict and a struggle to arrive. This conscious deliberate striving is always within the limits of a conditioned mind and in this there is no freedom. All effort to meditate is the denial of meditation. Meditation is the ending of thought. It is only then that there is a different dimension which is beyond time.'

PRACTICE

• Developing the third eye

The fourteenth path, joining together Chockmah and Binah, represents the third eye, the centre of psychic awareness, the opening of which is sometimes described as a result of attaining inner silence.

Meditate, focusing your attention on the centre of your head and the point between and just above your eyebrows. Keep your attention there, and whatever images, ideas, sounds or anything else that emerges, any thoughts, feelings, sensations or anything else that you become aware of, say to yourself: 'not this, not this' and return your focus to the chosen area.

When all else is silenced, become aware of a spiral (or spiralling effect) that originates in the area of this energy centre and spirals outwards, becoming smaller until it disappears, then another spiral instantly starts (or sometimes vice versa, spiralling towards you until it, as it were, passes through you and another spiral starts in the distance, heading towards you). This is quite difficult to describe but once you have the effect you will recognise it. You cannot make it happen except through silencing yourself and focusing your attention in this area. Don't use this for any purpose, but recognise that making this connection can strengthen your psychic abilities.

Opening the third eye (or ajna chakra) is said to confer spiritual freedom (the exact meaning of the fourteenth path). It is beyond all dualities, except that at the core of existence itself. Its opening confers upon an individual the responsibility of service – not service for any altruistic ends, or to bolster one's own feeling of well-being, but service for its own sake.

Imagine the sun rising in the right hemisphere of your brain and setting in the left. Then imagine the moon rising in the left and setting in the right. Keep this imagery going for several minutes, then watch for what images spontaneously appear.

ECSTASY AND INNER PEACE

Whenever we pray or meditate, we can distinguish two effects, ecstasy and inner peace. While they are not really separate and usually occur together in some combination or another, it us useful to be aware how we tend to focus on either ecstasy or inner peace. After a connection is made to ecstasy, the usual impetus is to express it outwardly, to share our 'high' with others. After we connect to inner peace, there is a tendency to hold on to it, to feel that outside influences will draw us away from our inner calm. Of course, this is often the case, but Kabbalists stress the importance of reversing these typical polarities. When we feel ecstasy, we can choose to draw it into ourselves and use its energies to illuminate and heal our inner world. When we experience inner peace, we can choose to live from the place and radiate our inner harmony into the world.

It is also important not to be goal-orientated in our meditative and contemplative work. If we meditate or pray with the overt intention of becoming more ecstatic or peaceful, our intention in itself can be a block to success. This brings us again to the importance in all developmental work of focusing on the next step. If we are goal-orientated we may miss our step or end up travelling the wrong path altogether. On the other hand, if we connect to our purpose, and then keep our attention on each step we need to make, we will more easily and successfully achieve our aim. If we were going to drive today from, say, London to Manchester, we would need to know where we are going, but to get there we have to pay attention to the road directly ahead of us and successfully negotiate every corner, roundabout, traffic light, and so on. Indeed, in focusing on the path and truly letting go of our attachment to our destination, we may even find we already have the ecstasy and inner peace we desire. Kabbalah stresses that to find these qualities while travelling the path is in itself the central aim of all our endeavours.

PRACTICE

• Arising from source

Shamans say that there are three different ways of using our attention. These closely parallel Kabbalistic thought on the subject. The first attention is when we put our attention on something. 'I see – whatever, I touch – whoever, I smell – whatever,' and so on. This corresponds to the bottom triangle on the Tree, particularly focused around Malkuth (or as we perceive it coloured through our experience of Netzach, Hod and Yesod).

The second attention is being aware of the totality of oneself. 'I am me, everything I do, and everything I am is me. I am I, a centre of pure self-awareness.' This is equivalent to the middle triangle on the Tree, particularly focused around Tiphareth, the heart centre.

The third attention is becoming aware that there is a source to all this attention. 'Not what am I doing or who am I being, but where does this attention arise?' While we cannot have direct experience of the Supernal Triad, we can contact it as the source of everything else we experience.

Where is your attention right now? Have you chosen to be consciously paying attention to what you are reading here, or has your attention just strayed to where it is, unconsciously? Right now, as you focus on your attention, it is conscious, but for all of us most of the time our attention is not conscious.

Focus your attention now on top left corner of this book and hold your attention there for a little while. It would be impossible for you to hold your attention there (or anywhere else) for all the time without becoming disconnected, sapped of your energy, and passionless. This is the experience of the first attention, where we are attending to something and our attention either becomes fixed on that something or it doesn't. (The lower triangle.)

Become aware now that at this moment you, yourself, are a totality. There is nothing missing. You are all that you are right now. Let this awareness come instantaneously. Don't focus on anything in particular; simply give your attention to the fullness of yourself. Don't focus on your head, the earth beneath your feet, don't focus on your breath or anything at all. Just let your attention rest on the undivided presence of yourself.

This is the second attention where we are not doing anything, not being anything, not focused on anything in particular, simply being aware of the undivided presence of oneself. Again become aware that, at this very moment, you are a totality. There is nothing missing. You are aware of this or you are not. You do not have to strive for anything or do any particular exercises, you just realise, by putting your attention here, that you are always here, now. You can't become more enlightened or spiritual than this, and you can't become less so, you are simply you, all you have been, are, and ever will be. This second attention is called self-remembering. (The middle, soul triangle.)

Deliberately choose to put your attention on your breathing. Notice how your inclination is that once you put your awareness on your breathing (or anything else) you lose contact with the second attention? You are no longer remembering that larger awareness. Notice how this happens, but don't strain to hold both attentions, just focus on what is happening right now in your awareness.

Now consider: who is doing this focusing? Is it someone trying hard to get it right? Someone who thinks they do not understand? Who is focusing? Is it the wise person who knows all this already? Someone who craves for a relationship and hopes this will make it happen? Is it someone happy? If you focus on what is happening right now in your consciousness, who is doing the focusing?

What are you focusing for? Because you have been told to do so? Do you desire to be more alert, more present, to learn how to become self-actualised? Be aware of your motive to focus. Now, if you look closely: from where, right now, is your attention emerging?

Not where is it going, but from where is it arising?

Where? Now where? Allow yourself to experience the source of your attention. Be aware of the pure consciousness in which everything arises, including all this witnessing of consciousness.

Who or what is this presence, this totality of being that emerges through your consciousness? Who comes alive inside you? Don't look for an answer, but instead look inside your looking. This is the third attention – awareness of the source of consciousness. (The Supernal Triad.)

7

KABBALISTIC HEALING

*The Tree of Life was impregnated with forces so harmonious and beneficial
that its leaves healed every illness and its fruits bestowed eternal life.*
Omraam Mikhael Aivanhov (*The Fruits of the Tree of Life*)

To heal something or someone is to make it whole as indicated by the
common root for the words heal and whole (the old English *hal*, to
make whole, and *haelen*, to restore to sound health). To bring
wholeness to something is to complement discord with harmony and
pain with wisdom, not to replace or somehow overcome the discord
and pain. To be whole does not mean to be perfect in any way, instead
it means to include everything, including our imperfections. To heal,
therefore, is to bring together the component parts of any system – be
it a human, animal, plant or inanimate system – in an including rather
than excluding way. When we do this we bring about true healing
rather than just the kind of healing that is concerned with fixing pain,
disguising discord or in some way treating the symptom rather than
the cause.

We are all fragmented, broken into pieces by the pressures of life, by
our fears, our pain and our sense of disconnection. It is only natural that
we wish to disconnect from such painful experiences. Sometimes pain
can be so bad we may yearn to disconnect from life itself. Pain can be
so acute it is all that you are aware of, as if nothing else but the pain
exists. You just hit your thumb with a hammer, for instance, and it is
throbbing. The pain is so intense it has 'taken over' your consciousness.
You cannot think of anything else – you rush around, cursing,
alternatively sucking your thumb, shaking it, frantically trying to change
your consciousness (stop the pain!).

When you are 'taken over' by the pain from a physical mishap as in
the hammer example, the pain is soon reduced to a manageable level.
Some physical pain is more chronic or acute, however. If, for instance,
you suffered from appendicitis, you would not be able to just make the
pain go away. You would need assistance from others, and even then
there would be no guarantee of success. It is important that we learn to
recognise those situations where we have the ability to heal ourselves,
those where we need to call on others, and those where we have to

contemplate the end of our life journey. There is a possibility that the condition may be incurable and death inevitable. This is not a sign to give up, though, more an incentive to continue with the healing process.

What is true for physical pain is also true for emotional and mental pain. It may arrive suddenly, with intensity – the shocking news that a loved one has died (we feel intense sorrow), that someone has committed a gross act of abuse against us (we feel intense anger). Emotional and mental pain may also be continuous, chronic, even obsessive – for instance, feelings about a forthcoming important meeting (we feel intense anxiety). Just as when you hit your thumb with a hammer and the intense sensation took over, we can all be just as easily taken over by intense emotional or mental reactions to events in our lives. In fact, these mental or emotional reactions can be more painful at their outset and much harder to shift than physical ones.

We also become fragmented when we feel a lack of spiritual connection in our lives. The classic 'existential crisis' is a good example of acute spiritual pain. Everything has been going fine when suddenly you start to ask yourself: what am I here for? what's the purpose of my life? isn't everything I've done so far meaningless, shallow, disconnected from any deeper significance? Spiritual pain can also be chronic in nature. For instance, some people experience, for much of their lives, that it is difficult to be here on the earth, incarnated in a physical body. They may expend much of their energy finding ways to 'bliss out', merge, become co-dependent, and avoid the responsibilities of life. They experience a kind of 'divine discontent', a deep compulsion to return to the oceanic bliss of the womb – or beyond.

Spiritual pain can affect us in many ways, and it can be equally as difficult to shift as mental, emotional or physical pain. Someone might be cured from a serious, life-threatening disease but it does not ensure she won't still feel angry. Someone else might discharge his anger in appropriate ways, but that would not ensure he finds meaning in his life. As said, to bring wholeness to something or someone, to heal them, is to complement fragmentation with harmony, not to replace or somehow overcome the unwanted difficulties.

PRACTICE

• Three body weights

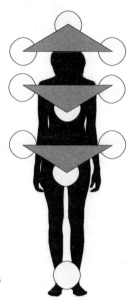

Diagram 19: Three body weights

These are three main weights in our bodies: the head, which sits on the thorax, which sits upon the pelvis. Experiment now with focusing your attention between these different body weights, using your breath to shift your focus between your head, your chest and your belly.

Get a sense of the three weights in your body – the biggest, pelvic weight supported through your legs by the floor; the middle, thorax weight supported by the pelvis, and the head supported through the neck by the thorax. Move your body a little, and as you do so get a sense of aligning the three weights. If you imagine a cord that comes out of the top of your head and pulls you up slightly, and another cord that comes out from your perineum – between your legs – and down into the earth, with a weight on it, pulling you down slightly, it helps to align the three weights. Try it.

Once you get a sense of these three weights, one resting on the other, you start to notice various effects. We all tend to hold back or push forward different body weights as we walk, which has an effect, not only on our walking, but on how we feel in ourselves. It is important for us to start to realise where we lead from, and where we hold back. It is not that one way of being is better than another. We have all learned the ways we lead and hold back from our life experiences. Much of this was learned in our earliest years, and then reinforced as we projected onto the world how we expect it to be. At the same time, the world has reinforced our patterns by mirroring this back to us.

What we do have is the choice to simply focus on our bodies and work at aligning our weights and observing how we react differently to different events in our lives. This way we start learning to respond rather than react, responding to our contact, whether painful or joyful, with the world, the environment, people, all the beings around us. We observe other people, too, and notice how we interact with different types.

Consider how the three body weights relate to the Tree of Life: the head corresponds to the top triangle, the thorax to the middle triangle, the pelvis to the lower one, all focused into the earth, corresponding to Malkuth on the Tree of Life. Through your own direct physical experience of being alive on the planet Earth, you can make a direct and easy inner connection with the Tree of Life. Just now, once again tune into the three body weights as before. Feel how gravity holds these three weights onto the earth, and feel the sphere of the earth beneath you. When you are aligned with the earth, it becomes one with your soul energy and feeds your psychic energy. It helps you to become less fragmented when you connect with this correspondence between your soul and that of the planet itself.

HEALER, HEAL THYSELF

The Tree of Life, being a map of the whole person, is an ideal model to use for healing, whether of ourselves or others. A 'whole healing' of any individual will include the whole Tree – body, personality, soul and Spirit. For the healing to be fully effective, it will also include the relationship of this individual with their external world. This 'whole healing' will act on many levels, from the physical, through the psychological, to the deepest levels of spiritual connection, dealing on the way with etheric, astral and other 'subtle' energies.

In this chapter we will initially focus on the ways of using the Tree as a healer of energy disorders and imbalances, then explore how the psychological work we do with the Tree of Life is also a form of healing. Some people object to this approach, suggesting that by working psychotherapeutically with Kabbalah we are reducing it to little more than another kind of psychotherapy. If this was the only work done, these objections might have substance. To be effective in our more abstract, sensitive and spiritual work, however, it us undoubtedly true that we need to be clear vessels for the reception and transmission of the energies engendered by such work. A thorough programme of therapy is one of the most effective ways of becoming such a clear 'vessel'. There are many examples of people in the esoteric and occult world who have not done this necessary preliminary work, and who thus become bloated with spiritual pride, psychologically disturbed, physically incapable or even downright 'crazy'. Their example, if it could be called that, can serve as a potent and timely reminder to those who wish to by-pass this necessary psychological growth and healing.

Kabbalah offers us a sure and certain way of developing all the parts of our being. Malkuth is involved with the senses, and the work in this sphere leads to an increase in sensory awareness and connection, improving our ability to 'be in the world' and manifest our True Will or Divine Purpose. Without direct work on our physical temple in Malkuth, we cannot fulfil our function for incarnating.

The work of Yesod involves the clearing out of repressed material and the integration of the resultant energies into the correct sphere. Clearing out the repressed material surrounding this sphere allows our unconscious energies to work more freely and strengthen the other spheres involved. It also aids our sexual balance and power. As Yesod is connected to both our personal and collective past, the psychological and direct healing work we do in this sphere helps release us from the ties that bind us, not only on a personal but also a collective level. Some Kabbalists believe that we carry emotional issues with us from past lives, and the work of clarifying Yesod helps release us from these ties as well.

Hod and Netzach involve the balancing of their polarity, that is, the balance of our thinking and feeling functions. This is affected most clearly through allowing the experience and expression of both spheres. The balance we need to achieve between all spheres on the Tree of Life is not a static balance of equality, but a living dynamic balance. To achieve this, we work to increase our contact with the spheres in which we are 'deficient' and refine the energies of the spheres with which we are more 'identified'.

The work of Tiphareth is the building of a strong centre for the directing of the personality, and for the strengthening of our connection to the soul energies represented primarily by Geburah and Chesed. The work of these two spheres, and those higher up the Tree of Life, is, in practical terms, to allow and experience their energies as they emerge, and to thoroughly ground any inspirational spiritual contacts that may be made. To effectively actualise our potential energy, we need a firm base.

PRACTICE

• The Healing Tree

In the following exercise we will be looking at how, through connecting to the Tree of Life, we can bring some healing energy into our own sphere of existence. It focuses particularly on the Middle Pillar. The spheres on the Tree of Life correspond to energy centres on the human body as shown in diagram 10 (page 62 above). Through finding their correspondence in our own bodies, we can use all the associated images and symbols to effect our healing.

Find a comfortable place where you can sit or lie in a relaxed fashion but without falling asleep. Spend at least five minutes focusing on your breathing. Do not force it or change it in any way, but keep to your own rhythm.

Now deepen your breathing a little and connect your out-breath with your in-breath. This means that once you have finished breathing out, immediately start breathing in, and once you have completed an in-breath, immediately breathe out. This connected breathing process is very easy to do yet very powerful.

Focus on yourself as a Tree of Life, overlaying the image of the Tree on your body.

Concentrate particularly on the Middle Pillar of Kether, Daath, Tiphareth, Yesod and Malkuth. Kether (the Crown) is at the very top of your head, Daath (Knowledge) is at the level of the throat, Tiphareth (Beauty) at the heart, Yesod (Foundation) the lower belly and Malkuth (the Kingdom) at the base of your spine. Move between the top and bottom of the Tree as it corresponds to your body, attempting as much as possible to get the whole picture.

As you breathe in, focus your attention on energy rising up the Middle Pillar, up the back of your body. As you breathe out, focus your attention on energy coming down the Middle Pillar and down the front of your body. Keeping your breathing connected as before, let this cycle of energy build up within you.

Determine where energy is needed in you to restore balance. You may already be aware of this place in your body, or you may like to simply ask yourself the question: where do I need healing?

Give yourself over to this place in your body, visualising energy there. On your in-breath imagine that the energy there becomes stronger and more balanced, on your out-breath that you let out all dis-ease and unbalance.

Allow yourself to relax in this place in your body and let go of all the tension.

See if there is a colour or image that will aid your balance, and simply imagine this colour or image sinking into this part of your body. Keep this up, letting the part of your body with which you are working be filled with the energy of the colour or image.

Now focus on your breathing again, directing your attention from this place in your body and return to the image of the Middle Pillar of the Tree of Life, then the whole Tree.

Take some time to be aware of your whole body, relaxed, feeling well and 'healed'.

Return to your normal waking consciousness and, in whatever way feels appropriate to you, thank the forces that have aided this healing process within your body. Affirm that your healing is part of the healing of the whole of life on our planet and beyond.

• Healing hands

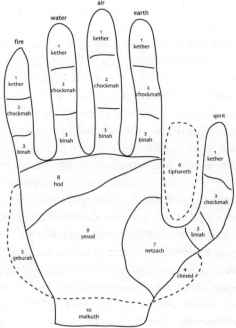

Diagram 20: Healing hands

Study diagram 20, which shows the correspondences of the Sephiroth to the various areas of the hand. Hold your hand out while looking at the diagram and use your other hand to touch the various places that correspond to the Tree of Life.

Using your existing Kabbalistic understanding, consider how all the different parts of the hand correspond to the spheres of the Tree of Life.

Do these attributions make sense to you? Could you devise a way either to test the correspondences involved, or to use them in a practical way?

DAATH AND HEALING

The sphere called Daath is not situated on the Tree of Life, thus it is not given a number and is sometimes called 'the sphere that is not a sphere'. Daath in Hebrew means knowledge and is the place of access to the dark side or reverse of the Tree. Traditionally Daath was seen in a very negative way, as it corresponds – on one level – to the false knowledge that is disconnected from the understanding of the Divine Plan. In this form it is essentially 'false knowledge'. However, since the opening up of the energies represented by the Tree of Life diagram brought about by the shifts in human consciousness in the last century, and particularly since the end of the Second World War, the positive aspects of Daath have become more apparent.

On an energetic level, Daath relates to the throat chakra, to the expression of spiritual knowledge. This expression can either be clear or distorted depending on how open this centre is within any particular human being. Daath is also a centre of generation and regeneration. Daath opens and represents the potential of clear expression when the two centres of the heart represented by Geburah and Chesed are in dynamic balance.

Of particular interest to us here is that Daath is the gateway to the reverse side of the Tree of Life. A 'negative' or 'dark' Tree exists behind the usual outwardly visible Tree of Life and is the world of the demonic, shadowy aspects or 'shells' of the positive energies represented by the front side of the Tree. There is no suggestion here that this 'negative' side of the Tree is evil – it is a necessary component of a complete system. Everything 'positive' has a 'negative' side. Peace is polarised with war, love with hate, joy with sorrow and so on.

There are many ways of using Kabbalah for healing, working with 'demons' being one of them. You may wonder what exactly is meant by demons here and if they really exist. From a practical Kabbalistic viewpoint, whether these 'demons' actually exist outside or whether they are figments of our imagination, or parts of us that we do not recognise as being part of us, this is a useful way of naming the negative forces and starting to understand how they operate. For example, when something goes amiss in one of our body systems, we might describe this in terms of the presence of a demon or demonic force. We do not have to believe in demons to understand that putting a name to them can help give the condition meaning, and enable changes to be made. Once the 'demon' has been named, the afflicted person is able to start communicating with it, find what needs to be expressed, and through various appropriate actions reduce or even remove the hold of the demon. We will further explore in the next practice what we might call 'healing through communicating with the demons'.

The tables in Appendices 4 and 5 detail the different parts of the body as they are attributed to the Tree. The disorders and diseases typical for each sphere or path on the Tree can be deduced easily from these tables. For example, if there was a disorder or disease originating in your liver (jaundice perhaps), it would show that the demons of the associated path (that from Tiphareth to Hod) were affecting your being. If you had a stomach ulcer it may suggest that a problem was occurring on the path joining Tiphareth to Netzach, which was allowing the attendant 'negative' energies (or demons) to manifest in this way.

If we consider the idea that demonic forces use your physical vehicle to come through into manifestation on the Tree of Life, one way of dealing with the resultant disorders and diseases is through contacting the appropriate positive force to counteract the intrusion of the demons. Thus, for instance, if the disease was associated with Hod (relating to the right kidney), the use of the positive attributes of this sphere will counteract the disease. If we wish to counteract a disease in Hod, we might wear the appropriate colour (orange) next to the diseased place, chant the name and invoke the corresponding deity (Elohim Tzabaoth), fill the room with the corresponding flowers, concentrate on relevant animals and gemstones – using all the correspondences to this part of the Tree of Life to bring more of the positive aspect of the path into the field of consciousness of the diseased person.

PRACTICE

• Facing a demon

It's important to remember the principle of inclusion when dealing with demons. We do not want to discard them or the energies they represent, however negative they appear. It is better to transform and absorb them, and, through including these so-called 'demonic forces', create an active balance within. All good systems of healing (and esoteric development) stress the importance of including these energies.

Create sacred space in the usual way and perform the Kabbalistic Cross (or equivalent). Stand in the centre of your circle, close your eyes and pay attention to your breathing. Don't force your breath, simply allow your own rhythm to flow.

Be aware of how you act differently in different situations, sometimes being in control, sometimes feeling out of control, sometimes liking the way you behave, sometimes not.

Focus on an aspect of your behaviour that you do not like to recognise in yourself. Fill this out in detail, and consider times when this behaviour takes over, as it were, how you tend to keep it hidden or suppressed.

Imagine that a demon affects this behaviour of yours that you don't like to recognise and would prefer to keep hidden . . . Allow an image for this demon and picture it standing in front of you. Look at the demon's image. What does it look like? How is it dressed? How old is it? Let the image clearly form.

If you are willing to explore this further, let yourself be aware of how you feel towards this demon.

(If you are not willing, close your sacred space, leave your temple and spend an hour or so performing mundane tasks. Don't judge yourself; there is a right time for everything. Trust in your own judgement.)

Are you willing to identify with this demon so you can explore it further? If you are, take a physical step into it, identify with it. Embody it – take up its physical posture, imagine taking on its form. Ask this demon: how do you feel? how do you see the world? what is your attitude?

As this demon: what is it you want? What is it you really need? Allow this need to fill you now. Move/dance to express this. Give it a voice. Feel it . . .

Allow this to build strongly, then choose for it to fade. Step back, clearly stepping out of the demon identification and into your own body. Take time to really feel this, to become yourself again. Breathe.

Look at the demon out there in front of you again. Give it a name.

How do you feel towards it now? Does this demon have any value in your life?

What would it be like if you were always identified with it?

What would it be like if it were gone altogether?

Would anything be missing if it didn't exist?

What is the quality, the good feelings trapped behind the hold of this demon?

When you are ready, shake off this demon, clearly and firmly sending it back to its own realm.

Close your temple, and engage yourself in some mundane everyday tasks for at least an hour. Later write about your experience in your Kabbalistic journal, particularly what you learned when answering the above questions.

THE PATH OF THE NOSE AND MOUTH

Diagram 21: The fourteenth path

The fourteenth path connects Chockmah to Binah. Before continuing, consider what you understand about Chockmah and Binah.

The fourteenth path is known as the illuminating path. Illuminating is the action from the verb to illuminate. Some extracts from the *Oxford English Dictionary* may help you understand what is meant by illumination:

1. To light up, give light to.
2. To give light to, or remove blindness from (the eyes), esp. fig. in religious sense.
3. To shed spiritual light upon; to enlighten spiritually.
4. To enlighten intellectually; to give understanding to.
5. To throw light upon; to make luminous or clear; to elucidate.
6. To make resplendent or illustrious; to shed a lustre upon.
7. To decorate profusely with lights, as a sign of festivity or in honour of some person or some event.

As the fourteenth path is so important in healing work, consider first how this path connects the first and second worlds (and does not figure in the third world of Yetzirah at all). Of course, for the first and second worlds of Atziluth and Briah, we remain in the transpersonal realms of the Supernal Triad. You can regard this path as the binding force of the universe, the bridge between spiritual Will and spiritual Love.

Daleth, the letter of this path, is the second double letter (Gimel is the first), and corresponds to the number 4. Note that there are four tastes (sweet, bitter, sour, salt). As well as being the Hebrew word for door, Daleth can also mean a gate or lid, specifically one that can be lifted up in order to reveal or deliver something. It is also sometimes described as the door into and out of the womb. Daleth is ascribed to the tarot card The Empress, also known as the daughter of the mighty ones. The Zohar describes Daleth as meaning impoverishment, a necessary stage in the preparation of oneself to 'make tikkun', that is to repair the fragmentation in your life. Considering that the traditional vision associated with the fourteenth path is the vision of fundamental holiness, I think it is becoming clear how important this path is for healing work, so now we are ready to deepen our understanding of the major physical correspondences to this path.

On the Tree of Life, both the internal and external structures of the nose and mouth are attributed to the fourteenth path, which also corresponds with The Empress tarot card and the letter Daleth. The fourteenth path is considered to be a primary path for healing, so we will next study it in more depth, firstly considering its attribution to the nose and mouth.

The primary concern of both the nose and mouth are the act of breathing. Many (even most!) systems of spiritual development attest to the importance of learning to breathe properly, or in a particular way. Often at the beginning of exercises, particularly in groups, I make a joke, telling the participants not to try breathing in any special yogic way but just allowing their own breath to enter and exit the body easily at its own rate. The hidden joke in this is that this is the most esoteric way to breathe, and, interestingly, it is the most difficult.

Spend a few minutes now just breathing, let the air enter your body, fill your lungs, then pass out again easily, without effort. As you do so, pay particular attention to any holding patterns that you become aware of in your body. Now place a hand on your belly and breathe in a way that causes your belly to expand and push your hand away; then, as you breathe out, feel your belly contract, and at the end of the breath use your hand to lightly push your belly in (and, as it were, the remainder of the air out). Then, as you breathe in again, feel your belly expand and push your hand outwards. Continue breathing like this for a few minutes.

Now place your hand on your chest and do the same, feeling your in-breath and out-breath alternately push your hand away and fall under the (light!) pressure of your hand. Do you habitually breathe from your chest or belly? Don't judge one better than the other, but notice which is your habitual pattern. Whether you usually breathe from your belly or chest, consider the other (i.e. if you tend to chest-breathe, then consider your belly and vice versa). What might you be holding on to in this part of your body?

Apart from breathing, the nose and mouth are also concerned with the senses of smell and taste. It is said that a dog has an olfactory sense somewhere in the order of thirty times stronger than that of humans, and some (rather surprising) creatures, for instance a moth, have thirty times greater olfactory sense than a dog. Salmon are said to find their way from the depths of the ocean back to a distant river, to their original spawning ground, through their sense of smell! Smell and taste are chemical senses, receptors in the nose and tongue responding to chemical stimuli. It is interesting to note that smells entering the right nostril and tastes affecting the right side of the tongue pass to the parietal lobe of the opposite, left side of the cerebrum, and vice versa. This tells us something of the functioning of the fourteenth path in the Yetziratic and Assiatic worlds.

Another function of the mouth is for eating. Many of our psychological functions have a parallel with eating (and eating disorders are not just common, they are pretty well universal, to some degree or another, with all human beings). He has bitten off more than he can chew; she finds that hard to swallow; the idea of doing that stuck in my throat; chew on that for a while; come on, spit it out . . . these and other similar well-known phrases apparently originate from eating analogies but are used to describe psychic functioning.

The Mass of the Holy Ghost, or the sacramental supper, takes place on the fourteenth path. On an esoteric level, this Mass involves the balancing of male and female energies and the acceptance within oneself of a deep sense of their ultimate unity. Some Kabbalists take this on a literal level and consider the Mass to involve the imbibing of commingled male and female essences. To smell, taste and ingest this elixir is said to confer magical powers and be the true meaning of the stone of the wise or elixir of life. The particular charge of the elixir is varied through the particular state of the emanations involved, for both the male and female. In Tantra, kalas is the name of the female emanations (or vaginal juices). Kala is a Sanskrit word meaning star and also perfume. At different times of the month (the cycle of existence) the kalas vary (after menopause as well as before). This is true also for male scent and bodily fluids. The perfect elixir is said to be sweet-smelling like the finest honey, and is the closest human equivalent to the emanations that pour from one sphere to the next on the Tree of Life in the creative process. This has particular relevance to the fourteenth path, which, joining as it does Chockmah and Binah, can be considered the primary holding force of the universe. Whether we take such practices as literal or symbolic, the essential message concerns treating our breathing, smelling and tasting, indeed all our sensory experiences, as being of the deepest spiritual nature. We are being asked to literally come to our senses and find ourselves!

PRACTICE

• Elemental breathing

Spend a few minutes just breathing. Let the air enter your body, fill your lungs, then pass out again easily, without effort. As you do so, pay particular attention to any holding patterns that you become aware of in your body.

Now breathe in the fullest way you can for a few minutes. As you breathe in, first feel your belly expand, then your chest, until you feel completely full of air in your whole body. Then effortlessly let the air out until you feel empty, and repeat the process. Do at least twenty of these full breaths and note any particular effects, immediately and for a short while afterwards.

There is a series of breathing exercises that connect different patterns of breathing with the five elements of spirit, fire, water, air and earth. There are different versions of this, but try experimenting with the following:

fire breath:	nose out, mouth in
water breath:	nose in, mouth out
air breath:	nose in, nose out
earth breath:	mouth in, mouth out
spirit breath:	mouth/nose in, mouth/nose out

After preparation, walk about in a relaxed fashion, being attentive to the different responses you have while experimenting with these different ways of breathing.

You might like to practise these elemental breaths at other times.

From both your experience, and your Kabbalistic knowledge, how could you attribute these five methods of breathing to the Tree of Life?

The Tree of Life in Counselling and Psychotherapy

The purpose of the Tree of Life is to help us sort out different aspects of our psyche so that we can more clearly work with heart energy as well as with intellectual knowledge. Indeed, the Tree of Life, through its cleverly designed visual structure, helps us make connections between apparently unrelated facts that then become gems of meaningful wisdom. So, for instance, as you learn to understand and develop the relationship between your different emotions, you find your relationship with other people's emotions becomes easier to handle. It doesn't necessarily make a teenager's angst or a partner's lack of interest any better, but you can change how you react to them. Your inner world changes so that you have your emotions rather than them having you. You *respond* to other people rather than just reacting to their difficulties.

With Kabbalah you don't have to believe in something or not. The Tree of Life is a structure that helps you sort things out for yourself. On top of that it helps you connect to a centre inside yourself where you are closest to the essence of yourself, your divine spark, or simply the deepest and most valuable aspect of yourself. When you connect with this, it vitalises your life, particularly your relationships, because at a deep core level you experience how everything is interrelated. Kabbalah doesn't show you anything new, it's more that as you work with it you uncover what was always there, a distinct individual who is at the same time inextricably linked to everyone else.

We have discussed earlier how Kabbalists agree with child development theories that there are various stages we go through in our development into adulthood, psychologically as well as physically. What happens to us at these stages sets the scene for how we (neurotically or healthily) function on various levels in later life. Kabbalists believe that our basic source of energy is through Yesod, which, if we did not carry the past within us, would give us access to a free-flowing, unlimited source of energy. Everyone, however, comes into life with issues to work on (and, sometimes, to work *through* – but not inevitably). What happens in our development is a result of soul transmitting these issues so we can have something to work with for our particular growth and development. These issues are 'deposited', as it were, round Yesod, blocking the free flow of energy.

As well as all the influences from the past, the other factor that affects us in the here and now is the future. Everything that is potential can happen in the future. The upper part of the Tree of Life represents the future; it is the potential we carry round in us, which is able to manifest at any moment. Most of the time, though, we are not aware of it. We might be so caught up with experiences from the past, or so busy in the present moment, we forget about our potential. It is still there, however, always manifesting. Indeed, we usually experience this potential through our intuition as it manifests itself in our thoughts, feelings or senses. We might have it as a flash, an inspiration, or an 'aha' experience. For instance, our potential shows itself through thoughts – we just know something. Or we might have it coming through as a feeling about something. We just feel this is right; it's not like a personal feeling, but is a deeper sense of feeling. Or we may have *a sense that* . . . whatever. We experience this sort of sensing when our inspiration or intuition is coming through our bodies or our sensations. Inspiration also comes through in dreams and images.

Kabbalah focuses on manifesting soul energy into everyday life. The danger for many 'spiritual seekers' is that they like it on the sun so much they never want to leave there. They become so involved in being the sun, being a light source, that they forget the shadows they cast. In terms of the solar system, in terms of our heart energy, if we stay just there, there aren't any shadows. Absolutely, and that's a wonderful place to experience. But often it is the shadows, the dark places, that reveal to us more things about how we are going to manifest. If

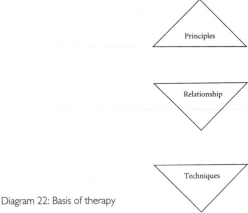

Diagram 22: Basis of therapy

everybody existed in a place of no shadow, there'd be no need for relationship, for contact, for service. We need places with shadows to remind us of our mortality *and* our totality.

There are many different kinds of therapies, and different aspects of all their practices may be related to the Tree of Life. Whatever the school or type of therapy, whether a talk-only type or one using hands-on techniques, there are three basic aspects to their practices (see diagram 22). These are the *principles* behind the work (the Supernal Triad), the *relationship* between the therapist and patient or client (the soul triangle) and the *methods and techniques* used (the bottom triangle). Through relating psychotherapy and counselling practice to the Tree of Life we can better understand the processes involved. Of course, there are many different schools of therapy but, generally, practitioners:

- do not judge, although they may interpret (Hod)
- they do not lead, although they may challenge (Yesod)
- they do not touch, although they do offer support (Malkuth)
- they work alongside the unfolding process of their clients, trusting in what manifests as being right for that person at that time (Netzach)
- they also generally work within the container of the therapeutic space, using the time of the session to be in deep relationship with their client (Tiphareth), involved and witnessing at the same time.

You can see already how the whole Tree of Life is engaged in the therapeutic process. Using the Tree of Life, a therapist can work in a truly integrative way, and not just offer a hotchpotch of disconnected techniques. The Tree is the perfect model or map for this work, for, through its simplicity and clarity, it can act as a central synthesising agent for methods and techniques, other systems, maps and models of consciousness development. Whatever methods are used, however, the principles behind the therapy remain basically the same. There is an attempt to share in an experiential understanding of the relationship between the therapist and client.

Different methods of psychotherapy and counselling concentrate on different aspects of the process. For example, Jungian therapists usually work up to Daath, concentrating on the dynamic between Chesed and Geburah (Love and Will archetypes) through the medium of dream analysis (Hod and Yesod). Traditional psychoanalysis works with the

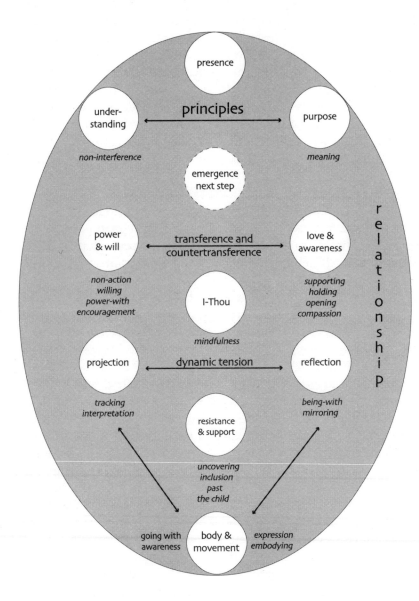

Diagram 23: Psychotherapy

lower Tree, attempting to normalise the personality (and at its worst denying the deeper or higher aspects of the psyche). This is the opposite pole from the worst forms of transpersonal therapies, which work up to Daath or above but not down into Yesod or Malkuth, potentially leaving their clients spiritually connected but totally ungrounded. The differences between approaches become clearer when related to the Tree of Life, which then offers us the possibility of integrating them so the common purpose becomes more apparent.

To use Kabbalah as a tool in therapeutic work, whether counselling, psychotherapy or other forms of one-to-one or group healing, it is vital the therapist has someone who can work with them in a supervisory capacity, to help them see what is going on in the work in terms of the model being used. If no such person is available then you can supervise yourself, but the work will lack the holding and challenging functions that are possible when working with the help of another.

Of most importance is the awareness of where and how the therapist and the client are relating or not in terms of the seven different planes of the Tree of Life, which represent different aspects of the psyche. For therapy to work it is important to be working on creating relationship at all times; to be establishing 'mindfulness' or focus; to make space for the individual experience of the client and the unfolding experience of his or her relationship with the practitioner.

To uncover and reveal the presence of soul around and within all aspects of our lives, including the light and the dark, is the common aim of transpersonal and spiritual psychotherapies and Kabbalah. This inclusive attitude allows an integration that is not forced, dogmatic or controlled but is free to find its own level wherever it manifests. Diagram 23 shows how some of the main issues dealt with in a psychotherapeutic practice can be related to the Tree of Life. Considering this diagram, we could, for example, look at transference and counter-transference, which are shown on the path or connection between the spheres attributed to the archetypes of Love and Will. Transference is a term used to describe how a client might project onto their therapist different feelings and ideas that they actually feel about someone else (usually a parent). Counter-transference is when the therapist does this back to the client. When such conditions occur, we could say that the client's 'Tree of Life' has triggered a response in the therapist's 'Tree of Life' and vice versa. This is really important for a therapist to notice because recognising this response tells them about their client's state at that moment. Even if you do not work in this field, it can be most useful and illuminating to watch for such interactions in your family or with friends. It then may be worth particularly noticing, for instance:

- the paired spheres: for example, watching the body/ shoulders/chest/arms etc. – how the other person's body is held, and where armouring is most apparent. Armouring is the term used to describe when a person's energy has become blocked and, as a consequence, they do not have free access to the parts of their body where this energy is trapped. You can watch for left/right differences to give you more information on the heart, whether love or will issues are involved and so on
- you can mirror the other person while visualising a coloured image of the Tree of Life between you, watching for changes in the image between you, offering information about the areas where you are clearly in contact and where your interaction is blocked
- paying attention to the paths allows access to more information. The associations and correspondences to the paths allow the 'promotion of connections' (between which spheres the path connects) and vice versa
- as the other person is describing imagery, dreams, and so on, you can place this information onto the Tree of Life.

Using the Tree of Life we can learn to go deeper into the process of our clients. For instance, imagine there is a person thinking she should brush her teeth every morning and she does not feel like doing it. On the surface this is a trivial matter (except for the probable dental bills that eventually will be involved, not to mention becoming toothless!). I've chosen something apparently minor on purpose, but of course the same principles would apply to more serious issues. If this person looks into her past (Yesod) she may find it is something to do with her parents' attitudes to life. They were always trying to make her brush her teeth, and her difficulty is her reaction, her resistance to that. Deeper than this, the issue might have something to do with the manifestation in her everyday life of her connection to spirit through the central, archetypal triangle on the Tree of Life. In her everyday life, all these issues, set in place right from birth or perhaps even before, will cause her to have neurotic responses to issues that will appear to be out of proportion and which will be disturbing and, at worst, debilitating. On the archetypal level we can see the 'presenting issue' has something to do with the interaction of the Love and Will archetypes within her that we connect to the Tree of Life via Chesed and Geburah, which also correspond to her parents. Something in her relationship to her father (Geburah) might have been damaged in some way, for instance.

From a worldly viewpoint, it has affected her ability to say yes to brushing her teeth. Why shouldn't she just say yes – after all, it's a sensible thing to do! What is behind that? Using the Tree of Life model we have made a correspondence that suggests it is something about her relationship to the archetype of Power (Geburah). Knowing this, she can look at it from this perspective and say, 'Well, how do I manifest that archetype? How can I bring that through more clearly?' She would not be doing this in order to be able to brush her teeth better, but so that the archetypal energy blocked around the resistance would be freed up and available to her again. If this is true for an issue such as tooth-brushing, how much more true – and powerful – might this way of looking at resistance and life issues of more central importance be to any individual.

WHOLENESS AND HEALING

'The Book of Splendour' describes how the Creator fashioned all the souls that would incarnate and then told them to go and manifest themselves. Many souls were appalled at this command and said they were happy to stay where they were, in the blissful heaven where they were created. The Creator replied that the whole point in their being created was to go into the world so they must do so. The souls, unable to disobey their Creator, unwillingly descended into bodies and came to the earth.

We all know how being in life can be very painful in so many different ways. There seems little or no point in bothering to incarnate in the first place, however, if we spend all our time trying to leave. The time to depart will come to us all soon enough. While here, let's enjoy life to the full, appreciate the opportunities it presents to us to learn and grow, and – perhaps most importantly in our modern world – learn to be here with respect for the planet itself and all the life forms it supports. Kabbalah, with its grounded, pragmatic approach to spiritual growth, is an excellent guide for such practice. We can work at bringing our spiritual insights, connections and experiences to earth, to illuminate not just ourselves but all sentient beings.

We all know how past experiences can affect our flow of energy, how repeating cycles of behaviour can sometimes cause us to fail to fulfil our deepest potential. The Kabbalistic approach gives us an opportunity to understand all our experiences as valuable, rather than looking at these developmental patterns as negative and restrictive. Of course, this does not mean that having been neglected, abused or mistreated is in itself valuable, rather that there is value in what we can do to learn from and change in ourselves through having had our unique life experiences.

Many people in the modern world suffer from what is sometimes called the 'crisis of meaning'. Particularly in the West but increasingly over the whole planet, many people live in an existential vacuum, where life has lost its meaning (beyond, at the best, the purely material). In this modern world, with its collective lack of meaning, there is much strife between people. The ecological state of the world is poor owing to the greed of some people and the mindlessness of others. There often seems to be such an appalling lack of care and understanding and so much imbalance, particularly in the interaction between people. Kabbalah offers to help with the healing of this 'illness' through assisting an individual to know herself or himself. To know oneself is to bring meaning back into life, which then creates a context for living a life in accord with others.

Some of our deepest spiritual connections foster the realisation that all life forms, not just human beings, are part of a totally interconnected and inseparable energy field. While most of us may spend a large part of our lives experiencing separation and disconnection, once we start to explore the deeper aspects of our being we discover the underlying truth of our connection. That doesn't make the alienation disappear, but it offers a new perspective from which to experience it. We may not be able to 'be there' all the time, indeed it may not be right for us to stay in such a state, but once we have the intimation of its existence, once we actually experience it in ourselves, there is no looking back. We have 'set our sights' on the clarity and connection that comes from such realisation and, when we remember, try to make each move we make a step in that direction. Working with the Tree of Life helps us remember ourselves a little bit more often.

The realisation that we are connected to everyone and everything else brings a different perspective on time and space where we can cultivate within ourselves a sense of 'global consciousness' that we can start to ground in our everyday lives. When we ground this awareness it helps us take actions that move the total collective consciousness forward along its positive evolutionary path. It is not an exaggeration to say that one small act made by one individual at one moment in time can make a profound difference. To care for others, both those immediately within our field of awareness and activity, and also all living and non-living things generally, is the way to ground this consciousness. When we care for our environment, both locally and generally, we are also grounding our deepest, psycho-spiritual consciousness. Every conscious act that includes such caring furthers the cause of global healing.

8

ANGELS, DEMONS, SEXUALITY AND SHEKHINAH

Behold, the human has become as one of us, and now may put forth a hand, and take of the Tree of Life, and eat, and live for ever.
Book of Genesis (adapted from 3:22)

Kabbalistic magic has been described as the mysticism or yoga of the West. While there are similarities, and the ultimate aim of complete self-realisation is the same, the major distinction is that Kabbalah focuses on coming to earth rather than transcending it. Kabbalah stresses that the world just as it is, although it may sometimes appear impure or valueless, is our most precious tool for transformation. You do not have to go somewhere else to attain self-realisation; instead you can uncover its abiding presence in the apparently mundane. Magic, in the Kabbalistic sense, is found within one's life as it is, in both its heights and its depths.

The philosophy of Kabbalistic magic says that the two most important powers in the human psyche are will and imagination, both properly tempered by the greatest cosmic force, love. Imagination is what we use to create the world in which we live, and will is the force by which we create it. In bringing these two forces together, a Kabbalist may affect events both in the immediate surroundings and beyond. While some Kabbalists, especially those of a mystical nature, sometimes deride Kabbalistic magic as being too involved with the use of power, all methods for transforming oneself and the world, whether considered spiritual, mystical or mundane, that change your inner reality and outer behaviour, may be considered valid approaches to self-realisation.

A medieval treatise called 'The Magic of Abra Melin the Mage' is based around the notion that to have 'knowledge and conversation of your guardian angel' (which will be explored further later on in the chapter), the equivalent to 'illumination', it is essential first to go into your depths, to face 'the demons of darkness', and bring them under your control. From a Kabbalistic perspective, we come to understand and experience that the light of Kether can be found shining in the darkest places and, when found, its light, brighter for being experienced in the darkness, may illuminate us.

The simplest definition of magic is that it is a way of making happen what you want to happen, using imagination (the intervention of spiritual beings) and will (the occult controlling principle). In his book *The Tree of Life*, Israel Regardie, accomplished magician and authority on ceremonial magic, says that through imagination 'we are capable of being united to the gods, of transcending the mundane order, and of participating in eternal life. Through this principle, therefore, we are able to liberate ourselves from fate.' Regardie goes on to reflect that 'it is a great mistake to consider imagination to be the same as fantasy and daydreaming. Imagination is the image-making faculty, an image creating power which when developed may prove of the utmost importance as assisting the soul in its forward journey.' What distinguishes magical imagination from daydreaming is that the imagination is being directed by the will. In *The Secret Doctrine*, Helena Blavatsky, founder of the Theosophical Society, writes of imagination that it is 'the mysterious power of thought which enables it to produce external, perceptible, phenomenal results by its own inherent energy', the will in action. Indeed, the act of will is a natural process, the very spark of life itself, and every choice or decision we make is an act of will.

The definition of magic most widely used in esoteric books is from Aleister Crowley, who defines it as 'the science and art of causing change to occur in conformity with your will', which is another description of making happen what you want to happen. Of course, to make magic work can be a complex task. To make happen what you want to happen, many different circumstances and conditions need to be taken into account. If what you want is, for instance, a bar of chocolate, you have to decide on the degree and kind of force to use; the shop is only a short distance away so you may decide upon walking as the kind of force, forward at approximately four miles per hour as the degree. You have to exert this force in the correct manner and through the correct medium – it would be no use walking in the wrong direction and up the garden path. This decided upon, you only have to apply your force to the correct spirit or agent – the shopkeeper – using a magical link, in this case money, and you have succeeded in your magic as you now have a chocolate bar to eat.

In this example, the spirit you have involved in your magic is a shopkeeper, the best kind of 'spirit' to invoke when you want to purchase something. You might not know exactly what they are or why they exist at all, but you can experience the presence of 'spirits'. Despite there being many different ideas and opinions about what the spirit world is, or whether it even really exists, the shared experience of magicians and shamans of all persuasions is that alongside our everyday reality there is a realm (or realms) of spirits populated by innumerable different types of entities. These range from the powerful to the weak, from the bright to the dim-witted, from benevolent through cheeky to downright malicious.

A Kabbalistic magician's power to communicate with a spirit, in either their world or ours, depends upon knowing the names, strengths, weaknesses and correspondences to the spirit in question. This knowledge enables you to call or dismiss spirits, and compel them to perform tasks for you. Thus in the example of summoning up a shop-keeper to acquire a bar of chocolate, your knowledge that a shopkeeper spirit will exchange a bar of chocolate for money enables you to communicate with the spirit and make your magic work. Learning the most appropriate means to communicate with a spirit is equally valid on the spirit plane as in our mundane realm, perhaps more so.

Magic is generally more oriented towards using the will rather than not and thus concentrates on developing our ability to choose. Some Eastern approaches to self-realisation suggest that it is better to simply accept things as they are and surrender to the unfolding nature of life. A Kabbalist will certainly choose to do just that at times, to let things be, wait and see what unfolds. The point is, however, that the magician has a choice in the matter, whether to act or not, and that is what defines magic as the ability to choose. The nineteenth-century Kabbalist Eliphas Levi, defining magic as 'the traditional science concerning the secrets of nature transmitted to us from the magicians of the past', is affirming that magic is a tradition, a science, natural and transmittable. Indeed, there is nothing unnatural about magic, as making happen what you want to happen is a basic human desire.

The real point of magic for a Kabbalist is to be able to shift your attention (or consciousness) beyond your everyday and ego-led limitations, to discover ways to make the right things happen for you, then to put this into practice. However strong your will may be, unless a link is made between the force of your will and the proposed object or condition to be changed, all attempts to make the required change will fail. However much you want to catch a fish, and even if the fish may want to be caught, unless there is a rod and line you can go on wishing (and fishing!) forever without success.

The magical link may be classified into three main groups depend-ing upon whether it involves (a) one plane and one person, (b) one plane and two or more persons, or (c) two planes. Group (a) involves changes brought about by a person to himself or herself. The instrument of the link already exists, therefore, in that all that happens is inside the magician. The necessary condition to make the link work is to inflame or elevate your will to the proper pitch so that your intent is put into action. Of course, the magic must still be in line with the greater nature of which we are all part. However strong your will may be, in the case of organic disease, for instance, your apparatus may be damaged beyond the art of nature to repair. It may be necessary in such a case to assist the internal 'spirits' through the 'purification' of medicine, the 'banishing' of diet, or some other extraneous means.

Group (b) includes all magical operations where the aim is to make happen what you want to happen upon objects or characters outside of your own inner control. The inner energy or will to make this happen still needs to be inflamed but now has to be externally expressed and imposed. For instance, should you wish to overthrow the leader of a nation, you might initially use words, as in speeches arousing feelings of discontent with the current leader. If all else failed, you might make the link by hiring the necessary assassin! But, of course (apart from all moral considerations) an assassin would not be suitable to deal with, say, your opponents in a local by-election. The strength of the agent used for the link has to be just right; too much force can be as useless as too little.

The third group of magical links (c), which involve two planes, requires a high degree of initiation and mystical understanding for, as Crowley put it in his work *Magick in Theory and Practice*, 'we see . . . that we can never affect anything outside ourselves save only as it is also within us. Whatever I do to another, I also do to myself.' For someone with the reputation of being a 'black magician' these words, perhaps surprisingly, convey a true understanding of the ethics by which a Kabbalistic magician will live.

Kabbalistic magicians sometimes use grimoires and spells to make their magic work, again acts that may sometimes be associated with magic of a less ethical nature than we we suggesting here, so it makes sense to check out what we mean by these words first. Grimoire is the name some magicians give to their book of spells. In the Disney movie *Fantasia*, the big old dusty tome that the sorcerer's apprentice opens to find a spell to use for cleaning is a grimoire. The fact that the spell takes the apprentice over and he loses control of the operation is a good warning about not using magical spells until you feel really able to deal with the consequences. As a grimoire is the place that a magician puts spells into, we could compare it to the 'grammar' of which 'spelling' is a part.

To create spells, a magician may use special magical tools that have a deeper inner purpose and significance than is sometimes apparent and which are intended to remind the magician of the deeper purpose of the work. For instance, sometimes a magician hangs a lamp above the altar to represent the light of pure soul, and to act as a reminder not to be too confident or clever, that some things are always unknown and beyond the understanding of even a magician. This lamp may be on the physical plane or in the imagination of the magician. A modern magician may also, for instance, use a clock or watch as a reminder of the passage of time, and as a timely reminder of the impermanence of all things.

So a grimoire is somewhere for a Kabbalistic magician to put their spells. The use of such spells depends on what the Kabbalist wants, how much they want it, and what they're willing to put into getting it. If you *spell* it correctly, what you want to make happen and the methods for achieving this will become clearer to you. Finding the right spelling of things isn't so easy, though. The spelling of 'things' for instance isn't what you see in the printed letters 't-h-i-n-g-s' but what the word conjures up in your awareness. A dog is most definitely not what you see in the letters 'd-o-g' and, more than that, may represent many different connections and associations for different people (and of course different associations for the same person).

Good magical practice is to make a spell, set the magic in motion, and then let it go and not worry whether or not the spell has worked. In other words, the best way to make a spell work is to forget all about it. The spell will only work, though, if you concentrate your intent strongly enough before you forget it. The notion is that by consciously forgetting your spell, it will be more active in the unconscious and therefore stir up enough energy to make it happen. This does work, the only issue being that you cannot control when the spell will actually come into operation. Of course, this is also not a problem because it means you have to trust to nature, which is always the best magic.

Carlos Castaneda suggests that the best way to activate your intent is to speak it out loud. This is true, the only problem being that you must have stored enough personal power to be able to voice your spell clearly enough. You collect personal power every time you act from your centre of intent (paradoxically, whether the specific intent comes to fruition or not). This suggests, therefore, that the old saying 'practice makes perfect' is magically correct. It is worth remembering that spells work best when the magician is not attached to the desired outcome, a somewhat strange and yet basic paradox at the heart of magic.

CONTACT WITH 'EXTRA-DIMENSIONAL' BEINGS

All cultures throughout our planet's history have described beings and creatures that exist in other realities or dimensions in parallel with and sometimes interpenetrating our world. In the view of some mainstream psychologists, these 'extra-dimensional' beings are the impersonal forces of nature, which we personalise so we can attempt to gain control over them. According to some more far-sighted psychologists and those aware of the work of the New Physics, however, these beings are representational of real forces. Looked at superficially, our world is composed of atoms and molecules, which arrange themselves to create the different life forms we directly perceive. If we examine this basic atomic reality under an electron microscope, we enter the world of subatomic particles. This is a level of existence where different laws apply, but it is no less real simply because we cannot see it on a mundane level. The same applies to the 'levels of existence' that we cannot perceive with our usual senses but which are, despite this, no less real.

As our work in Kabbalah progresses and we wish to use the Tree of Life for our healing, we start to meet 'other beings'. At first sight this may appear strange, even ridiculous, until we consider the nature of these 'extra-dimensional' beings. Any being or entity outside of ourselves can be considered this way, including other human beings. Whether these 'beings' actually exist outside or whether they are figments of our imagination, projections or parts of us that we do not recognise as being part of us, we all have the experience that they exist.

All the beings that inhabit our world, including animals, plants and all living and so-called non-living things, are apparently outside of us and we meet with them primarily in Malkuth. At a deeper level we meet 'astral' entities that inhabit the lower spheres on the Tree. These 'astral beings' include those we meet in dreams, astral projections, fantasies and visualisations, and include all symbols and thought-forms. Tiphareth, while primarily associated with our own essential selves, is also the sphere for contact with our Guardian Angel. Whether these angels exist outside of us matters little in practical terms; when we contact Tiphareth we find such beings in attendance. Then, on even deeper levels of the Tree we may 'contact' Archangels and, if we reach the Supernal Triad, we may have contact with the Deity or some aspect of it.

Daath is the unnumbered sphere that resides in the Abyss between the Supernal Triad and the lower Tree. It is said to be the access point to the reverse side of the Tree where all the demons that bring 'dis-ease' into our lives exist. Again whether these 'demons' merely represent aspects of our own shadow nature and inhabit the dark recesses of our being, or whether they are actual entities with a life of their own, is an irrelevant issue. We can communicate with them and affect our relationship with them as if they are real.

The question arises why anyone would want to make contact with astral entities, Archangels or any other 'being' of this type, particularly demons! To answer this question we have to return to our definition of healing as making something whole. If we are to be whole, to include rather than exclude all our energies, one way of achieving this is through making contact with all the forces within our universe. We are usually quite willing to include the 'good guys' – if I suggest that you talk to your Guardian Angel you would probably have little resistance (assuming you believed it possible). On the other hand, once we discuss communicating with demons we are entering the realm of the shadow, which includes those parts of ourselves that we would rather not face.

Any aspect of our being and our energy that we exclude from our awareness becomes part of our shadow, which has been usefully described as being like a big bag we drag round behind us. The more shadow we have, the more we are excluding, the heavier our bag becomes and the more it restricts our free movement. Conversely, the more material from this 'shadow bag' we can dredge out, face, deal with and integrate into our conscious being, the lighter the bag becomes and the more energy we have available to fulfil our life functions, from the loftiest sense of Divine Purpose through to the everyday functions that help us survive in the world.

If we do not face our anger over, say, a poor work situation, this suppressed anger and the associated anxiety will become part of our shadow. If we find ways of facing and expressing the anger, we will no longer be pulled down by the weight of it, and will free our energies, perhaps to make a life-enhancing decision about the work. On the other hand, if we do not express our anger, it will get pushed deeper and deeper down into the shadow bag until we are no longer even aware of its existence. As a result there will be tension and holding patterns in our body, which will cause pain and disease later in life. We might start smoking tobacco to alleviate the stress from denying the anger; we might over-eat in an attempt to suppress the attendant feelings.

We can then say that our behaviour opens us up to the influence of the corresponding demonic force. For instance, a demon whose presence brings 'cancerous misgrowth of cells' might be allowed a foothold in the physical body, and lead to severe illness and death. We do not have to believe in demons to understand the process of what is happening. Perhaps what we are dealing with is a personification of the suppressed material in an individual's subconscious. Whatever we believe, however, what we can do is to encourage this person to start communicating with their demons or 'suppressed energies', find what they need to express, and through various appropriate actions, dispel the demons through releasing the pent-up anger. Thus we can heal through 'communicating with the demons'.

GODS, GODDESSES AND OTHER DIVAS

Gods and goddesses are natural phenomena caused by activities of some sort that we may be able to recognise in ourselves (for example, the anger of the gods, the love of the gods, etc.) but operating on a higher plane, invisible to our usual perceptions. They are of the same nature as us, but they are not the same as us. In other words, there is a correspondence between gods and humans. It seems therefore, from a practical viewpoint, of little value to get caught up with trying to make specific correspondences. If I want to invoke, say, Horus, I will do best to realise 'he' corresponds to the whole Tree of Life and consider which aspects of 'his' being I want to contact. This is true for all such deities.

The name of a god of goddess is the magical formula that can set its energy in motion. Invocation is calling up this energy inside you; evocation is calling it up outside yourself. Gods and goddesses are then living entities, or should be considered as such, so they should be treated with the same respect you would give to your best friends. Then, like best friends, they will assist you in your magical work and be available in times of great need. The difference between how you interact with a god or goddess as opposed to a spirit is basically the same as the difference in your interaction with a best friend as opposed to a shopkeeper.

The divine forces columns in the correspondence tables in Appendix 4 are worth studying in some depth. Of course, all gods and goddesses relate, through their different aspects, to many or all of the spheres. For instance, the energy described by the 'god-name' Isis can be attributed to Binah as the mother goddess, to Tiphareth for her beauty and harmonising features, to Netzach as goddess of love and nature, to Yesod as the moon goddess, to Malkuth as a virgin, and so on.

Pay particular attention to the 'names' of the Hebrew deities associated with each sphere. The divine forces most appropriate to the paths are the individual Hebrew letters themselves. Each of these can be used, not so much as 'god-names' but as a *formula* (composed of particular Hebrew letters) that does correspond to the spheres. On a practical level these are useful formulae, therefore. It is important to stress, also, that to use these formulae does not suggest any allegiance to any particular set of religious beliefs.

To pronounce the divine names, intone the names in a low voice, vibrating, as deep as you can get, and stretch the words, particularly the vowels. Let the sound fill up your body (and imagine the sound stretches to the furthest reaches of the universe). Not to worry if you don't get them exactly right, the intent is what really matters.

eheieh	air – hair – ee – air (silent 'r')
ihvh	yo – hey – vow – hay
ihvh elohim	. . . el – oh – hu – eem
ue	oo – ai
el	el
elohim gebor	. . . geb – or
ihvh aloah	. . . al – oh – ah
ihvh tzaboath	. . . t – za – boh – at
elohim tzaboath	. . .
shaddai el chai	shad – ai – el – shy
adonai ha-aretz	ad – on – aye – ha – ah – retz

The Hebrew names for Archangels are also sometimes useful. For most practical work, however, you may find the suggestive titles for the archangels and archdemons shown in diagram 24 of more immediate value. Looking at the diagram now, reflect on the archangel and archdemon names given there, and how you understand them in the light of your existing Kabbalistic knowledge.

Remember also that the connection between the Archangels and the four quarters is very relevant because through using such correspondences you bring the energy of the Archangels right to earth. Different Kabbalists have different attributions for these forces, but generally the following correspondences are effective:

- in the east: Raphael, the angel of illumination, lighting up your life
- in the west: Gabriel, the angel of healing, eradicating all your ills

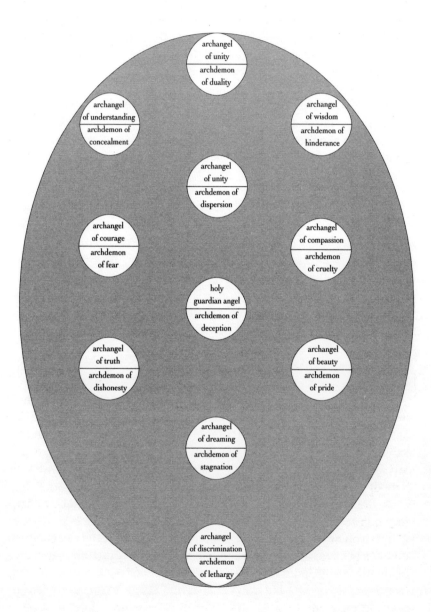

Diagram 24: Angels and demons

- in the south: Michael, the angel of grace, offering you love in all you do
- in the north: Auriel, the angel of strength, supporting your most difficult activities.

If each morning upon awakening, and/or each night before sleep, you call upon these Archangels to be present in your life, you can create a very powerful connection to their energies.

Finally, do not become caught in any gender trap where the Archangels are involved, because they exist in a realm that is beyond gender (as we know it anyway). Archangels are neither male or female; some people like therefore to exchange (at least sometimes) the male-sounding Archangel names for female ones: Raphaella, Gabriella, Michaella, Oriella.

THE HOLY GUARDIAN ANGEL

Knowledge of and conversation with your Holy Guardian Angel is a description used by some Kabbalists to describe the process of full and deep contact with the energy of Tiphareth. It is as if this energy is so refined, in comparison to the human realm, that we can only describe it with words that are inaccurate and describe the actual force itself as a Guardian Angel that may take many different forms (if it takes a form at all). This Angel may appear as a dove, a light, an angel, an inner guide, a radiant and wise old person, but however it appears it is a link between you and your innermost connection to the spiritual realms.

The next practice involves work to contact your Guardian Angel and to embody the energies that this 'being' represents. I have chosen the term Guardian Angel because it is fairly neutral and preferable to words like 'inner guide'. We know this 'energy' exists, and many people manage to make contact with their 'angel', but the mystery of what it 'actually' is has not been solved. I suggest you don't try to work it out in any way, but simply trust that there is a 'Guardian Angel' energy, whatever it actually means, and that it is yours to contact. You don't have to believe in any particular system or religion or sets of beliefs to do this – our 'angels' are not concerned with such matters. They are simply there to help and befriend us when needed. Call on your Angel when the time is right but don't expect him or her to appear unless it really is appropriate.

If you learn the name of your Angel, do *not* reveal it to anyone at all – it is your most precious secret, for with the name of your Angel you can summon this energy at any time. The name of your Angel is, in fact, for you the word of greatest power. This is because by knowing your Angel's name you can then summon this energy at will.

PRACTICE

• Contacting your Angel

In a previous practice, you visited a Temple of Inner Silence. This is the same temple where, for this exercise, you will meet your Guardian Angel. If you do not recall how to create such a visualisation, look it up now (page 121). Follow the same instructions as before until where you enter the temple. Once inside, take some time to really feel your body connecting strongly with your inner divinity, being infused with healing energy.

Then, when you feel ready, silently stand before the altar, and in whatever way feels appropriate to you, invoke the presence of your Guardian Angel and take time to really feel the presence of your Angel. Feel alert and alive as you silently contemplate your Angel's presence in your temple.

Specifically ask your Guardian Angel to be with you throughout your Kabbalistic work and in your life generally.

Engage your Angel in dialogue if it seems right for you, asking about any issues that currently concern you. Listen carefully to anything and everything your Angel tells you, whether it is in words, pictures, movements, or in any other way.

When it is time for you to leave, thank your Guardian Angel, confirm you will meet again, then in your own time, turn and leave the temple.

Once outside, open yourself to the impact of the day, feel a gentle breeze on your cheeks and listen to the singing of birds.

Fairly rapidly, with ease and a light spring in your step, return to where you started your journey.

In your own time, open your eyes now and bring your consciousness back to your room.

Very firmly and distinctly guide yourself back into everyday reality, perhaps writing about your experience in your journal. Remain conscious of the subtle presence of your Guardian Angel who is with you at all times.

HOW TO TELL ANGELS FROM DEMONS

Sometimes people worry when they do visualisations or pathworking such as the one just described that they will be in contact with a 'demon' instead of an 'angel'. The best way to check on this is through the quality of the communication – that the message, although it may be firm and challenging, will have the feeling of support (and is not judgemental or a put-down, a sure sign not so much of a demon but of an intrusive superego).

Angels can be described as messengers of the Deity, and some of them have the specific function of being 'guardian spirits'. Perhaps each of us has our own unique Guardian Angel, perhaps we have more than one, perhaps we may share one with other people – humans have contemplated these questions throughout the centuries with no firm or definite conclusions. As said earlier, it is the practice that is most important. You can choose to believe what you will, your Angel will be present for you at appropriate times.

Originally for Jewish people, angels (Hebrew = mal'akh) were seen as the shadow side of the Deity, and only later did they become messengers or intermediaries. Other religions have always seen the beneficial side of these 'divine spirits', however. Angels are generally said to possess subtle bodies, but there are many different versions of angels so perhaps they have many different forms of subtle body too. They take up a position between gods and humans, which is why they often act as messengers or intermediaries. They are not complete in the way humans are – they are parts of the Deity but not a 'complete image' of the Deity like us.

Demons are generally seen as 'inferior beings' or sometimes even as fallen angels. The distinction between angels and demons is not (nor has it ever been) truly clear-cut, however. Consider, for instance, the word 'genius', which actually means an attendant spirit. These attendant spirits are also known as 'genies' (who generally rarely behave like 'good angels'!). A person with extraordinary talents or powers is said to 'have a genius' for whatever they are good at – in other words they have a 'demon' (or is it 'angel'?) assisting them. Sometimes the term 'daimon' is used to distinguish such a force from more 'negative' and partial demons.

Perhaps it is all down to 'who has who'! If you 'have' an angel or demon working for you then you are in control of it; on the other hand, if it 'has you' you are under its power and not in touch with your free will. In that case it will little matter what you call it, angel or demon, the important thing will be to free yourself from your attachment or identification with it.

Demons might just be embodiments of our psychological complexes and physical problems. The way to deal with them is the same, whatever we believe them to be. And as we gain control over them, and they become 'our friends', then we find what we originally perceived as demonic may in fact have been angelic all along.

The bottom line is to remember that your sense of what is right or wrong for you is of primary importance. Only you can decide if a message or piece of advice is meaningful and true for you. You can use your Kabbalistic knowledge to check the validity of the contact, however:

- all messages from the Guardian Angel are ultimately positive rather than negative towards you. They are never judgemental (although they can be serious and severe), but reflect the attitude of a kind and loving parent figure (rather than a pompous or uncaring authority figure).
- use Netzach and Malkuth: does it feel right, and do you have a sense of a real contact with your Angel?
- use Hod and Malkuth: if you are genuinely discriminating about this contact, you will know in your body if it is real.

One of the most powerful 'extra-dimensional beings' in our human culture is what we call 'the devil', often depicted as the very personification of evil. The devil represents for us, individually and collectively, what we repress, positive and negative, and what we fear particularly. To connect with the devil is to let go to these feelings, thoughts, and sensations that hold us back from our fullest inheritance. It is no wonder, therefore, that the force of this energy has been literally demonised in such a way. Part of our work as Kabbalists is to redeem this energy in ourselves, an energy that paradoxically brings with it the deepest sense of ethics and value, being truly rooted in the earth.

The devil is only evil insofar as we have been conditioned to be fearful of the life force itself. That is not to say that evil does not exist, and we might consider, for instance, that when people intentionally set out to be cruel to or to harm others they are being evil. If so, then it is the intention of the person that is evil, not the life force itself. This is a way to distinguish between white and black magic – not by the acts of the practitioners (which might be identical) but the intent behind their acts.

Kabbalists believe that while the intoxicating, primal and raw energy of life can be dangerous, it is far less dangerous than fearfully holding ourselves back from living life to the full. Understood thus, the devil represents not evil but the raw energy of life, which cuts through convention and traditional morality to create a space for creativity to blossom. To build a relationship with the energies represented by the devil is to break down old structures, to laugh, play and celebrate the dance of life.

If you become frightened or freaked out by any such encounter, there are various ways to protect yourself. Particularly effective is to imaginatively surround yourself in a deep blue egg-shaped aura, and imagine the blue egg around you is covered with millions of tiny stars (like the night sky). On the surface you can see, these stars transmit positive energies towards you; on the outside of the egg there are mirrors rather than stars, and these reflect away from you and back to their source any negative energies directed towards you. You will feel completely safe in such a blue egg. If the fearsome figure does not then disappear, simply imagine an upright flaming white pentagram over its body and, if it is negative, this will dissolve its form and make it depart.

PRACTICE

• Ritual to embody the angel's energy

Perform the Kabbalistic Cross (or equivalent).

Stand in the centre of your circle with eyes closed.

Connect to the ground: imagine you have roots that connect you deeply into the earth.

Visualise the energy of the earth flowing up your legs, into your lower body, your genitals and lower abdomen, and as you do this, get a sense of openness and freedom pervading you.

Visualise energy rising up into your belly, your solar plexus and whole trunk, and as you do this feel your centredness in life, how you are rooted in earthly existence.

Visualise energy rising up into your heart, and see your heart glowing with energy. As you do this, feel yourself filled with courage and compassion.

Visualise energy flowing from your heart, down your arms and into your hands. Without opening your eyes, physically reach out with courage and compassion. Feel yourself reaching out to your Guardian Angel. Feel how courage and compassion in your heart gives you the power to link with your Angel.

Staying connected with your Angel, visualise energy rising up into your throat and mouth, and into your voice. Feel this connected energy giving you the power to speak out your truth.

Without opening your eyes, make a sound to express your connection with your Angel (don't force it, keep making the sound until you feel complete).

Visualise energy rising to your eyes. Open your eyes and see the truth of who you are and where you are.

Close your eyes again, and visualise the energy ascending to the top of your head. Feel the presence of your Guardian Angel.

Become the Tree of Life: your roots deep in the earth, your trunk filled with energy, your branches stretching up into the sky, connecting with the light of the sun and stars.

Draw down the energy of the sun and stars into your body and bring this energy right down to earth (keep this up for as long as you feel is right).

Bring energy right down into your roots, taking up a posture expressing who you are, your own truth when you are connected to your Guardian Angel.

Following the energy in your hands and legs, let them lead you forward into the rest of your life.

To complete your ritual, ground yourself back on your own power spot. Be aware of your inner stillness, your centre, your individual integrity.

GRACE

Grace is like a favour bestowed, something you have not exactly earned but merited through acts of tikkun or service. This merit depends upon the relationship between your own soul and deity or whatever mechanism it is that bestows grace, because something does, whatever we believe about its origins. Kabbalists have differing opinions about this (which probably depends upon their experience of the bestowal of grace), but generally agree that the experience of grace suggests the direct link between Kether and Tiphareth in harmonious balance with the link between Chesed and Geburah. The cross created by these two paths is an inverted Calvary cross, suggesting something of the willing sacrifice (and intent) necessary to create the conditions for the bestowal of grace.

Grace is a result of goodwill, not something that is a right, obligation or a concession. Many Kabbalists believe that grace is individually allotted, and is therefore another way of describing your appointed fate or destiny. Remember that the Kabbalistic view of fate, however, does not imply any preordained, destined outcome. Fate depends upon the act of your intent; in other words, we create our own fate at each and every moment. Grace is the result of a moment of balance.

Grace is also, of course, intricately bound up with tikkun. In this sense, it is the divine operating through people to regenerate and redeem them, and through them, the fragmented world. For Christian Kabbalists grace can be imparted through a priest passing on the sacraments or through the mediation of the Virgin Mary. This suggests the path between Tiphareth and Yesod, in dynamic balance with the path from Netzach to Hod, forming an upright cross, the Christian totem.

Some more esoteric Kabbalists believe that grace is a permanent force, having its origin in the soul. It is attained through the raising of the personality triangle and the lowering of the soul triangle; when they meet, the personality triangle flips over, as it were, and the two triangles then form a hexagram, its sixth (highest) angle being infused with light from the Supernal triangle.

KABBALISTIC SERPENT POWER

The Kabbalistic 'serpent power', also known in the East as kundalini, is always ready to uncoil and bring illumination to an individual who activates it. Kabbalists describe this serpent as coiled around the Tree of Life, which can only release its full potential when the serpent is activated on all the planes. When this serpent power or 'dragon energy' is activated, it brings an inner excitement, a joyous thrilling sensation throughout the body, taking the breath away. It can move mountains! It is sometimes referred to in such a way in descriptions of very exciting sexual encounters. This is a true mystical experience of connectedness with universal energy. It is not a substitute or 'dangerous short cut' but an experience, available to every man and every woman, that allows them to experience themselves as living centres of energy, as 'stars' no less. By following their true course through the heavens, stars are not bounded but are free to express themselves in their own, individual and unique way.

You can have this experience, but don't try to do anything with it beyond letting it infuse you with its strength, and cleanse you. It can really transform your life, but don't push it too hard; it must come as it comes. You can truly connect to the magical energy of love and fully understand why all the best magicians have maintained that love is the central, overriding energy in the universe.

It is true for all aspects of energy, but particularly relevant to sexual experiences, that you can only release the quantity of energy that you have built up in the first place. If you are not sufficiently excited (that is, if you have not built up enough energy), however hard you try you will not reach a climax. Conversely, once you pass a certain level of excitement there is, so to speak, 'no going back' and climax becomes inevitable. It is when we 'let go' in this way that we release our energy in a full and satisfying orgasm. When the charge is high enough to get you to the peak experience, you enter spiritual or 'transpersonal' realms where energy is available for your Kabbalistic work.

It is important to remember that just because there are left and right hand pillars on the Tree, it does not mean the system is in any way based on a patriarchal or dualistic view of life. Some Kabbalistic writers have insisted on referring to the two pillars as male and female, a dichotomy that is not part of the original map, and only leads to confusion. Of course duality exists, but maleness and femaleness exist on both sides of the Tree.

PRACTICE

• Male and female polarities

Study diagram 25 to see a different way of understanding male and female polarities corresponding to the Tree of Life.

Reflect on the meaning of these attributions in the light of your growing Kabbalistic understanding.

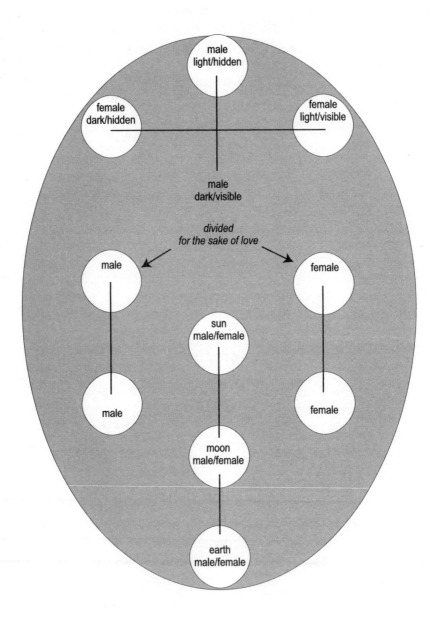

Diagram 25: Male and female energies

SHEKHINAH, GRACE AND UNITY

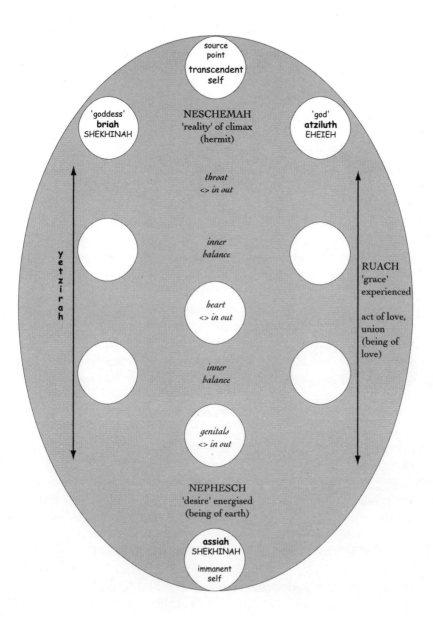

D iagram 26: Reality, grace, desire

The Deity in the Kabbalistic tradition is both male and female (see diagram 26). The female aspect of the Deity is sometimes called Shekhinah, and her mysteries are central to an understanding of Kabbalah and Kabbalistic healing. Shekhinah is essentially sexual in her manifestation. She is said to enter the bed of a couple who are having loving sexual intercourse and bring them the greater depths of ecstasy that such a union can produce. For Kabbalists the sexual act is a divine sacrament, and it is said that if sexual union is not achieved on this deep level, it obviates even the highest spiritual attainments. It is believed that a loving sexual act can bring both partners closer to the Deity than any other ritual. Indeed, by coming together with this understanding, a couple may emulate the original creative act of the Mother–Father Deity, thus again emphasising the identity between the macrocosmic and microcosmic worlds.

The union of the mother and father aspects of the Deity takes place in Atziluth and Briah, the first two Kabbalistic worlds. The third and fourth worlds of Yetzirah and Assiah are then seen as the fruits of their union. The father-god involved here is Eheieh, the primary force of Kether, while the mother-goddess is Shekhinah, the essence of Binah who is also, in her manifest form, seen as the indwelling spiritual presence of the created world in Malkuth.

At the moment of orgasm, Shekhinah, sometimes known as the Holy Spirit, comes into the participants. The female partner may identify with this Spirit while the male partner may take her within himself. They are both then able to use the presence of Shekhinah to clarify their energies and make them fit vessels for further spiritual and material work. This is an essential aspect of our healing, for by coming together sexually we may bring a new wholeness to our lives. (This is not to say someone living alone, or with a homosexual orientation, cannot make a similar connection, for each of us has both male and female sides within us.)

The third world of Yetzirah is particularly affected by such work. Inner balance is achieved both on the level of Hod and Netzach (thoughts and feelings) and Geburah and Chesed (Will and Love). Outer balance is increased through the heightening of our energies in Yesod (the sexual centre in the human body), and also the throat (represented on the Tree by the unnumbered sphere called Daath). The connection – both energetically and sexually – between the throat and the genitals is well-known, and can lead to the clearer expression of spirituality on the mundane plane of Malkuth.

We only speak of levels of energy for convenience and so that our usual linear language can at least approximately describe the actual multi-dimensional experience. Workers in the field of healing know from their experience that if they affect one level of energy, this effect will carry through to other levels. In practice, therefore, if we can change our relationship to energies in the third world of Yetzirah, this healing will be transmitted through to the other worlds. This is the reason why visualisation, for instance, can be so powerful a healing tool. It works directly on the astral level, but any changes that occur there are mirrored on the etheric level, then directly affect the physical world.

Similarly, if we work directly on the physical plane we can effect change on the subtler planes of energy. The different levels of energy are really more clearly understood as a continuum that connects the densest physical world with the subtlest spiritual realms. If we dance until we drop in our Kabbalistic movement work, we are affecting our subtle energies through direct physical action. If we meditate and pray we may directly affect our physical world through indirect, inner processes. However we effect a healing, however, it is most important that we are aware of this continuum of energy, which not only connects all our different levels of energy but also connects us to everyone and everything else. This knowledge gives us an awesome connection to the deepest sources of energy and also brings the attendant responsibilities. If we use our inner understanding wisely, we realise all our actions affect the whole, and may effect a whole healing as discussed above, not only on a personal but also on interpersonal and collective levels.

The Zohar says: 'And they flowed in a straight path through all the spheres, until they came to that one place which collects them all into a union of male and female, and that one place is called the foundation, for it is the life and breath of all worlds.'

'They' are the potent male and female energies, Eheieh (the masculine, transcendent element of God) and his holy bride, the Shekhinah (the feminine, immanent element of God). They correspond to the famous Shiva and Shakti in Indian traditions.

Shakti is the Goddess, the eternal female partner. Some systems say that men often fail to recognise their human partner as the Goddess, and then use her to gratify their senses. As a man you can learn instead to worship her, or the Goddess in her, and turn your senses from gratification of selfish desires to an expression of devotion. Kabbalists are not quite as formal or severe, for in their estimation, 'every true marriage is a symbolical realisation of the union of God and the

Shekhinah'. Knowledge, in its deepest sense, always means the actual-isation of a union, be it that of wisdom and understanding, or that of Eheieh and Shekhinah. Thus a sublime erotic quality of knowledge is restored.

The Zohar states: 'Each soul and spirit prior to its entering into this world, consists of a male and female united into one being. When it descends on this earth the two parts separate and animate two different bodies. At the time of marriage, the Holy One, blessed be He, who knows all souls and spirits, unites them again as they were before, and they again constitute one body and one soul, forming as it were the right and left of one individual. And when They are conjoined together, They appear to be only one body.'

Kabbalah teaches that men and women are created equal but have been divided from one another, and within themselves. Sex is considered a holy sacrament that can bring the divided back together. The Kabbalistic practice of tikkun stresses that the vessels God used during creation were broken and our work in life is to repair these vessels. Sex undertaken in a loving context is a powerful method for such repair.

Particularly important is sexual contact between a couple in a loving relationship, traditionally on Friday nights when, during sex, the feminine aspect of God manifests and helps bring extra energy to the love-making. To make a baby, the Kabbalah teaches that the couple should focus their attention on God during their love-making and open themselves to being a channel for the manifestation of a new soul. Any and all other procedures – which might include candle-lighting, prayer, ritual chanting, bathing for purification, and so on – are considered useful extras but the real focus is on two people coming together to create a new being, thus mirroring God's original creation.

Kabbalistic magic adds an extra dimension by pointing out that the 'offspring' of a sexual union are not necessarily physical children. A couple holding the intention of making a baby will hopefully succeed in their wish, but what if another intention is held by the couple instead? The basis of sexual magic states that any intention held at the moment of union is empowered by the sexual energy and may be brought to fruition.

Kabbalah stresses that parental responsibility to the new soul does not end with the procreative act, but should include the upbringing and guidance of the child to adulthood, helping the child to feel at one with himself or herself and not fragmented within. Thus the work of 'repairing the vessels' is not just accomplished through sex but through a life of dedication to the power of love and unity.

VENUS APHRODITE

In the last chapter you learned of the importance of the fourteenth path in healing. The fourteenth path is like a strengthening bar across the top of the two outer pillars, connecting transpersonal Will and transpersonal Love, our deepest sense of Purpose with our spiritual Awareness. The celestial attribution for this path is Venus, with its symbol the familiar 'female' sign of a circle above a cross. The shape is similar to the Egyptian ankh, which corresponds to love, life and sexuality, all aspects of the goddess Venus (the Roman version of Aphrodite). The Romans considered Venus as one of the most sacred of

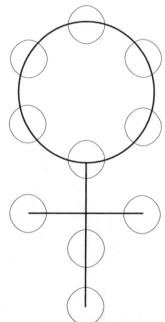

Diagram 27: The Venus tree

all deities and the word veneration used to mean specifically worship of Venus. Also venia, the Latin word for grace, means to be in the goddess's favour. The symbol also stands for copper in alchemy, and copper is associated with Venus. There is also a connection between shrines to Venus being placed on high mountains (similar to the path being at the top of the Tree).

As well as standing for Venus and woman generally, the symbol also represents the whole Tree of Life (see diagram 27). This creates an interesting correspondence: the whole Tree can be seen as a manifestation of the connection represented by this path. The circle and cross are said to represent respectively complete awareness and balanced manifestation. The symbol, then, is perfect for the Tree of Life.

When we consider the eleventh sphere we find, using this symbolic representation of the Tree, that its central position is emphasised. It is also interesting to note the close proximity of Daath to the fourteenth path.

The process of fragmentation described above is the origin of the separation of the male/animus aspect of psyche from the female/anima aspect. This is understood in Kabbalah as the process whereby the Shekhinah is separated from its source (the difference between Shekhinah in Binah and in Malkuth). Again the concept of exile is useful; it is as if the Shekhinah is, in this sense, our innate and innermost sense of our divinity, wanting to reunite with its source. The Creator is apparently absent, however, and the desire for contact with this absent one underpins much human behaviour, from the loftiest attempts at mystical experience, through myths and images of the quest involved in the human life journey, to the most mundane sexual encounters.

Kleinian and other psychological theories concerning the loss of a loved one, or the loss of the infant's sense of unity with its mother, are descriptions of this essential human separation, leading to much of the controlling repressive material (such as anxieties about death, guilt, depressive and self-denying stances) deposited at Yesod. The Kabbalist longs for the reunification of the exiled Shekhinah with its creative source; indeed, the human condition is underpinned by the desire for this reunification. To co-operate with tikkun is to mend (or repair) what has become broken; as individuals we try to make amends for our perceived wrongdoings that have led to us being separated or exiled from our source. A major part of the healing or reparative process is to accept our condition as is, without guilt, and understand sin not as wrongdoing but as error. Again, to reach perfection means to accept the psychic and physical reality of what is.

PRACTICE

• Reunification of the four worlds

One of the ways that tikkun can take place is through the reunification of the IH (father–mother) aspect of tetragrammaton with the VH (son–daughter) aspect. Lay out the sixteen court cards of the Thoth Tarot pack (or whichever equivalent pack you use) thus:

I	H	V	H
knight wands	queen wands	prince wands	princess wands
knight cups	queen cups	prince cups	princess cups
knight swords	queen swords	prince swords	princess swords
knight discs	queen discs	prince discs	princess discs

Meditate upon what you have learned about the process of tikkun so far. How can the sixteen Tarot cards be seen to represent this process?

How can you understand this in terms of your own life experience, both as a developing baby and infant and as an adult now?

It is said that the greatest reparation is found through sexuality. Genital energy is then seen as not only procreative but also reparative. How have you acted this out in the past? How can you act upon this in the future?

Meditate upon the well-known phrase: 'as above, so below', and the Kabbalistic concept: 'Kether is in Malkuth, and Malkuth is in Kether, but after another manner.' How do you understand these phrases now?

Practise tikkun!

Devise some practical work you can undertake to further your understanding and practice of tikkun.

9

THROUGH THE ASTRAL TO THE HEART

God is manifest in gathering: harmony: consideration: the Mirror of the Sun and of the Heart.

Aleister Crowley (*The Book of Lies*)

The fifth plane of the Tree of Life, that of the spheres Netzach and Hod, while attributed to the 'higher' astral realms, is also of particular significance psychologically as Netzach and Hod relate to feeling and thinking respectively. From an esoteric viewpoint, however, when we connect to the fifth plane we are moving into the deeper layers of the Astral, those where more 'fixed' astral forms are located. The Astral energy in Yesod is fluid – the stuff of which dreams, fantasies, images are made and which is constantly changing. If those images (whatever their source) are repeatedly called upon, eventually they become 'semi-permanent' – they act as if they are real. It must be emphasised, however, they are as illusionary as more fleeting images and, because of their apparent greater solidity, more easy to get hooked into. These 'higher Astral' images include those created by religions, by mass movements on social and political levels, and by groups working over an extended period. We only have to consider the power of the Christian Cross or the Swastika to understand how powerful such images might become, a power that can be used for good or ill. We can more easily become over-attached to these images, and fall prey to their glamour.

We can understand glamour most effectively from a psychological perspective. Glamour is the state we enter when we become over-attached to either our thinking or our feeling function. We all know people who are 'in their heads' and unable to express their feelings; or people who are 'all over the place' emotionally and who seem to have poor thinking abilities. It is important to stress in both these cases, and all possible manifestations of these attachments, that while it is essential we should free ourselves from attachments of this kind, we have the attachments in order to learn something. If you happen to be 'mentally identified' it is important you clear this attachment, but *not* at the expense of your thinking abilities! Usually the work would more correctly involve bringing up or elevating your connection to your feeling function until it is as well developed as the thinking function. That way you grow through inclusion rather than exclusion, through heightening consciousness rather than lessening it. Obviously the same would be true in reverse for someone who is 'emotionally identified' – they should not lessen their feelings, but increase their mental abilities.

However 'high' we become, however 'deep' our initiations, without the ground beneath us and without our bodies, thoughts and feelings through which to express ourselves, our work amounts to very little. The myth of Hercules and Antaeus illustrates the physical aspect of this very well. Hercules was fighting Antaeus and yet, although he was much stronger, each time he threw Antaeus to the ground, Antaeus rose up stronger. Eventually Hercules understood what was happening – Antaeus was a true child of the earth, so each time he was thrown to the ground, he was nourished by the earth (his mother), and rose up strengthened. Hercules eventually won the fight by holding Antaeus up in the air until he lost all connection with his ground and died.

The moral for us in this myth is to allow ourselves to be nourished by the earth and not to hold ourselves in the air, in ungrounded postures, values or belief structures. All our Kabbalistic work needs to start from and return to ground, for there we are nourished by our connections.

Working up the Tree of Life, the fifth plane is the first one where there are two spheres. Every plane with two spheres is focusing primarily on a polarity between two apparently opposing but actually complementary energies. Our work on such planes is in balancing and synthesising all the opposites within and around us. The principal polarity within us (and our world) is the archetypal polarity between Love (Chesed) and Will (Geburah). These archetypes manifest through polarities such as male and female, anger and forgiveness, lust and aversion, power and weakness or vulnerability, spirituality and sensuality, idealism and practicality, toughness and sensitivity, discipline and spontaneity, freedom and order, and so on. It cannot be over-stressed that both poles of any polarity are equally essential.

Many of these polarities manifest in our personalities and daily lives through the interaction between Netzach and Hod. Each of us, then, through our personal connections to these spheres, creates our own mythology of opposites. There can then be situations where only one of the pair of opposites is obviously manifest, the other being under-developed or repressed. For example, you might be very obviously a thinking person but not at all emotional (as far as can be obviously seen). Alternatively, there can be a direct 'here and now' conflict between any two opposites, for example, between a feeling you have to go for a walk and your thought that it is too cold outside.

It is possible to hold both opposites through an inclusive act. Yes, I will go out and I will wrap up warm. Yes, I will use an aerosol and I will ensure it is an environmentally safe one. An act of will, the taking of a direct choice, is always the key; choice not as 'either this or that' but moving to a place outside of the original opposites that can include both, then moving back into the situation with clearer awareness. This way you learn to develop the connection between Hod and Netzach, and start building a centre from where you can truly contact Tiphareth.

To solve a problem at its own level is impossible; you always need to move to a separate, 'witness' space from where, with a clear perspective, you are able to make the correct choice. Consider the following activity before continuing.

PRACTICE

• Towards the clearest space

Focus your attention on the lower spheres of the Tree of Life and how they manifest in your life.

Identify two opposing parts in yourself, or parts in a current conflict situation, and listen to each concerning what they want and need at this time.

Move to the clearest inner space you have available to you, look back upon these two parts and their wants, consider what each needs, then ask yourself: 'What would it be like if these two parts came together?'

Act appropriately upon this.

The same process can be used to deal with conflicting 'parts' on a global level as well as on this individual level. Try this activity again, but this time choose a current world conflict. See if you can really identify with the opposing forces and hear the voice of each. See the point of view of each side. Then move to a new, third position outside of the conflict and ask the question: what would it be like if these two parts come together? You might not be able to get a complete picture or a total answer, but what you do understand in this way can help resolve the conflict, and you will now be able to send out a positive energy pattern that adds to the healing of the conflict.

Working with the Subtle

Once we start working with subtler energies than the merely physical, it is important we protect ourselves from unwanted 'astral' intrusions. You may have previously learned how to psychically protect yourself using the visualisation of a blue egg around your body. You now have to strengthen and deepen this procedure, which involves imagining your body as a brightly shining Tree of Life. If you find this difficult, just allow yourself to 'get a sense' of it being there. Then imagine you are completely surrounded on all sides by an egg of dark blue light, which is covered with millions of brightly twinkling stars, rather like a very clear night sky. These stars transmit positive energy into your aura, allowing the passage from outside of beneficial energies. Finally, imagine that what you see as stars, from the outside looks like millions of tiny mirrors. These tiny mirrors reflect back to their source any negative or harmful energies that come in your direction.

Practise this technique as often as you can, including when walking down the street, in bed, and so on. If you do this, the protection will build up, and after a while you will only need to repeat the exercise occasionally, if you feel or imagine any harmful energies are coming your way, or before doing an important piece of work. Certainly practise it at least once before attempting the activities in the following section.

PRACTICE

• Astral exercising

These exercises involving astral energies need to be practised with clear consciousness. Before doing them, it is best not to intake any drugs (including tea and coffee!) or food for at least a couple of hours. If you experience any difficulty, make a note of it and pass on to the next procedure.

1. Simply stand up and move your left arm to the left. As you do so imagine your 'astral double' moves its left arm to the right. Repeat a few times.

Now move your right arm to reach upwards. As you do so imagine your 'astral double' moves its right arm straight out to the side. Repeat a few times.

Devise other techniques with a similar intention: moving a part (or all) of your body in one direction and imagining your astral double moves the same part of your body elsewhere. You may find your astral body can move in directions and over distances that you cannot achieve with your physical form!

When you have finished, stand with your feet about a foot apart, knees slightly bent, take a deep breath, then as you slowly and easily breathe out, put your right forefinger onto your lips (as if making a 'shhh'/'be silent' gesture) and stamp your left foot. After completing all 'astral separation' exercises, always close in this way. It ensures your astral double is back in place, realigned with your physical form.

2. Let any memory from your past arise in your consciousness. Note any associated images, sounds and feelings. Really re-experience whatever it is you are remembering right now, as if it is happening again.

Pay particular attention to how you feel in your body when this memory is experienced. Connect with this as strongly as you can.

Exaggerate any body postures, sensations, movements, gestures associated with this experience . . . then exaggerate them even more.

Now allow an image to emerge in your mind that represents this experience. Don't judge or censor the image, just let it emerge. Pay attention to this image, study it in detail. Don't just focus on the central components or theme of the image, look around the edges too.

Consciously choose to change the image in any way that seems appropriate. Let your imagination have free rein with this, and consciously choose to change the image until it is as you choose it to be – maybe less threatening, more healing, more pleasant, totally different – whatever is appropriate for your image.

Say to yourself, 'I am in control of this image, it is not in control of me.'

Imagine the changed image in front of you, as brightly lit as possible, then draw its energy into your body. Really feel this new, positive energy filling you with its life-enhancing qualities.

This exercise is an effective healing technique.

3. Simply smell whatever is in your current environment. If you cannot smell anything specific, then imagine what things around you would smell like if you could smell them.

Imagine your sense of smell expands outwards, so that you can smell the scents of the location in which you live, then the city, then the country.

Smell something on the other side of the planet.

Smell the scents somewhere in the far reaches of outer space.
Finally, smell your own heart.

THE SPIRIT AND THE SPARK

In an earlier chapter we described Kether, at the top of the Tree of Life, as being the Universal Spirit that is common to everyone and everything. Tiphareth is then seen as the spark of that Spirit that can be found at the heart or centre of each individual. For each of us it is our individualised bit of Spirit and, as such, can be related to the individual soul. In other words, Tiphareth is the personal self, the self-aware 'I', which is a reflection of the Spiritual Self into human consciousness. Another way of describing this is to say that the Universal Spirit projects a small portion of self-consciousness, Tiphareth, which may grow in self-awareness, intelligence, the power to act, and so on. This growth will proceed most effectively under the combined nourishment of energies coming directly from the Spirit and those from the fertile soil of an earthly existence.

The paths that converge on Tiphareth from higher up the Tree of Life bring energies or 'qualities' such as love, joy, truth, beauty, courage, freedom and wonder, to each individual being. While the overall quantity of these energies is the same for all of us, we each have a different combination of these qualities with which to work in our life. These qualities, similar to archetypes, flow through Tiphareth into the personality and then become diffused into everyday experience.

It is obviously in our interests to connect more clearly and thoroughly with these qualities so they can have more expression in our lives. One way of strengthening their flow is through contact with Tiphareth. Thus it is vitally important that we learn to dis-identify from our personalities and build a strong centre. Of equal importance, however, is the need to work actively on clarifying our personalities. We can then become better 'receptacles' or 'containers' for these spiritual qualities and become more able to express them for our own good and the good of our planet. We then connect back to Malkuth, the earth, without which our work remains ungrounded and, from the point of view of active service for the planet, worthless.

HEART ENERGY

If you look once more at diagram 11, the Tree of Life overlaid on a human body (p. 63), you see that Tiphareth corresponds to the position of the heart in the centre of the chest. Physically our hearts may be slightly off-centre, but energetically speaking our hearts are right in the middle. Both Eastern and Western systems agree on this, and the 'anahata' or heart centre of the Eastern chakra system corresponds directly to Tiphareth.

To understand the working of this heart energy within our human bodies, we need to understand that Tiphareth has a dual aspect 'hidden behind it'. This dual aspect is represented on the Tree of Life by Geburah and Chesed, which relate to the Archetypes of Will and Love respectively. The heart centre is, therefore, in reality a trinity. For this reason, for the heart centre to be truly open in an individual, there has to be a balance of Love and Will. Other energy centres may open partially or in a distorted way. The heart centre, however, is more of an 'on–off' affair: it is open if there is balanced energy between Chesed and Geburah, closed if there is not.

If the heart is totally closed and never opens it stops the free passage of energy through Tiphareth and will eventually lead to heart-death through becoming clogged up or blocked. If the heart remains open all the time, never able to close even when appropriate, it will eventually lead to heart-death from too much energy being channelled there, usually experienced as a heart attack. A connected and effective heart centre chooses to open or close as appropriate to the situation at hand, being able to heal itself and others, but also able to protect its body from unwanted intrusions.

The heart is associated with 'higher' feelings such as altruistic love and compassion. Given the current state of our planet, and given the dangers from having an imbalance at this level of energy, it is vital we learn to respect our hearts and live our lives from this clearer space. When we connect with our heart energy, we express ourselves with greater understanding and harmony and are able to 'speak from the heart'. We become more able to manifest our creative potential for wholeness, using this energy to heal ourselves, other people and our relationship with our environment. We bring love back into our vision of the planet and our purpose for being here. We learn that when we truly accept who we are, we can experience and express our inner wisdom. When we 're-member' our hearts in this way, and connect with Tiphareth, our own fulfilment fosters the well-being of our planet.

When we connect with our heart energy, when we are working on our personal and spiritual development, we are adding to the total pool of consciousness around our planet. If we are aware of this process, we can see that, in essence, by doing this work we are manifesting love. Love is the energy that divides us but only so that we can have the opportunity of coming together again to experience the joy of union. We are born out of an undifferentiated unity – we are one with everything but, because we are one, we cannot experience it. As we grow and develop in life we become more and more differentiated; we become more unique and individual, more ourselves.

From this differentiated position we are able to experience love, for we are able to join with other people and other beings. Of course this includes sexual union, but it also includes all the other ways in which we can join harmoniously with others, whether for brief, passing moments or for lifetimes. Alive on our planet Earth, we are all developing on the same Tree of Life. Every conscious act of love increases the chances of us reaching our common goal, the manifestation of peace and joy.

We are divided for the sake of love and when we realise this we can honour both our separateness and our moments of togetherness. This is true self-love, when we accept ourselves for who and what we are without complaint or criticism. This is, in fact, the only place from where we can truly grow and realise our own unique purpose for incarnation. Paradoxically, accepting the truth of who and what we are does not stop us from growing but instead accelerates our development until we can echo the words that the great Kabbalist Jesus is reported as saying in the Gospel of John: 'I and the Mother–Father Deity are as One.'

PRACTICE

• The strong heart

The following exercise is a 'development' of the Kabbalistic Cross; it is not intended to replace it, but rather to adapt it to deepen your connection with heart. The exercise strengthens your heart energy and your connection to your heart centre. To strengthen your heart in this way is an essential task for a Kabbalist intending to make a firm and potent connection to Tiphareth.

Relax and centre yourself in the ways that work best for you. Imagine that a line of white light comes from your heart and stretches out before you into the far distant reaches of space. Spend some time visualising this light as strongly and as clearly as you can.

Touch the centre of your chest with your right hand. Imagine that the white line of energy you projected into space returns and is concentrated in your heart. Focus your whole being in the centre of your chest.

Remove your hand from your chest and relax.

Next imagine that a line of white light comes from your heart and stretches out behind you into the far reaches of space. Visualise this light as strongly and as clearly as you can.

Touch the centre of your chest with your right hand. Imagine that the white line of energy now returns and is concentrated in your heart. Focus your whole being in the centre of your chest.

Remove your hand from your chest and relax.

Imagine that a line of white light comes from your heart and stretches out above you into the far reaches of space. Visualise this light as strongly as you can.

Touch the centre of your chest with your right hand. Imagine that the white line of energy now returns and is concentrated in your heart. Focus your whole being in the centre of your chest.

Remove your hand from your chest and relax.

Again imagine that a line of white light comes from your heart, this time stretching off to your right and off into the far reaches of space. Spend some time visualising this light as strongly and as clearly as you can.

Touch the centre of your chest as before, imagine that the white line of energy returns and is concentrated in your heart. Focus your whole being in the centre of your chest.

Repeat again, this time imagining the line of white light stretching off to your left.

Touch the centre of your chest as before, imagine that the white line of energy returns and is concentrated in your heart. Focus your whole being in the centre of your chest.

Remove your hand from your chest and relax.

Now imagine that a line of white light comes form your heart, travels down through your body, and right into the very centre of the planet. Visualise this light as strongly and as clearly as you can.

Touch the centre of your chest as before, imagine that the energy returns and is concentrated in your heart. Focus your whole being in the centre of your chest.

Repeat the above procedure with your left hand, again imagining the light going off in the six directions — in front, behind, above, to the right, left, then below you — each time concentrating it back into your heart.

Finally, place both your hands flat on your chest and simply be aware of the strength of your heart. Realise how you are able to both radiate energy out from your heart centre, and focus right in on your heart.

A PATH WITH HEART

Diagram 28: The nineteenth path

The nineteenth path plays such a central role in the work of a Kabbalist that it is worth special attention. It connects two of the three spheres that are attributed to heart, Chesed and Geburah, two spheres that are located on the same plane of the Tree (diagram 28). When there are two spheres on the same plane, it suggests that the path connecting them must be concerned with the balancing of energies.

The best activity for developing the heart centre is to develop feelings of the heart, such as compassion, forgiveness and tenderness. Reflect now on how you experience such feelings in your life. For instance, who do you need to open your heart to and forgive? To forgive someone who has hurt you in some way can be a supreme act of heart. To forgive them does not mean you have to forget the injustice, abuse or whatever it is that has hurt you, however. It is important you remember so that you can take back your energy from the event. It may seem paradoxical at first, but to remember is a vital component for forgiveness because it opens the channel between Love and Will.

In the physical realm (or the fourth world), the nineteenth path corresponds to the chest, or thorax, which is the upper part of the human body and is situated between the neck and the abdomen. It is formed by twelve vertebrae, twelve pairs of ribs, the sternum (breast-bone) and associated muscles and fascia, and is separated from the abdomen by the diaphragm. Present within the thoracic cavity are the chief organs of the respiratory system and certain components of the circulatory and digestive systems. The lungs occupy lateral regions of the thoracic cavity, and are more properly ascribed to other paths (if you do not know which ones you might like to look them up in the correspondence tables). The heart and oesophagus are enclosed in a compartment known as the mediastinum, which also corresponds to the nineteenth path, and are attributed to the lymphatic system and spleen. The functions of the thorax include protection of the enclosed organs, support for the bones of the shoulder girdle and upper extremities, and expansion and contraction of the thoracic cavity during respiration.

The lymphatic system, composed of widely spread and structurally distinct tissues, is involved with immune defences. Its organs filter foreign substances and cell debris from blood, and store lymphocytes, the most common type of white blood cell. It is a one-way transport system closely associated with the circulatory system. In the circulatory system, when blood passes through a capillary network, about one percent of the liquid leaving the capillaries is not reabsorbed by the capillaries and remains as excess tissue fluid in the spaces between the capillaries and the cells of the particular tissue. This fluid must be returned to the circulatory system in order to maintain the proper volume of blood in the body, thus the importance of lymphatic drainage, a technique used by many modern massage therapists.

The lymphatic system consists of lymphatic capillaries that absorb the excess tissue fluid. There are two major lymphatic ducts. The larger of the two is the thoracic duct, which serves the legs, the trunk of the body, the left arm, and the left side of the neck and head. The right lymphatic duct is smaller in diameter and serves only the right arm and the right side of the neck and head. Contractions of the skeletal muscles of the body exert pressure on adjacently located lymph vessels and move the lymph fluid along. The lymph vessels also have valves that ensure the unidirectional flow of the lymph.

PRACTICE

• The nineteenth path in the body

After preparation, turn your attention into your body and let emerge a sense of the lymphatic system as it exists throughout your whole physical form. How does your lymphatic system feel – energised or sluggish, active or passive?

Now spend at least fifteen minutes in energetic activity, such as high-energy dancing, or walking or whatever it is for you that raises your physical energy.

Visualise and connect with your lymphatic system again: has anything changed?

The lymphatic system defends the body against diseases through accessory lymphoid organs such as lymph nodes, the spleen, thymus, tonsils and adenoids. Lymph nodes are small masses of cells located at intervals along lymph vessels. While flowing through the lymph vessels, lymph trickles through one or more lymph nodes, which ingest any bacteria, red blood cells, toxins and cellular debris that are present in the lymph, filtering it of impurities. The lymphatic system can be affected by several disorders, for instance, lymphatic vessels can become blocked as a result of injury, inflammation, surgery or parasitic infection. The spleen is the largest organ of the lymphatic system and is associated with the circulatory system, involved in the formation of antibodies and the removal of cell waste products and worn-out red blood cells.

Most vertebrates have a spleen, but it is not essential to life from a medical viewpoint, thus stressing, for us, its importance on an energetic level. The spleen has a special function regarding the connection between the third and fourth worlds, being the organ where energy transfer happens between the astral and etheric bodies. Although in humans the spleen is located in the abdominal cavity below the diaphragm, behind and to the left of the stomach, its functioning is closely associated with the energies of this path. With regard to the nineteenth path, connecting as it does the spheres of Love and Will on the Tree of Life, it is clear how this path has its attribution to the lymph, as the balancing of Love and Will has a direct effect on astral and etheric well-being.

FOUR WORLDS OF HEART

Now we can consider how the nineteenth path manifests in the four worlds. For the first and second worlds of Atziluth and Briah, we remain in the transpersonal realms of the Supernal Triad, so the energies at work are more subtle and potential rather than active. This path is a lower reflection of the fourteenth path (which connects Chockmah and Binah) representing the binding force of the universe, the bridge between Spiritual Will and Spiritual Love. The nineteenth path is a lower reflection of this force, the bridge between personal will and love.

The primary attribute, the Hebrew letter, in this case is the letter Teth

(ט), which means a serpent. If you draw a purple-coloured letter Teth, you can use it to stimulate your imagination when you meditate upon it in a dimly lit room. You can use the purple Teth on a door to enter other worlds, and of course, as with any of the sacred letters, you can try making and holding the shape of the letter Teth with your body, noticing what feelings, thoughts, sensations or any other responses you have when holding this shape. You learned how to undertake these practices in an earlier chapter.

As well as meaning serpent or snake, Teth in Hebrew also means a worm or a dragon, and is related to words associated with slithering and crawling. It is associated also with the concept of resistance and protection. The Zohar says this letter invokes the beginning of goodness and the ending of errors (an important step in the process of tikkun). The Sepher Yetzirah calls Teth the secret of all activities of spiritual beings. In 777, Aleister Crowley writes for this letter and path: 'Teth is a serpent, as is very obvious from the shape of the letter . . . It being the house of the Sun, the idea is to emphasise the identity of the Star and the Snake.'

Once we are investigating paths that connect spheres that are themselves in the third world of Yetzirah (as Chesed and Geburah are), we also have to pay particular attention to the shadow side of the path. The legendary being attributed to this path is a gorgon, which is described in early Greek mythology as a monster of the underworld. In later tradition the Gorgons were three sisters named Stheno, Euryale and Medusa. Originally all very beautiful women, they were transformed into ugly monsters, with writhing snakes for hair, claws of bronze, staring eyes, and ugliness capable of turning anyone who looked at them into stone. The hero Perseus killed Medusa by cutting off her head while looking at her indirectly in the mirror of his shield. The winged horse Pegasus sprang from the blood that spurted from her neck. Perseus used Medusa's head to petrify Atlas but he later gave the head to Athena, who put it in the centre of her shield.

It is vital to balance any shadow work through connecting also to the brighter creatures associated with the path, and in this case the associated extra-dimensional beings are Archangels. Contact with these entities is closely linked to your contact with your true identity, your soul.

PRACTICE

• The experience of blessings

The vision associated with the nineteenth path is the experience of blessings.

After preparation, draw or paint a representation of what the experience of blessings means to you.

Alternatively, write about all the blessings you have received in your life.

Allow yourself to experience your blessings.

We experience Tiphareth through our embodiment of its energies. The following activity will help you to experience Tiphareth in your body and in your life. Read through the directions and procedures carefully and ensure you clearly understand what is required before actually doing it.

PRACTICE

• Experiencing Tiphareth

Have your lamen with you (or if you haven't constructed one, have an object – it could be anything, even a book! – that represents your intention to find out more of yourself and manifest this energy in life).

Create a clear circle in which to work. Your circle will enable you to define the boundaries for your work. It will also, in the case of this ritual, act as a container for your invocation of energies from the 'higher' spheres on the Tree of Life.

Find the centre of your circle, then stand quietly while sensing the outer boundaries of the circle.

Make your intention clear: to embody the energies of the Tree of Life.

Do something that for you represents your connection and communion with the earth. (You may, for instance, want to stamp your feet, prostrate yourself three times, touch the ground in all directions, etc.).

Do some vigorous activity (movement, dance or any other activity that shifts you from your usual, everyday state of awareness and raises your energy). Start your activity gently so as not to overstrain your body, then keep at it until you feel you cannot do any more. Then continue for at least another minute or two. (I don't want you to strain yourself here but the more you put into this movement to raise energy, the more you will get from the procedures that follow.)

Stand at the centre of your circle facing north, and gather all your forces and energies. Place your lamen at the centre then step out of the circle, turn around and face back into it.

Project into the circle your desire to connect with Tiphareth. When you feel ready, step into the circle, pick up your lamen and hold it over your heart centre.

Imagine
  – a bright white light hovering over your head
  – draw this white light down into your heart
  – as the white light reaches your heart it glows like a bright yellow sun in the centre of your chest. This yellow light fills up all the space around you, pervading all directions with bright yellow light.

Imagine white light above your head again
  – visualise it flowing down into your yellow heart
  – then feel this light flow down into your lower body, your genital area, your legs, then into and around your feet. A bright purple energy pervading all of your lower body, connecting you to the ground beneath you
  – feel the presence of your feet on the floor, supported by the earth.

Keep the sense of the white light flowing down from above your head, down through your glowing yellow heart, down into a purple light where you are in contact with the ground
  – imagine you are surrounded by a deep and intense blue aura surrounding and protecting you
  – affirm that this blue light brings you fully into manifestation, so that all that you are is here right now.

Again feel the presence of the white light above your head, down through your glowing yellow heart, down to the purple light in your lower body and where you contact the ground
  – be aware of the blue aura surrounding you
  – ask yourself: how can I manifest my connection to spirit? As a soul what is my next step here on earth? What practical steps can I take in my life, now or in the near future, to manifest this energy to which I am connecting?

When you feel ready, close the circle by standing at the centre, feeling the stillness pervading you, then shouting and stamping your feet, affirming your intention to fully close your magical circle.

After such an intense experience, remember how useful it is to write about your experience in your journal, paying particular attention to your next step(s) in manifestation.

• Solar consciousness

The previous ritualised way of connecting to heart energy is very powerful but takes considerable time to perform. The following exercise offers a simple and effective way of connecting with Tiphareth whenever and wherever you like. It may sound a little complicated at first, but once you become familiar with it, you will find it is easy to reduce it to the basic elements and it can then be undertaken in a few moments. It is a particularly important exercise, so please only practise it with the right attitude and in the right space.

Sit upright, relaxed but attentive, and pay attention to your breathing without altering it or forcing it in any way. Spend a few minutes watching how the air flows in and out of your body in a natural, easy way.

Be aware of what is going on inside your body. Be as fully aware of your body as you are able to be.

Ask yourself: Who is aware of my breathing? Who is aware of my body? Who is aware?

Now imagine a sphere around this body awareness and that you step back out of it. Vividly imagine in front of you a sphere that contains your body awareness. It is called Malkuth.

Consider your feelings. Are you feeling happy, sad, or what? Spend some time looking at your feelings.

How do you feel? Be aware of how your feelings change all the time. For instance, you may be sad one minute, happy the next. Be as fully aware of your feelings as you are able. Ask yourself: Who is aware of my feelings?

Now imagine a sphere around this feeling awareness and that you step back out of it. Vividly imagine in front of you a sphere that contains your awareness of feelings. It is called Netzach.

Consider your thoughts. What are you thinking right now? You are probably thinking about this exercise, but what other thoughts are coming in and out of your awareness? Watch the flow of these thoughts for a while without getting caught up in them.

Your thoughts come and go almost as if they are independent of you. Be as fully aware of your thought processes as you are able. Ask yourself: Who has these thoughts?

Now imagine a sphere around your thoughts and that you step back out of it. Vividly imagine in front of you a sphere that contains your awareness of thoughts. It is called Hod.

Focus on these three spheres of awareness – your sensations in Malkuth, feelings in Netzach, thoughts in Hod. Who is focusing on these spheres?

Ask yourself: Who am I? Who is it that experiences all these sensations, feelings and thoughts?

Allow yourself to experience fully this part of you that has sensations, feelings and thoughts but is more than any or all of them. This is solar consciousness, the experience of Tiphareth.

You can choose to be separate or non-attached to the contents of your personality. You can also choose to go into any of these spheres of awareness when it is appropriate for you to do so. Choose now to re-enter your personality and take some time to bring yourself back into everyday consciousness. You can do this through concretely expressing your connection to Tiphareth. What do you wish to do to express clearly your connection to your heart?

AFTERWORD

One of the most exciting aspects of Kabbalah is that the more you use it, the more interesting and useful it becomes. As you delve further into practical Kabbalistic work, the Tree of Life becomes alive in your consciousness. It lives with you in everything you do: increasing your awareness, deepening your connection to soul energy, giving you assistance in manifesting who you are and what you want to be in life. Only practical experience can show you the true value of Kabbalah.

After reading this book you may think Kabbalah is not for you or that it is an interesting path but not one you choose at this time. Kabbalah is definitely of little value to someone unless they feel personally connected to it. On the other hand, having found something here to interest you, you may wish to continue your study and practice of Kabbalah:

- simply to know more about it so you can decide whether you wish to go further into its mysteries and revelations
- to foster your individual growth and development
- to add new skills, and develop your work in your own field
- to become a Kabbalist, using the Tree of Life as a major tool in your path towards self-realisation.

It is possible to make Kabbalah a dry, intellectual study, and if that is what you desire and enjoy all well and good. I would like to stress again, however, the importance of practice. Without it, you will be missing the excitement and meaning that is found when the Tree of Life shines in your everyday life and lights up the path towards your goals whatever they may be. Kabbalah is of equal value for those travelling the simplest, most mundane path as it is for those attempting the loftiest peaks of attainment. The practical Kabbalah is for everyone who wishes to partake of its splendours.

A lot can be gleaned from reading books on Kabbalah and related subjects, particularly those books that offer you practical suggestions and exercises. Reading is best accompanied by experiences so that you can connect what you read with your own process. The books in the Bibliography and Further Reading section are a good place to start. My book *The Complete Guide to the Kabbalah* is an excellent practical guide, encapsulating twenty years of practical work with the Tree of Life.

There are an increasing number of people who either teach

Kabbalah or share their insights about Kabbalah with others. I would suggest that if you decide to attend or join any ongoing groups, you do not make a commitment until you have experienced what they offer. Anyone who asks you to do otherwise is probably to be avoided. Be wary also of any group leaders who ask you to follow their teachings or practices to the exclusion of your reading other books or following any other course of study that interests you. Kabbalah is not intended to be an exclusive system – indeed, part of its value is its ability to interrelate with other systems.

I offer individual tuition in Kabbalah, basing the work on your own life experience and needs, not through applying a set formula without regard to who you are. I also run group courses on Kabbalah and related subjects. If you would like details of these ventures please write to me care of my contact details, which you will find near the end of the book.

Whatever your feelings about Kabbalah, may your search for inner wisdom and understanding be fruitful, and may you come to a self-realisation that nurtures both your own individual experience and expression and that of the planet as a whole.

APPENDIX 1

USING THE PRACTICES IN THIS BOOK

The practices in this book offer you the opportunity to connect with Kabbalah in an experiential way. You might like to try some out immediately you come to them, or you may prefer to leave them until you are feeling more in the mood. If you are reading this book while travelling, for example, you may prefer to wait until you are home before attempting a practice. It is always worth reading through a practice, though, even if you do not intend to do it (then or later). It may not be as powerful as actually performing the practice, but it will at the very least give you a flavour of the practical Kabbalah.

Before starting any of the practices, ensure you have enough time to complete the practice without being disturbed. Take up a comfortable position, either standing, sitting or lying as appropriate to the practice, and, with a straight but not stiff spine, close your eyes and take a few deep breaths. Be aware that you are a unique individual choosing at this time to perform this practice. You are then ready to start the practice. Take your time going through the instructions to the practice – it is better to err on the side of slowness rather than to rush things.

It may be necessary to read the practice through a few times to familiarise yourself with what you have to do. This will help you to focus, so do not begrudge this time. If you find any particular practice especially useful or meaningful to you, you can always repeat it more than once. Repetition of a practice can, in fact, multiply its power in helping you realise more about yourself.

You might like to share the experience of the practices with someone else, each of you alternately acting as guide and speaking the words and directions for the other person. If you do this, remember to respect the other person's process, and to speak slowly and distinctly, allowing him or her time to do whatever is required.

Some people find it particularly helpful with longer visualisation and meditation practices to tape-record the instructions, which then enables them to relax more deeply as they follow the directions being played back to them. If you choose to do this, you will find it is best to read the words slowly and leave ample spaces between each section for you to experience what is being suggested. After a little preparation, you will find the speed of delivery that best suits your own process.

It is a good idea to keep a record of your work with the Tree of Life in a journal or workbook as, apart from anything else, it helps you to ground your experience. This simply means finding ways of expressing what you have learned in your everyday life. A practice in Chapter 1 may make having a Kabbalistic Journal in which to record your work more real for you (see p. 11). Mostly, however, have fun with the practices – taking a light approach can help you both connect with the work and keep a perspective on it, and be willing to adapt the exercises to your own way of working.

PRACTICE

• The Kabbalistic Cross

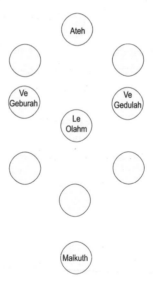

Diagram 29: The Kabbalistic Cross

The Kabbalistic Cross exercise is useful because it connects us with the Tree of Life through our physical form; it aligns our energies and balances our auras; and it acts as a barrier or protection device to stop unwanted intrusions into our space. The small effort required in becoming familiar with this procedure, which can then be used daily if so desired, is well worth it.

*

Following the instructions below, start to practise the Kabbalistic Cross on a daily basis. It need only take a few minutes once you are familiar with it. Re-read this even if you are already familiar with and using the Kabbalistic Cross. Note well not to rush such work – be clear with each stage before moving on to the next. It is better to go too slowly than to go too fast.

Relax and centre yourself. Stand upright, attentive but not stiff. Pronounce each word slowly and with as much resonance as possible.

Touch your forehead with the forefinger of your right hand and say: *Ateh* ('for thine'). Be aware of your innermost connection to deity.

Move your finger down in a straight line to touch just above your genital area and say: *Malkuth* ('is the kingdom').

Be aware of your whole body.

Visualise this straight line down the front of your body and all the subsequent lines you draw as bright, shining, silver-white light, which permeates your astral, etheric and physical bodies.

Touch your right shoulder, and say: *Ve geburah* ('the power').

Be aware of your power.

Drawing a line across to touch your left shoulder, say: *Ve gedulah* ('and the glory').

Be aware of your love energy.

Clasping your hands together over your heart, visualise a shining white cross inscribed over your body. Say: *Le olahm* ('unto the ages').

Be aware of exactly where you are (here), exactly at this moment (now).

Extend your arms out so you are standing as a cross, and say: *Amen*.

Stay standing for a while, feeling the energy to which you've connected permeating your physical and psychic space.

THE SACRED ALPHABET

The Hebrew Alphabet is a sacred alphabet, just as Sanskrit is in the East, for instance. As explained in Chapter 3, each Hebrew letter is a symbolic representation of a cosmic principle and has a specific meaning and a number attributed to it. There are twenty-two letters in the Hebrew alphabet and they are related to the twenty-two paths on the Tree of Life. They represent different states of consciousness that are created when the cosmic principles represented by the spheres are connected through human awareness. The letters then represent the essence or principle behind these connections.

As well as being used to 'make up words', the letters of the alphabet have a deeper, inner significance. In English the letters U-N-I-T-Y make up the word 'unity', which can be applied to a particular state of consciousness. The equivalent Hebrew word is 'Achad', made up of the Hebrew letters A-Ch-D, that is Aleph, Cheth and Daleth. (Remember, Hebrew actually runs from right to left, so more properly this should read D-Ch-A!) All of the letters also has a numerical equivalent and other meanings that can help us understand more about the word. So the three letters of 'achad' add up numerically to thirteen, thus asserting a connection with all other words that also add up to thirteen. This is explained in the section on gematria in Chapter 3.

The three letters also tell us more about 'achad = unity' through their own individual meanings. Aleph means an ox and is also the first letter of the alphabet. Cheth means a gate and daleth a door. We may interpret this in many ways, but for instance we could say the message is thus: that unity is a great strength and comes at the beginning of everything. Indeed, its strength is so great it needs a gate to keep it from coming through the door into our dualistic lives, otherwise, like an 'ox in a china shop'(!), it would destroy our nice neat world. Whether that is to be desired or not is a philosophical matter.

For the work presented in this book, you do not need to understand Hebrew at all. If you are interested in the Hebrew alphabet, however, you will find many correspondences to the letters in the tables in Appendix 4. So, using the tables in the usual way, you would find, for instance, that the letter Beth is numbered 2, and corresponds to the 'magician' tarot card, the left brain, the colour grey, frankincense, the beech tree, an owl and so on. The intuitive connections that can be made through this – and the increased awareness that flows through these connections – can be most illuminating.

The letters can be used for healing, as a correspondence themselves, and through using the shape and form and sound of the letter in your healing work. For instance, visualising the shape of a Hebrew letter over the corresponding diseased area of a body can aid the flow of healing energies. They are powerful tools for such work and should be used with respect.

Aleph	א	Lamed	ל
Beth	ב	Mem	מ
Gimel	ג	Nun	נ
Daleth	ד	Samekh	ס
He	ה	Ayin	ע
Vau	ו	Pe	פ
Zain	ז	Tzaddi	צ
Cheth	ח	Qoph	ק
Teth	ט	Resh	ר
Kaph	כ	Shin	ש
Yod	י	Tau	ת

APPENDIX 3

STANDARD
SYMBOLS

The astrological symbols used in this book are fairly standard. They are:

Aries ♈ Taurus ♉ Gemini ♊ Cancer ♋ Leo ♌ Virgo ♍
Libra ♎ Scorpio ♏ Sagittarius ♐ Capricorn ♑ Aquarius ♒ Pisces ♓

Earth ⊕ Sun ☉ Moon ☽ Mercury ☿ Venus ♀ Mars ♂
Jupiter ♃ Saturn ♄ Uranus ♅ Neptune ♆ Pluto ♇

Planetary symbols are composed of seven basic components:

- *point or dot*   . the self, simple consciousness, beingness
- *circle*   ○ complete awareness, everything
- *crescent*   ☽ receptivity and transmission of energy
- *arrow*   ↗ movement, creativity, response
- *horizontal line*   - feminine, passive energy
- *vertical line* | masculine, active energy
- *cross*   + male and female union, balanced
                       manifestation.

Each of the symbols can be understood according to how it is made up of these component parts. For instance, the symbol for Mercury is composed of a crescent, circle and cross: receptivity (the crescent) passing down through awareness (the circle) into manifestation (the cross). It is worth exploring all these symbols in a similar way.

THE CORRESPONDENCE TABLES

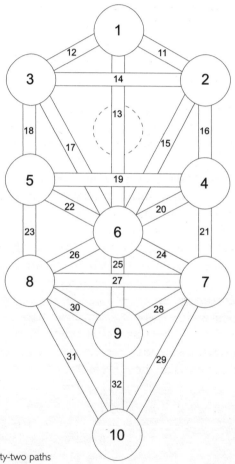

Diagram 30: The thirty-two paths

The correspondence tables contain a plethora of images, ideas, concepts, experiences and so on that correspond with the spheres and paths of the Tree of Life. These include: the human system, the body, colours, Tarot cards, Hebrew letters, trees, flowers, animals, etc. Diagram 30 indicates the thirty-two paths. Many items are traditionally attributed to each sphere and path – indeed, one could ultimately ascribe everything in the universe to the Tree of Life. This is part of its value, and what makes it a wonderful compendium of universal symbols. With all correspondences, however, the most important thing is to make your own connections. So, for instance, if your experience is that a willow tree and goldfish are more appropriate correspondences for Malkuth than the oak and rabbit, then these will be your personal correspondences for working that sphere.

The whole point of using correspondences is to be able to relate your experience into the Tree, then see some relationship of this with the whole Tree. As well as working with individual correspondences, it is also useful to stretch ourselves to see why certain correspondences have a more 'universal' application. For example, in Western Europe anyway, most people seem to find the oak tree is a good correspondence for Malkuth = Earth. Why should that be? On the other hand, correspondences can become rather dated. Traditionally the jackal was attributed to Hod, for instance, because in the ancient world it was considered sacred to Mercury, the planet of Hod. In our modern world, however, we may not have much contact with jackals and think that, for instance, a fox is a better correspondence because of its mercurial nature.

The tables in this book include many updated correspondences that are more relevant to our modern world. They are the result of many years work by myself and other Kabbalistic students. Hopefully, many (if not all) of them make sense to you, and can be used appropriately for your Kabbalistic work. Let me stress again, however, that nothing in the Kabbalah is fixed and as time passes these correspondences may change again. Also, as stated above, you may find ones that better suit your psyche. For now, however, use the given correspondences as a good starting point for your explorations.

The paths also have a 'dual' aspect to them in that they can be seen from 'below upwards' or from 'above downwards'. For example, the path joining Malkuth to Yesod can be seen as both: from Yesod to Malkuth (down) representing your subjective experience of repressed subconscious material being held in your body (experienced as tensions, physical ailments, 'armouring', etc.); or from Malkuth to Yesod (up), the first path for going deeper into the Tree, as representing your subjective experience of connecting with your subconscious realms (experienced primarily through dreams and your conscious work on your past conditioning etc.).

The paths may also be understood in relation to one another. For instance, the paths joining Hod to Tiphareth and Netzach to Tiphareth, when 'balanced' together, represent the subjective experience of the integration of mind and feelings through the connection to Self (Tiphareth).

*	Spheres and paths	Hebrew letters	Hebrew names of letters	English equivalent	Numerical value	English letters
1	Kether			Crown		
2	Chockmah			Wisdom		
3	Binah			Understanding		
D	Daath			Knowledge		
4	Chesed			Mercy		
5	Geburah			Judgement		
6	Tiphareth			Beauty		
7	Netzach			Victory		
8	Hod			Splendour		
9	Yesod			Foundation		
10	Malkuth			World		
11	joins 1–2	א	aleph	ox	1	A
12	joins 1–3	ב	beth	house	2	B
13	joins 1–6	ג	gimel	camel	3	C, G
14	joins 2–3	ד	daleth	door	4	D
15	joins 2–6	ה	he	window	5	H
16	joins 2–4	ו	vau	nail	6	U, V
17	joins 3–6	ז	zain	sword	7	Z
18	joins 3–5	ח	cheth	fence	8	Ch
19	joins 4–5	ט	teth	serpent	9	T
20	joins 4–6	י	yod	hand	10	I, Y
21	joins 4-7	כ	kaph	palm of hand	20	K
22	joins 5–6	ל	lamed	oxgoad	30	L
23	joins 5–8	מ	mem	water	40	M
24	joins 6–7	נ	nun	fish	50	N
25	joins 6–9	ס	samekh	support	60	S
26	joins 6–8	ע	ayin	eye	70	O
27	joins 7–8	פ	pe	mouth	80	P
28	joins 7–9	צ	tzaddi	fish-hook	90	X, Tz
29	joins 7–10	ק	qoph	back of head	100	Q
30	joins 8–9	ר	resh	head	200	R
31	joins 8–10	ש	shin	tooth	300	Sh
32	joins 9–10	ת	tau	cross	400	Th

*	Spheres and Paths	Physical structure	Inner body components
1	Kether	crown	consciousness
2	Chockmah	L side of head	left brain
3	Binah	R side of head	right brain
D	Daath	throat	throat, thyroid
4	Chesed	L shoulder	L adrenal
5	Geburah	R shoulder	R adrenal
6	Tiphareth	breast bone	heart, thymus
7	Netzach	L arm and hand	L kidney
8	Hod	R arm and hand	R kidney
9	Yesod	sexual organs	sexual organs
10	Malkuth	base of spine, feet	body as whole
11	joins 1–2	L eye, L ear	L eye, L ear, pituitary
12	joins 1–3	R eye, R ear	R eye, R ear, pineal
13	joins 1–6	backbone	spinal cord
14	joins 2–3	nose, mouth	nose, mouth
15	joins 2–6	L front of neck	arteries, oxygenated blood
16	joins 2–4	L rear neck	posterior pituitary, endocrine overall
17	joins 3–6	R front of neck	veins, deoxygenated blood
18	joins 3–5	R rear neck	anterior pituitary, endocrine overall
19	joins 4–5	upper chest (breasts)	lymph, spleen
20	joins 4–6	L upper back & sides	L lung
21	joins 4–7	L mid back & sides	large intestine (descending), rectum
22	joins 5–6	R upper back & sides	R lung
23	joins 5–8	R mid back & sides	large intestine (ascending/transverse)
24	joins 6–7	L lower back	stomach
25	joins 6–9	solar plexus	solar plexus
26	joins 6–8	R lower back	liver, gall bladder, pancreas
27	joins 7–8	navel, mid belly	small intestine
28	joins 7–9	L lower abdomen	L inner sexual system
29	joins 7–10	L leg	L skeleton, bones, muscles
30	joins 8–9	R lower abdomen	R inner sexual system
31	joins 8–10	R leg	R skeleton, bones, muscles
32	joins 9–10	perineum, buttocks	bladder, skin

*	Spheres and paths	Human system	Divine forces	Archangels
1	Kether	the self	Eheieh	Metatron
2	Chockmah	spiritual will/purpose	Ihvh	Ratziel
3	Binah	spiritual love/awareness	Ihvh Elohim	Tzaphkiel
D	Daath	'the next step'	Ue	
4	Chesed	love/ awareness	El	Tzadkiel
5	Geburah	will/power	Elohim Gebor	Khamael
6	Tiphareth	personal self/centre/ 'I'	Ihvh Aloah	Raphael
7	Netzach	feeling	Ihvh Tzabaoth	Haniel
8	Hod	thinking	Elohim Tzabaoth	Michael
9	Yesod	subconscious/sexuality	Shaddai El Chai	Gabriel
10	Malkuth	body (as whole)/senses	Adonai Ha-Aretz	Sandalphon
11	joins 1–2	[connections between	[the sacred	[angels work
12	joins 1–3	systems in spheres]	alphabet is	the paths]
13	joins 1–6	"	ascribed to	
14	joins 2–3	"	the paths]	
15	joins 2–6	"		
16	joins 2–4	"		
17	joins 3–6	"		
18	joins 3–5	"		
19	joins 4–5	"		
20	joins 4–6	"		
21	joins 4–7	"		
22	joins 5–6	"		
23	joins 5–8	"		
24	joins 6–7	"		
25	joins 6–9	"		
26	joins 6–8	"		
27	joins 7–8	"		
28	joins 7–9	"		
29	joins 7–10	"		
30	joins 8–9	"		
31	joins 8–10	"		
32	joins 9–10	"		

*	Spheres and paths	Physical disorders
1	Kether	lifelessness, soul-less, etc.
2	Chockmah	left brain disorders
3	Binah	right brain disorders
D	Daath	thyroid disorders, metabolic rate
4	Chesed	adrenalin – flee (stress, muscular waste)
5	Geburah	adrenalin – fight (stress, virilism)
6	Tiphareth	heart failure & disease, thymus, immunosystem disorders
7	Netzach	kidney disorders
8	Hod	kidney disorders
9	Yesod	sexual disorders
10	Malkuth	death
11	joins 1–2	optical defects, ear disorders, hearing, balance, seeing
12	joins 1–3	optical defects, ear disorders, hearing, balance, seeing
13	joins 1–6	spinal disorders, sensation disturbance
14	joins 2–3	nasal & mouth disorders, vibrational recognition
15	joins 2–6	stroke, coronary thrombosis, arteriosclerosis
16	joins 2–4	inner growth disorders
17	joins 3–6	thrombosis, clotting
18	joins 3–5	outer growth disorders
19	joins 4–5	defence disorders, widespread disorder
20	joins 4–6	numerous disorders (e.g. bronchitis, pneumonia, asthma)
21	joins 4–7	various disorders (incl. emotional)
22	joins 5–6	numerous disorders (e.g. bronchitis, pneumonia, asthma)
23	joins 5–8	various disorders (incl. emotional)
24	joins 6–7	various disorders (incl. ulceration)
25	joins 6–9	nervous disorders
26	joins 6–8	various (liver, e.g. jaundice; pancreas, e.g. diabetes)
27	joins 7–8	various (incl. emotional)
28	joins 7–9	reproductive disorders
29	joins 7–10	skeletal disorders (e.g. rheumatism, arthritis, gout)
30	joins 8–9	reproductive disorders
31	joins 8–10	skeletal disorders (e.g. rheumatism, arthritis, gout)
32	joins 9–10	skin diseases, cystitis, etc.

*	Spheres and paths	Colours	Celestial attributions	Alternative esoteric titles
I	Kether	white	pluto	vast countenance
2	Chockmah	grey	neptune/zodiac	crown of creation
3	Binah	black	saturn	the great sea
D	Daath	lilac	uranus/asteroids	the abyss
4	Chesed	blue	jupiter	majesty
5	Geburah	red	mars	justice
6	Tiphareth	yellow	sun	the child
7	Netzach	green	venus	the beauty of nature
8	Hod	orange	mercury	active science
9	Yesod	purple	luna	the fulcrum
10	Malkuth	sky blue	earth/elements	the gate
11	joins 1–2	light grey	air	the holy spirit
12	joins 1–3	mid grey	mercury	the messenger
13	joins 1–6	pale yellow	luna	the virgin
14	joins 2–3	dark grey	venus	the wife
15	joins 2–6	pale blue	aquarius	the mother
16	joins 2–4	grey–blue	taurus	the child priest
17	joins 3–6	pink	gemini	the twins emerging
18	joins 3–5	crimson	cancer	the grail
19	joins 4–5	purple	leo	the magical union
20	joins 4–6	olive green	virgo	the secret seed
21	joins 4–7	blue–green	jupiter	the father of all
22	joins 5–6	orange	libra	the sexually united
23	joins 5–8	red–orange	water	the water redeemer
24	joins 6–7	yellow–green	scorpio	the redeeming belly
25	joins 6–9	mauve	sagittarius	the pregnant womb
26	joins 6–8	gold ochre	capricorn	the erect and glad
27	joins 7–8	brown	mars	the conquering child
28	joins 7–9	bright green	aries	the ruler
29	joins 7–10	silver	pisces	the elder witch
30	joins 8–9	bright orange	sun	the playing gods
31	joins 8–10	pale pink	fire	the emerging goddess
32	joins 9–10	black	saturn	pantacle of the whole

*	Spheres and paths	Pathworking and the places of power
I	Kether	the innermost temple
2	Chockmah	the celestial spheres
3	Binah	the great sea
D	Daath	the rainbow bridge
4	Chesed	the temple of love
5	Geburah	the temple of power
6	Tiphareth	the mountain of the soul
7	Netzach	the garden of beauty
8	Hod	the house of spells
9	Yesod	the secret valley
10	Malkuth	the meadow of delights
11	joins 1–2	scintillating path, facing the creator
12	joins 1–3	transparent path, seeing of visions
13	joins 1–6	uniting path, realising spiritual truth
14	joins 2–3	illuminating path, fundamental holiness
15	joins 2–6	constituting path, substance of creation
16	joins 2–4	eternal path, pleasure of paradise
17	joins 3–6	disposing path, foundation of faith
18	joins 3-5	influential path, understanding causality
19	joins 4–5	activating path, the experience of blessings
20	joins 4–6	intelligent path, knowledge of existence
21	joins 4–7	conciliatory path, transmitting divine influence
22	joins 5–6	faithful path, increasing spiritual virtue
23	joins 5–8	stable path, increasing consistency
24	joins 6–7	imaginative path, renewal and change
25	joins 6–9	tentative path, the alchemical processes
26	joins 6–8	renovating path, life force in action
27	joins 7–8	exciting path, the nature of existence
28	joins 7–9	admiral path, understanding the depths
29	joins 7–10	corporeal path, the formation of the body
30	joins 8–9	collecting path, celestial arts and astrology
31	joins 8–10	perpetual path, regulating the creation
32	joins 9–10	administrative path, directing life energies

*	Spheres and paths	Aromatic oils	Herbs
1	Kether	almond	camomile
2	Chockmah	frankincense	rosemary
3	Binah	myrrh	comfrey
D	Daath	eucalyptus	balm of gilead
4	Chesed	cedarwood	borage
5	Geburah	cypress	borage
6	Tiphareth	rose	hawthorn berries/bay/heartsease
7	Netzach	patchouli	couchgrass/verbena
8	Hod	rosemary	couchgrass/sage
9	Yesod	lavender	damiana
10	Malkuth	sandalwood	meadowsweet
11	joins 1–2	melissa	hyssop/eyebright
12	joins 1–3	cardamom	hyssop/eyebright
13	joins 1–6	sage	red clover
14	joins 2–3	clove	elderflower
15	joins 2–6	marigold	lime blossom
16	joins 2–4	pine	yellow dock
17	joins 3–6	jasmine/ylang ylang	marigold
18	joins 3–5	thyme	thyme
19	joins 4–5	calamus	echinacea
20	joins 4–6	camphor	coltsfoot
21	joins 4–7	basil	pilewort
22	joins 5–6	clary sage	coltsfoot
23	joins 5–8	camomile	bayberry
24	joins 6–7	peppermint	peppermint
25	joins 6–9	bergamot/hyacinth	passiflora
26	joins 6–8	nutmeg	dandelion
27	joins 7–8	fennel	fennel
28	joins 7–9	geranium	nettle/black cohosh
29	joins 7–10	juniper	bogbean
30	joins 8–9	cinnamon	raspberry leaf/blue cohosh
31	joins 8–10	hyssop	yarrow
32	joins 9–10	marjoram	sarsaparilla/rue

*	Spheres and paths	Flowers	Trees	Magickal instruments and symbols
1	Kether	lotus/almond	almond	crown/cauldron/lamp
2	Chockmah	orchid	beech	penis/body/word
3	Binah	lily	alder	vagina/cloak/cup
D	Daath	ivy	magnolia	incense/bell/oil
4	Chesed	tulip	birch	wand/sceptre/crook
5	Geburah	peony	rowan	sword/spear/scourge
6	Tiphareth	yellow rose/gorse	holly	lamen/rosy cross/altar
7	Netzach	red rose/grasses	apple	lamp/girdle/dagger
8	Hod	pansy	hazel	spells/book/chain
9	Yesod	iris/violet	willow	perfumes/sandals
10	Malkuth	clover/meadowsweet	oak	circle/triangle/crystal
11	joins 1–2	daisy	spruce	dagger/fan/stick
12	joins 1–3	primrose	ash	wand/caduceus
13	joins 1–6	buttercup	maple	bow/arrow/veil
14	joins 2–3	bluebell	sweet chestnut	girdle/shield/lotus
15	joins 2–6	marigold	pine	censer/starcharts
16	joins 2–4	cowslip	cypress	crown/pentagram
17	joins 3–6	honeysuckle	sycamore	tripod/egg/flower
18	joins 3–5	nasturtium	cherry	furnace/grail/chariot
19	joins 4–5	sunflower	fig	heart/reins/elixir
20	joins 4–6	rosebay willowherb	walnut	lamp/wand/bread
21	joins 4–7	anemone	plane	sceptre/wheel
22	joins 5–6	dahlia	palm	equal cross/scales
23	joins 5–8	harebell	lime	christian cross/wine
24	joins 6–7	snowdrop	yew	scythe/poisons
25	joins 6–9	hyacinth	cedar	alchemical items
26	joins 6–8	foxglove	aspen	elixir/lamp/horns
27	joins 7–8	nettle	horse chestnut	sword/tower/fire
28	joins 7–9	geranium	elder	sceptre/orb/flag
29	joins 7–10	poppy	elm	magic mirror/blood
30	joins 8–9	crocus	bay	lamen/talismans
31	joins 8–10	dandelion	balsam poplar	wings/stars/pyramid
32	joins 9–10	daffodil	hawthorn	pantacle/salt/temple

*	Spheres and paths	Animals	Legendary beings	Magickal visions and powers
1	Kether	swan	dryad	union with self
2	Chockmah	owl	lemur	vision of self
3	Binah	whale	siren	vision of wonder and sorrow
D	Daath	vulture	chimera	dominion over darkness
4	Chesed	dolphin	sphinx	vision of love
5	Geburah	horse	dwarf	vision of power
6	Tiphareth	spider	fairy	vision of harmony
7	Netzach	dove	faun	vision of triumphant beauty
8	Hod	fox	elf	vision of splendour
9	Yesod	cat	vampire	vision of machinery of universe
10	Malkuth	rabbit	gnome	vision of guardian angel
11	joins 1–2	tiger	sylph	fearlessness
12	joins 1–3	monkey	apeman	healing/casting spells
13	joins 1–6	camel	ghost	clairvoyance/dream control
14	joins 2–3	bee	harpy	enchantment/love potions
15	joins 2–6	human	succubus	actualising true will
16	joins 2–4	cow	banshee	inner voice/physical strength
17	joins 3–6	magpie	incubus	control of double/prophecy
18	joins 3–5	crab	nereid	past life recall
19	joins 4–5	lion	gorgon	dialogue with other beings
20	joins 4–6	crow	apparition	invisibility
21	joins 4–7	blackbird	lemur	divination
22	joins 5–6	elephant	nymph	equilibrium and balance
23	joins 5–8	snake	mermaid/man	skrying/body-will
24	joins 6–7	scorpion	lamia	necromancy/mediumistic abilities
25	joins 6–9	peacock	centaur	transmutation/vision of peacock
26	joins 6–8	goat	satyr	fascination/casting evil eye
27	joins 7–8	gnat	dragon	talismanic arts/creating disorder
28	joins 7–9	sheep	minotaur	power of consecration
29	joins 7–10	dog	werewolf	bewitchments/casting illusions
30	joins 8–9	butterfly	willowisp	power of acquiring wealth
31	joins 8–10	hawk	salamander	evocation/transformation
32	joins 9–10	crocodile	ghoul	astral vision/geomancy

*	Spheres and paths	Tarot attributions	Esoteric titles of tarot cards
1	Kether	4 aces	
2	Chockmah	4 twos/knights	
3	Binah	4 threes/queens	
D	Daath	—	
4	Chesed	4 fours	
5	Geburah	4 fives	
6	Tiphareth	4 sixes/princes	
7	Netzach	4 sevens	
8	Hod	4 eights	
9	Yesod	4 nines	
10	Malkuth	4 tens/princesses	
11	joins 1–2	fool	the spirit of the aethyr
12	joins 1–3	magus	the spirit in the temple
13	joins 1–6	priestess	priestess of the silver star
14	joins 2–3	empress	daughter of the mighty ones
15	joins 2–6	star	daughter of the firmament
16	joins 2–4	hierophant	magus of the eternal
17	joins 3–6	lovers	children of the voice
18	joins 3–5	chariot	magus of the triumph of light
19	joins 4–5	lust/strength	children of the dragon flame
20	joins 4–6	hermit	prophet of the eternal
21	joins 4–7	fortune	ruler of the forces of life
22	joins 5–6	adjustment/justice	spirit of inner truth
23	joins 5–8	hanged man	spirit of the mighty waters
24	joins 6–7	death	lord of the great transformation
25	joins 6–9	art/temperance	the bringer forth of life
26	joins 6–8	devil	lord of the gates of matter
27	joins 7–8	tower	priest of the divine fire
28	joins 7–9	emperor	son of the morning
29	joins 7–10	moon	priestess of the crescent gate
30	joins 8–9	sun	son of the world fire
31	joins 8–10	aeon/judgement	spirit of the primal fire
32	joins 9–10	universe	great one of the night of time

*	Spheres and paths	Spiritual fire/wands	Key words Mental air/swords	Emotional water/cups
1	Kether	revelation	illumination	ecstasy
2	Chockmah	dominion	peace	love
3	Binah	virtue	sorrow	abundance
D	Daath	recognition	conflict	vitality
4	Chesed	completion	truce	luxury
5	Geburah	strife	defeat	disappointment
6	Tiphareth	victory	science	pleasure
7	Netzach	valour	futility	debauch
8	Hod	swiftness	interference	indolence
9	Yesod	strength	cruelty	happiness
10	Malkuth	oppression	ruin	satiety
11	joins 1–2	wholeness	stimulating	expressive
12	joins 1–3	wilful	quick	unpredictable
13	joins 1–6	intuitive	clear	centred
14	joins 2–3	unconditional	tolerant	forgiving
15	joins 2–6	realisation	bright	flowing
16	joins 2–4	channel	establishing	compassionate
17	joins 3–6	integrating	balancing	changeable
18	joins 3–5	questing	focused	secretive
19	joins 4–5	affirming	certain	passionate
20	joins 4–6	introspective	discriminating	sober
21	joins 4–7	change	opportunistic	courageous
22	joins 5–6	idealistic	logical	observing
23	joins 5–8	patience	reflective	stoical
24	joins 6–7	liberation	recognition	fear
25	joins 6–9	harmony	ingenious	optimistic
26	joins 6–8	vitality	original	unrestrained
27	joins 7–8	purifying	motivated	cathartic
28	joins 7–9	discipline	analytical	stable
29	joins 7–10	receptive	reflective	explosive
30	joins 8–9	celebrating	spontaneous	joyous
31	joins 8–10	seeing	perceptive	detached
32	joins 9–10	fulfilling	plenty	exciting

*	Spheres and paths	Physical earth/discs	Key words Qualities (virtues)	Distortions (vices)
1	Kether	refinement	unity	confusion
2	Chockmah	change	purpose	illusion
3	Binah	works	silence	greed
D	Daath	clearing	expression	dispersion
4	Chesed	power	alignment	bigotry
5	Geburah	worry	courage	restriction
6	Tiphareth	success	devotion	pride
7	Netzach	failure	unselfishness	lust
8	Hod	prudence	truthfulness	dishonesty
9	Yesod	gain	independence	idleness
10	Malkuth	wealth	discrimination	inertia
11	joins 1–2	energetic	original	impractical
12	joins 1–3	graceful	talented	deceptive
13	joins 1–6	pure	contemplative	rigid
14	joins 2–3	embracing	sharing	possessive
15	joins 2–6	sensual	guiding	ungrounded
16	joins 2–4	enduring	traditional	arrogant
17	joins 3–6	synthesising	choosing	unreliable
18	joins 3–5	moving	explorative	elusive
19	joins 4–5	beautiful	limitless	selfish
20	joins 4–6	sufficiency	separated	escapist
21	joins 4–7	extremist	gambling	compulsive
22	joins 5–6	aligned	adjusting	judgemental
23	joins 5–8	stiff	passive	victim
24	joins 6–7	structured	changing	refusing
25	joins 6–9	regenerative	productive	dualistic
26	joins 6–8	expressive	fearless	debauched
27	joins 7–8	releasing	opportunistic	apathetic
28	joins 7–9	solid	materialistic	authoritarian
29	joins 7–10	resting	cyclical	imbalance
30	joins 8–9	radiant	active	insensitive
31	joins 8–10	cautious	planning	critical
32	joins 9–10	integrating	beginning	scattered

*	Spheres and paths	Sepher Yetzirah	Crystals and jewels	Drugs and intoxicants
I	Kether	admirable I†	diamond	–
2	Chockmah	illuminating I	pearl	–
3	Binah	sanctifying I	jet	psilocybin
D	Daath	–	coal	belladonna
4	Chesed	cohesive I	amethyst	opium
5	Geburah	radical I	ruby	cocaine
6	Tiphareth	mediating I	topaz/rose quartz	LSD
7	Netzach	occult I	sapphire	marijuana
8	Hod	absolute I	citrine	hashish
9	Yesod	pure I	quartz	alcohol
10	Malkuth	resplendent I	crystal	com/wheat
I I	joins I–2	scintillating I	chrysophase	psilocybin
12	joins I–3	transparent I	agate	ayahuasca
13	joins I–6	uniting I	opal	DMT
14	joins 2–3	illuminating I	jacinth	cannabis
15	joins 2–6	natural I	garnet	hashish
16	joins 2–4	triumphal I	lapis lazuli	sugar
17	joins 3–6	disposing I	agate	MDMA
18	joins 3–5	influential I	emerald	LSD
19	joins 4–5	spiritual I	onyx	ginseng
20	joins 4–6	wilful I	cornelian	ethyl oxide
21	joins 4–7	conciliating I	jade	cocaine
22	joins 5–6	faithful I	chrysolite	tobacco
23	joins 5–8	stable I	aquamarine	vervain
24	joins 6–7	imaginative I	beryl	heroin
25	joins 6–9	tentative I	topaz	psilocybin
26	joins 6–8	renovating I	turquoise	cannabis
27	joins 7–8	exciting I	garnet	mescaline
28	joins 7–9	constituting I	bloodstone	amphetamine
29	joins 7–10	corporeal I	moonstone	opium
30	joins 8–9	collecting I	sunstone	alcohol
31	joins 8–10	perpetual I	tigers eye	heartsease
32	joins 9–10	administrative I	pearl	coltsfoot

†Intelligence

*	Spheres and Paths	Demonic animals & beings	Kliphoth (demons)	English names of demons	Demons of hidden paths
1	Kether	star	Thaumiel	twin gods	
2	Chockmah	dog	Ghagiel	hinderers	
3	Binah	ass	Satariel	concealers	
D	Daath	vampire	Belia'al	worthless ones	
4	Chesed	goat	Gha'agsheblah	breakers	
5	Geburah	elephant	Golachab	burners	
6	Tiphareth	horse	Thagirion	disputers	
7	Netzach	hen	A'arab Zaraq	dispersers	
8	Hod	cock	Samael	deceivers	
9	Yesod	snake	Gamaliel	obscene ones	
10	Malkuth	peacock	Lilith	averse energy	
11	joins 1–2	sylph	Oriens	air demons	Amprodias
12	joins 1–3	wizard/witch	Samael	deceivers	Baratchial
13	joins 1–6	lemure/ghost	Gamaliel	obscene ones	Gargophias
14	joins 2–3	succubus	A'arab Zaraq	dispersers	Dagdagiel
15	joins 2–6	nymph/siren	Bahimoron	bestials	Tzuflifu
16	joins 2–4	gorgon/minotaur	Adimiron	bloody ones	Uriens
17	joins 3–6	apparition	Tzalalimiron	clangers	Zamradiel
18	joins 3–5	vampire	Schichiriron	black ones	Characith
19	joins 4–5	dragon	Schalenbiron	flamers	Temphioth
20	joins 4–6	mermaid/man	Tzaphiriron	scratchers	Yamatu
21	joins 4–7	incubus	Gha'agsheblah	breakers	Kurgosiax
22	joins 5–6	fairy/harpy	A'abiriron	clayey ones	Lafcursiax
23	joins 5–8	undine/nereid	Ariton	water demons	Makunofat
24	joins 6–7	lamia/hag	Necheshthiron	brazen ones	Niantiel
25	joins 6–9	centaur	Necheshiron	snakey ones	Saksaksalim
26	joins 6–8	satyr/faun	Dagdagiron	fishy ones	A'anonin
27	joins 7–8	fury/chimaera	Golachab	burners	Parfaxitas
28	joins 7–9	erinye	Ba'airiron	the flock	Hemetterith
29	joins 7–10	werewolf	Nashimiron	malignants	Qulielfi
30	joins 8–9	willowisp	Thagirion	disputers	Raflifu
31	joins 8–10	salamander	Paimon	fire demons	Shalicu
32	joins 9–10	ghoul/gnome	Satariel	concealers	Thantifaxath

*	Spheres and paths	Egyptian deities	Hindu deities	Greek deities	Roman deities
1	Kether	Ptah	Brahma/Shiva	Zeus/Gaia	Jupiter
2	Chockmah	Isis	Shiva/Vishnu	Athena/Poseidon	Neptune
3	Binah	Ta-urt	Bhavani	Cybele/Demeter	Cybele/Saturn
D	Daath	Typhoon	—	Hades/Kronos	Uranus
4	Chesed	Amoun	Indra	Zeus	Jupiter
5	Geburah	Horus	Vishnu	Ares	Mars
6	Tiphareth	Ra	Krishna	Apollo/Helios	Apollo
7	Netzach	Hathor	Bhavani	Aphrodite/Nike	Venus
8	Hod	Thoth	Hanuman	Hermes	Mercury
9	Yesod	Shu	Ganesh	Zeus/Selene	Diana/Hecate
10	Malkuth	Osiris	Lakshmi	Persephone	Ceres
11	joins 1–2	Maat	Maruts	Dionysus	Jupiter/Bacchus
12	joins 1–3	Thoth	Vishnu	Hermes	Mercury
13	joins 1–6	Isis	Chandra	Artemis/Hecate	Diana
14	joins 2–3	Hathor	Lalita	Aphrodite	Venus
15	joins 2–6	Nuit	Maruts	Athena	Juno
16	joins 2–4	Osiris	Shiva	Hera	Venus
17	joins 3–6	Merti	[Twins]	Castor/Pollux	Janus
18	joins 3–5	Hormaku	Krishna	Apollo	Mercury
19	joins 4–5	Horus	Vishnu	Demeter	Venus
20	joins 4–6	Horpakraat	Gopis	Attis	Vesta/Adonis
21	joins 4–7	Amounra	Indra	Zeus	Fortuna
22	joins 5–6	Maat	Yama	Themis	Vulcan/Minerva
23	joins 5–8	Tum	Soma	Poseidon	Neptune
24	joins 6–7	Typhon	Yama	Kronos	Mars
25	joins 6–9	Nephthys	Vishnu	Apollo/Artemis	Diana/Iris
26	joins 6–8	Set	-	Pan/Priapus	Pan/Bacchus
27	joins 7–8	Mentu	Krishna	Ares	Mars
28	joins 7–9	Osiris	Shiva	Zeus	Mars/Juno
29	joins 7–10	Anubis	Vishnu	Poseidon	Neptune/Diana
30	joins 8–9	Ra	Suriya	Helios/Apollo	Apollo
31	joins 8–10	Rahoorkut	Agni	Prometheus	Vulcan/Pluto
32	joins 9–10	Sebek	Brahma	Athena/Gaia	Saturn/Ceres

*	Spheres and paths	Nordic deities	Runic world	African deities	Buddhist meditations
1	Kether	Wotan	ond/buri	Obatala	indifference
2	Chockmah	Odin	borr	Onse	joy
3	Binah	Frigga	bestla	Ododua	compassion
D	Daath	Ing	ljossalfheimer	Olorun	illusion
4	Chesed	Wotan	odhin/hamr	Jakuta	friendliness
5	Geburah	Thor	vili.hugr	Ugun	death/rebirth
6	Tiphareth	Sol/Balder	ve/hamingja	Chango	buddha
7	Netzach	Freya	embla/hamr	Ifa	the gods/nature
8	Hod	Odin	askr/hugr	Aje	analysis/elements
9	Yesod	Odin	fylgja	Iyemota	dharma
10	Malkuth	Freya	la/laeti/litr	Ile	sangha/body
11	joins 1–2	Odin	daeg	Orungan	wind
12	joins 1–3	Odin	os	Osanyin	yellow
13	joins 1–6	Odin	is	Ochu	food
14	joins 2–3	Freya	cen	Ododua	dark blue
15	joins 2–6	Ymar	haegl	Ugan	purple corpse
16	joins 2–4	Vanir	ur	Ife	beaten corpse
17	joins 3–6	Alcis	eh	Ibeji	white
18	joins 3–5	Valkyrjur	eoh	Ojehun	worm-eaten corpse
19	joins 4–5	Freya	wyn	Manamana	gnawed corpse
20	joins 4–6	Frigga/Hel	beorc	Ile	divided corpse
21	joins 4–7	Heimdallr	man	Chango	bloated corpse
22	joins 5–6	Tyr/Mani	tir	Egungun	liberality
23	joins 5–8	Njordhr	lagu	Olokun	hacked corpse
24	joins 6–7	Ullr	eoh	Aidowedo	water
25	joins 6–9	Forseti	rad	Ochumare	skeleton
26	joins 6–8	Nonins	nyd	Elegba	limited aperture
27	joins 7–8	Thor	thorn	Ugun	putrid corpse
28	joins 7–9	Aesir	feoh	Iyemota	bloody corpse
29	joins 7–10	Odin/Freya	gyfu	Adirana	conduct
30	joins 8–9	Sol	sigil	Orun	light
31	joins 8–10	Ing	ing/ger	Zangbeto	fire/breath
32	joins 9–10	Nornir	peorth/ethel	Odun	peace/earth

*	Spheres	Christian deities	Life of Jesus	Social issues
1	Kether	god 3-in-1	ascension	equality/justice
2	Chockmah	father god	proving	direction/leadership
3	Binah	virgin/mother Mary	resurrection	inclusion/support
D	Daath	Satan	crucifixion	law and order
4	Chesed	gentle Jesus	trial	health
5	Geburah	strong Jesus	arrest	wealth
6	Tiphareth	Christ the son	christhood	council
7	Netzach	healer Jesus	miracles	social services
8	Hod	messiah Jesus	teaching	education
9	Yesod	holy spirit	early years	therapies
10	Malkuth	Magdalene/church	birth	housing/nutrition

*	Spheres	Chakras energy centres	Cosmic levels	Neurological circuits
1	Kether	sahasara	space/subatomic	VIII: neuroatomic
2	Chockmah	ajna	space/subatomic	VIII: neuroatomic
3	Binah	ajna	space/subatomic	VIII: neuroatomic
D	Daath	visuddhi	DNA	VII: neurogenetic
4	Chesed	anahata	galaxy	VI: neuroelectrical
5	Geburah	anahata	galaxy	VI: neuroelectrical
6	Tiphareth	anahata	sun/atoms	V: neurosomatic
7	Netzach	manipura	planets/molecules	II: territorial
8	Hod	manipura	planets/molecules	III: semantic
9	Yesod	svadisthana	moon/cells	IV: socio-sexual
10	Malkuth	muladhara	nature/bodies	I: biosurvival

*	Spheres	Seven ways	Tree of power	Levels of consciousness
1	Kether	[origin]	incarnate will	spiritual/transpersonal
2	Chockmah	[origin]	purposeful will	spiritual/transpersonal
3	Binah	[origin]	collective will	spiritual/transpersonal
D	Daath	[transcendence]	no will	unfolding/negative
4	Chesed	love	good will	archetypal form/soul
5	Geburah	will	strong will	archetypal force/soul
6	Tiphareth	ritual	skilful will	archetypal focus/soul
7	Netzach	beauty	emotional will	higher astral/personality
8	Hod	science	mental will	middle astral/personality
9	Yesod	devotion	unconscious will	lower astral/personality
10	Malkuth	action	manifesting will	etheric/physical

*	Spheres	Gardening	Music	Actors/ musicians	Transcendental morality
1	Kether	inspiration	form	performance	great work
2	Chockmah	intent	intent	communication	devotion
3	Binah	awareness	spirit	relationship	silence
D	Daath	sowing	drone	the play/music	openness
4	Chesed	waiting	colour	support	obedience
5	Geburah	germinating	colour	production	energy
6	Tiphareth	bursting forth	repetition	director/conductor	centredness
7	Netzach	weeding	harmony	players	unselfishness
8	Hod	feeding	melody	writers	truthfulness
9	Yesod	watering	harmonics	company	independence
10	Malkuth	harvesting	rhythm	stage	scepticism

*	Spheres	Hebrew Adepts	Magickal grades	Magickal formulae	Process of creation
1	Kether	Messiah	ipsissimus	lashtal/aumgn	point
2	Chockmah	Moses	magus	viaov	line
3	Binah	Enoch	master of temple	babalon	triangle
D	Daath	—	babe of abyss	[demons]	[breathe]
4	Chesed	Abraham	exempt adept	ihvi/agape	solid
5	Geburah	Jacob	major adept	agla/alhim	motion
6	Tiphareth	Elijah	minor adept	abrahadabra	consciousness
7	Netzach	Noah	philosophus	ararita	bliss
8	Hod	Aaron	practicus	inri	knowledge
9	Yesod	Joseph	zelator	alim	being
10	Malkuth	David	neophyte	vitriol	fulfilment

Court cards and the elements

Knight of Wands	fire of fire	LIGHTNING
Queen of Wands	water of fire	SUN
Prince of Wands	air of fire	RAINBOW
Princess of Wands	earth of fire	EARTH FIRES
Knight of Cups	fire of water	RAIN
Queen of Cups	water of water	SEA
Prince of Cups	air of water	POOL (LAKE)
Princess of Cups	earth of water	RIVER
Knight of Swords	fire of air	GALES
Queen of Swords	water of air	CLOUDS
Prince of Swords	air of air	ATMOSPHERE
Princess of Swords	earth of air	CLEAR SKIES
Knight of Discs	fire of earth	MOUNTAINS
Queen of Discs	water of earth	SEASHORE/ PLAINS
Prince of Discs	air of earth	FIELDS (MEADOW)
Princess of Discs	earth of earth	ROCKS/ CAVES

BODY SYSTEMS AND THE TREE OF LIFE

The following listing, arranged under the different body systems, helps locate the connections between the Tree of Life and the human body. It also introduces some other connections with the internal body systems, namely functions, associated energy centres, connected body parts and endocrine system connections, and a key word or two to connect it to the 'ego or soul state' that corresponds. It is intended to further your understanding of Kabbalistic healing, and also to help you deepen your connections between your body and the Tree of Life. Use it wisely!

THE CENTRAL NERVOUS SYSTEM

Functions:	Experience, response, communication and integration
	Expression of life principles, ideals, purpose, revelation
Energy centres:	Crown and mid-head chakras
Body parts:	Head and back
Endocrine:	Pituitary (L eye), pineal (R eye)
Ego/soul state:	Infinity & illumination

Tree of Life	Human Body
1: Kether	life force, energy, consciousness
2: Chockmah	left brain
3: Binah	right brain
path joins 1–2	left eyes, ears, pituitary
path joins 1–3	right eyes, ears, pineal
path joins 2–3	nose, mouth
path joins 1–6	spinal cord
path joins 6–9	spinal cord, (solar plexus)

THE ENDOCRINE SYSTEM

Functions:	Energy and growth. Survival and expression
Energy centre:	Throat chakra
Body parts:	Neck, shoulders and arms, endocrine system

Endocrine: Thyroid and whole system

Ego/soul state: Inspiration & intuition

Tree of Life	Human Body
4: Chesed	left adrenal
5: Geburah	right adrenal
0: Daath	throat, thyroid
path joins 2–4	posterior pituitary and overall system
path joins 3–5	anterior pituitary and overall system

THE CARDIOVASCULAR AND RESPIRATORY SYSTEMS

Functions: Energy exchange, quality of life, defence and transport
Transformation and love

Energy centre: Heart chakra

Body parts: Thorax

Endocrine: Thymus

Ego/soul state: Individuation

Tree of Life	Human Body
6: Tiphareth	heart, thymus
path joins 2–6	arteries, oxygenated blood
path joins 3–6	veins, deoxygenated blood
path joins 4–5	lymph, spleen
path joins 4–6	left lung
path joins 5–6	right lung

THE DIGESTIVE AND EXCRETORY SYSTEMS

Functions: Ingestion, digestion, absorption, discrimination and
elimination. Processing and clearing of desires

Energy centre: Solar plexus chakra

Body parts: Abdomen

Endocrine: Pancreas

Ego/Soul State: Imitation

Tree of Life	Human Body
7: Netzach	left kidney
8: Hod	right kidney

path joins 4–7	large intestine (descending), rectum
path joins 6–7	stomach
path joins 5–8	large intestine (ascending and transverse)
path joins 6–8	liver, gall bladder, pancreas
path joins 7–8	small intestine
path joins 9–10	bladder, skin

THE REPRODUCTIVE SYSTEM

Functions:	Connection, propagation, balance
	Manifestation of energies
Energy centre:	Sacral chakra
Body parts:	Inner and outer sexual organs
Endocrine:	Gonads
Ego/soul state:	Impulse

Tree of Life	**Human Body**
9: Yesod	sexual organs
path joins 7–9	male: left seminal vesicle, vas deferens
	female: left uterine tube, ovaries
path joins 8–9	male: right seminal vesicle, vas deferens
	female: right uterine tube, ovaries

THE LOCOMOTOR SYSTEM

Functions:	Support, movement, expression
	Grounding, will-to-live (hereditary, genetic, cultural)
Energy centre:	Base chakra
Body parts:	Legs, feet, skeletal and muscular systems
Endocrine:	Adrenals
Ego/soul state:	Instinct

Tree of Life	**Human Body**
10: Malkuth	body as whole
path joins 7–10	left skeleton, bones, muscles
path joins 8–10	right skeleton, bones, muscles

BIBLIOGRAPHY AND FURTHER READING

The following books are recommended further reading for those of you who wish to continue your studies of the practical Kabbalah. You will obtain most understanding from those in the first section, but all the other listed titles contain some Kabbalistic knowledge or connection and are highly recommended.

THE STUDY OF PRACTICAL KABBALAH

Andrews, T. *Imagick*, Llewellyn, 1989
Crowley, A. *The Qabalah of Aleister Crowley (inc. 777)*, Weiser, 1973
Crowley, V. *The Woman's Kabbalah*, Thorsons, 2000
DuQuette, L. *The Chicken Qabalah*, Weiser, 2001
Feldman, D. *Qabalah*, Work of Chariot, 2001
Fortune, D. *The Mystical Qabalah*, Benn, 1970
Gonzalez-Wippler, M. *A Kabbalah for the Modern World*, Llewellyn, 1987
Halevi, Z. *The Work of the Kabbalist*, Gateway, 1984
Hoffman, E. *Opening the Inner Gates*, Shambhala, 1995
Kaplan, A. *Sepher Yetzirah*, Weiser, 1990
Knight, G. *Practical Guide to Qabalistic Symbolism*, Weiser, 1978
Kramer, S. *Hidden Faces of the Soul*, NK, 2000
Levry, J. *Lifting The Veil*, Rootlight, 2002
Love, J. *Quantum Gods*, Element, 1976
Malachi, T. *Gnosis of the Cosmic Christ*, Llewellyn, 2005
Parfitt, W. *The Complete Guide to the Kabbalah*, Rider, 2001
Regardie, I. *The Tree of Life*, Weiser, 1972
Schaya, L. *The Universal Meaning of the Kabbalah*, Penguin USA, 1974
Scholen, G. *On the Kabbalah*, Schochen, 1965
Schulman, J. *Kabbalistic Healing*, Inner Traditions, 2004

BOOKS ON MAGIC, TAROT, AND ASSOCIATED SUBJECTS

Alli, A. *All Rites Reversed*, Falcon, 1988
Casteneda, C. *Tales of Power*, Penguin, 1976
Castaneda, C. *The Art of Dreaming*, Aquarian, 1993
Crowley, A. *The Book of Thoth*, Weiser, 1971

Crowley, A. *Magick*, Weiser, 1973
Crowley, A. and Harris, F. *The Thoth Tarot Cards*, various editions
Douglas-Klotz, N. *Prayers of the Cosmos*, Harper & Row, 1990
Ellis, N. *Awakening Osiris*, Phanes, 1988
Grant, K. *Nightside of Eden*, Muller, 1977
Heaven, R. *The Journey To You*, Bantam, 2001
Hillman, J. *The Soul's Code*, Bantam, 1997
Johanson, G. and Kurtz, R. *Grace Unfolding*, Bell Tower, 1991
Johnson, D. *Body, Spirit & Democracy*, North Atlantic, 1994
Masters, R. *The Way of the Lover*, Xanthyros, 1988
Narby, J. *The Cosmic Serpent*, Tarcher, 1998
Needleman, J. *Lost Christianity*, Element, 1993
O'Regan, V. *Pillars of Isis*, Aquarian, 1990
Parfitt, W. *Walking through Walls*, Element, 1989
Regardie, I. *The Complete Golden Dawn*, Falcon, 1984
Wanless, J. *New Age Tarot*, Merrill-West, 1987
Wilson, R. *Prometheus Rising*, Falcon, 1983

GLOSSARY OF TERMS

Abyss	The gulf between the phenomenal world of manifestation (Chesed and below) and its noumenal source (the Supernal Triad). Only through crossing the Abyss can we realise our innermost spiritual nature
Adam	Man, literally 'red earth' or 'first blood'. 'Adam Kadmon' is the prototype of all human creatures (male and female)
Adept	An initiate who has reached a deeper level of understanding
Adonai	Lord, the personal 'deity within', or the Holy Guardian Angel (of which each manifest creature has at least one)
Ain	Nothing, the void. The outermost of the three veils
Ain Soph	Limitless, the void beyond the known universe represented by the Tree of Life. The middle of the three veils. Sometimes described as the Kabbalistic name for God because it is beyond manifestation and non-manifestation and cannot be limited in any way
Ain Soph Aur	Limitless Light, the innermost of the three veils from which the spheres are formed
Anima	An archetypal soul image embodiment of the reflective, feminine nature of man's subconscious
Animus	An archetypal soul image, embodiment of the creative, masculine nature of woman's subconscious
Assiah	The fourth world of material manifestation, of humans and other manifest beings
Atziluth	The first world of creative essence, the realm of the Mother–Father Deity
Barakah	Grace, divine blessing bestowed when 'desire' and 'reality' are united
Binah	Understanding, the third sephirah, relating to Saturn. The first sphere beyond the Abyss. (Sometimes erroneously called 'reason', a patriarchal misunderstanding)
Briah	The second world of receptive essence and pure spirit, the realm of Archangels

Cabala	*See* Kabbalah
Chesed	Mercy, Love, the fourth sephirah, relating to Jupiter
Chiah	The part of the soul associated with the second world. It is described as the life force, divine will, and source of action
Chockmah	Wisdom, the second sephirah, relating to Neptune, the sphere associated with Spiritual Purpose
Daath	Knowledge, the 'eleventh' sephirah or 'the sphere without a number', the gateway to the 'hidden' Tree behind the visible one, relates to Uranus
Deity	A God or Goddess. A spiritual being embodying one or several aspects of divine essence
Demon	An evil spirit, or unbalanced force
Eden	The 'garden' of 'unity' to which we return when we realise divine 'union' here on earth
Eheieh	Hebrew word meaning 'I am that I am'. The divine name associated with Kether
Elements	There are four basic elements (fire, water, air, and earth), which are realms, or divisions of nature. They are the basic modes of existence and action, and the building blocks of everything in the universe. A fifth element, spirit, is said to bind together and govern the lesser four
Elohim	Usually translated as 'God', the word is composed of a feminine singular with a masculine plural, thus expressing the uniting of male and female principles
Eve	The 'first woman'; the inner aspect of all humans (male and female) through which we come to know ourselves
Geburah	Strength, judgement, the fifth sphere, relating to Mars
Gematria	Kabbalistic numerological system where words having the same numerical value are said to be essentially identical. A meditational and revelatory technique
Great Work	An alchemical term summarised in the words 'Know Thyself'
Hod	Splendour, the eighth sephirah, related to Mercury, the sphere of thinking
Immanence	Belief or experience that the divine is already manifest in all things and is to be found within (cf. transcendence). The Way of the Kabbalah is essentially biased towards immanence
Kabbalah	To receive, and by implication also to reveal. A

	practical system for understanding ourselves and our relationship with our world
Kavvanah	Conscious meditation or prayer
Kether	Crown, the first sephirah, related to Pluto, transmits the influences from 'trans-mundane' realms
Kliphoth	The plural of 'kliphah', meaning 'shells' or 'otherness'. The shadow side of the sephiroth on the Tree of Life, the kliphoth are the realms of 'demons'
Maggid	Any trans-mundane entity with whom the Kabbalist communicates; also a spiritually advanced human being
Magic	Any intentional act is an act of magic, which has been described as the art of causing willed change. A world view that gives precedence to immanence rather than transcendence. (Sometimes spelt with a 'k' at the end to distinguish it from conjuring)
Malkuth	Kingdom or bride, the tenth sephirah, related to earth, the total manifestation of all matter
Mysticism	Any method designed to bring the practitioner closer to union with their higher Self is mystical. A world view that gives precedence to transcendence rather than immanence
Nephesch	The part of the soul located in Yesod, which is described as the Lower Unconscious. Contains primal instincts, fundamental drives and animal vitality. Sometimes associated with the astral body
Neschamah	The highest part of the soul, its highest aspiration, associated with the Supernal Triad, or specifically Binah
Netzach	Victory, the seventh sephirah, related to Venus, the sphere of feelings.
Otz Chiim	The Tree of Life in Hebrew (sometimes Etz Chaim, depending upon transliteration method)
Qabalah	See Kabbalah
Qliphoth	See Kliphoth
Ruach	Spirit. Patriarchally related to 'air' and 'reason'; originally – and correctly – related to 'water' and the womb out of which all life, male and female, appears
Sephirah	Number, emanation, sphere, container. The name given to each of the eleven emanations of cosmic manifestation on the Tree of Life that underlie the

	whole of existence
Sephiroth	The plural of Sephirah
Shekhinah	The female embodiment of spiritual power
Supernals	The Supernal Triad: the three Sephiroth above the Abyss, therefore beyond material manifestation. The source of all creation
Tarot	The 'tarot' of anything is its spiritual essence, its connection with the wheel of manifestation. Particularly related to the seventy-eight images (or cards) of the tarot pack that act as a compendium of all human knowledge and understanding
Tetragrammaton	IHVH, the four-lettered name of the Deity, commonly referred to as Jehovah. Tetragrammaton contains a complex formula relating to cosmic union and the manifestation of the elements. Only after the creation is fully manifest is the term IHVH used for 'God' in the Bible
Tikkun	Repair, reparation or restoration of the original Unity through acts of awareness and service; the purpose of incarnation
Tiphareth	Beauty, the sixth and central Sephirah on the Tree of Life, related to the sun, and to the central core or heart of each individual
Torah	The five books of Moses (the first five in the Bible) and sometimes, beyond that, meaning the spiritual laws of the Jewish tradition; in a more esoteric sense, a description of the interaction between oneness and duality
Transcendence	Belief that experience of the divine is separate, not-manifest and is to be found through acts that separate us from mundane reality (cf. immanence)
Tree of Life	The ten sephiroth and the twenty-two connecting paths. All forms – manifest, unmanifest, animate and inanimate – mirror this structure. It is not merely a diagram of representation of reality but a device (or 'doorway') to bring us into closer relationship with reality
Yesod	Foundation, the ninth sephirah, related to the Moon, astral and sexual energy. Also the place where unresolved subconscious material is 'deposited' in the individual and collective psyche

| *Yetzirah* | The third world of formation, realm of Angels |
| *Zaddik* | A person who is well-versed in the path, a spiritual guide |

HOW TO CONTACT
THE AUTHOR

If you want to contact Will Parfitt, including for details of current courses, workshops, and his distance learning programme in Kabbalah, Will's website can be found at: http://www.willparfitt.com

You can email him at: will@willparfitt.com

and his mailing address is:
Box 1865,
Glastonbury,
Somerset BA6 8YR,
UK.

If you write to Will and want a reply, please enclose a stamped and addressed envelope or, if from overseas, an international reply coupon.

INDEX